With Doctors Johnson and Brock's world class and unmatched insight, you will go on a journey of self-discovery through the lens of four temperaments. Through this powerful framework you will learn about the essence of who you are, your gifts, and your potential greatness. You will also learn potential challenges due to your temperament to help you anticipate and eliminate blind spots and recurring challenges. You will also learn better ways to understand people different from you and help enhance their lives and enrich your relationships. This book can be a powerful pathway to fuel personal growth, a contribution to success, and personal fulfilment. Enjoy your journey with them. I have for 18 years and counting.

~ Joseph Hastreiter, B.A., CPA, Vice President, EWH Small Business Accounting

What's Your Temperament? creates a foundation, a compass, a positive way of looking at life. Johnson and Brock's temperaments have given me a framework by which I understand and orient my life. Life is all about relationships. This book sheds light on how I understand myself and look at both differences and similarities among my fellow humans. Read it and understand and create your relational foundation!

~ Tim Jorgensen, fly fish guide

Doctors Johnson and Brock provide insights into personality temperaments, which provides valuable information in understanding ourselves and others. Learn about positive dimensions of your personality and areas you can work on to improve your relationships with others. Lots of practical examples for understanding the four temperaments in both personal and professional relationships.

~ Dr. Dan Feaster, Executive Director and Psychotherapist with the Samaritan Counseling Center of Southern Wisconsin

WHAT'S YOUR TEMPERAMENT?

*Identifying and Enhancing
Your Personality Strengths*

Ron Johnson, Ph.D., Deb Brock, Ph.D.

What's Your Temperament?
Identifying and Enhancing Your Personality Strengths

Copyright © 2022 by Ron Johnson, Ph.D., Deb Brock, Ph.D.

All rights reserved. No part of this book may be reproduced or transmitted in any form or by any means without written permission of the author.

ISBN 978-1-7354289-1-8

Published by Midlands Psychological Associates,
Lodi, Wisconsin.

Midlandspsychological.com
brockandjohnson@frontier.com

Cover Photo by Deb Brock: The GgantijaTemples, Island of Gozo, Malta.

Other works by the authors available through Midlands Psychological Associates:

Balls: Men Finding Courage to be Honest

Friendly Diagnosis: What is Right With Me!

I Want to Tell You How I Feel: How to Know What You Feel, Express How You Feel, and, How to Listen to Others.

Mantalk: How Men Express their Feelings

Seen and Not Heard: Effective Parenting with Fewer Words and More Action

The Positive Power of Sadness: How Good Grief Prevents and Cures Anxiety, Depression, and Anger

4-8-12: Managing Difficult Children

Dedication

We dedicate this book to our daughters, Jennifer Joy, and Kristin Karin (rest in peace, Sweetheart), as they have loved us and inspired us to love others and inspire others.

Appreciations

Special appreciation to the following readers and editors, all good and longtime friends: Dan Feaster, John Ganahl, Joseph Hastreiter, Tim Jorgensen, Jeff and Kathy Laudin, Dave Michael, and Scott Savage.

Contents

Foreword 1
Introduction. 5
1 The Player Personality 27
2 The Caretaker Personality 57
3 The Analyst Personality. 77
4 The Lover Personality 97
5 Challenges for Players 123
6 Challenges for Caretakers 153
7 Challenges for Analysts 181
8 Challenges for Lovers 211
9 Maturing Your Temperament 243
10 Connections and Conversations 271
Appendix: Johnson Temperament Indicator. 319
Annotated Bibliography. 323

Foreword

In *What's Your Temperament?* you will see yourself and people you know numerous times, both in familiar and surprising ways. These sightings will sometimes be amusing, sometimes disturbing, but always insightful in challenging you to understand your strengths of personality and mature beyond them. The authors' hope is for this book to make a profound positive difference in your life. It has in mine.

I am honored to provide the forward for this important book, a work that will undoubtedly make significant enhancements to many lives, including yours. As a lifelong student of personality in all its complexity I find this work to be immensely helpful in quantifying the important aspect of *temperament* as these authors have done. Equally, the authors have succeeded in presenting useful ways of enhancing life, both personally and interpersonally. Their approach to psychology in general, and personality in specific is positive and practical, but also grounded in solid psychological research and theory that stands apart from simplistic self-help books and unduly pedantic psychology.

My relationship with Drs. Johnson and Brock spans 25 years during which we have listened to each other, challenged one another, and loved one another through life's inevitable crises, difficulties and celebrations. As a serious student of personality type and its application to personal lives, interpersonal lives, and business, I am attuned to anything that adds to my knowledge of understanding and application. In their asking me to write this forward, they do so from my broad and deep (albeit a bit unorthodox) experience working with personality assessments and helping myriad people apply the learning to their lives and work. For 35 years I've worked as a consultant and coach to individuals, leaders, and organizations, striving as Drs. Johnson and Brock do, to provide people with an understanding through which they can make good sense of their lives. My own understanding of personality has largely been in the realm of personality type as understood through tools such as the Myers-Briggs Type Indicator, The Pearson-Marr archetype Indicator, the Strong Interest Inventory, and other instruments. My degree in Business Education and several certificates in Training and Development in Business and Industry, have given me a practical, common-sense approach to helping others, which is what Drs. Johnson and Brock have done in this work.

My first encounter with them was when they were speaking at a professional group about this important aspect of *temperament*, specifically the four personality temperaments that are discussed in this book. We were attending a meeting of the Madison Association of Psychological Type, MAPT. It was Valentine's season and Ron was addressing the "R-Word". He stammered it out, "We are going to talk about R-r-r-relationships tonight," as he admitted that the whole concept of relationships was not one of his strengths. He then went on to note that one of the four temperaments he would be discussing was that of a "lover," namely someone who is particularly oriented towards human connections and all that makes up a relationship. I immediately resonated with this "lover" temperament just as much as I was intrigued and bemused by the "caretaker" temperament that he personified. I had a hard time getting my head around a "caretaker," someone who values the care of property more than the care of relationships. Since I have been interested in differences of personality, primarily through personality type theory, Ron's suggestion that there was another way of understanding our differences immediately intrigued me. "Hmm, I thought, not everyone regards relationships in the same way!" Being the "lover" that I am, I was immediately attuned to what he was saying and knew that I wanted to establish a r-r-r-relationship with this guy. Not only did I learn about my lover nature, I also learned about my "secondary temperament," which Brock and Johnson call a "player," someone they describe as seeking experience in life, whether physical, emotional, or intellectual. As the years progressed, I learned about the complexity of the fourth of the temperaments, "analysts," who seek to make the world a better place by finding and solving problems. These four temperaments: Lover, Player, Analyst and Caretaker, identified by Drs. Johnson and Brock have impacted my life and my work by providing insight into the wonderful differences of us all.

Johnson and Brock's whole approach to temperament and the larger matter of self-understanding and understanding of others is built on a foundation of looking "for what is good about you" rather than the things that might be wrong. While they have four chapters dedicated to presenting the typical ways people with these four temperaments feel, think, act and relate, they do not shy away from the challenges that each one has, things that are discussed in another four chapters. In the later chapters they look at "maturing in one's temperament" which means "adding to one's own nature" some of the aspects of the other temperaments.

This book, *What's Your Temperament?* cuts through the complex and confusing models of personality to provide an eloquent understanding and appreciation of how our differences in temperament impact well-being, happiness, and success. This book is an essential guide to knowing yourself, and all those fascinating, gratifying, enticing others you run into on life's path. It offers the wisdom that comes from their 100 plus years of experience, strong education, rich personal journeys, and hearts opened with joy, sorrow, and love.

Reading though this book I found it profound, simple and easy to apply. I discovered nuggets of insight that I was surprised had not appeared to me from my decades of studying personality. I have applied these new insights to my clients, family, neighbors, and colleagues. These include answers to questions that humans have struggled with for eons, such as "if you love someone, won't you automatically like them?" As a lover my immediate answer has always connected loving and liking, but Brock and Johnson have forced me to consider that liking and loving are not the same.

As you peruse *What's Your Temperament*, you will learn the basic personal, relational, and spiritual characteristics of these four temperaments and see deep and practical applications that understanding temperament can bring to you. I found myself thinking, "Now I know why my neighbor's behavior drives me crazy. He is probably a caretaker" and "I see why my child has been such a challenge for me. He's an analyst" and "I know why my wife and I are such good companions. She and I both share the lover temperament". As much as I have understood differences in personality for so many decades, Brock and Johnson have helped me learn even more ways to understand myself and others and truly value our differences." I am confident you will find your own nuggets to aid you in your relational journeys.

Unlike much clinical and popular psychology, *What's Your Temperament?* focuses upon what is good with people, not what is wrong. This is the banner flag of the work that Drs. Johnson and Brock do in their book, which reflects how they look at people. Importantly, their book focuses on what we differing types need to learn to fully individuate, as the great Dr. Carl Jung described 100 years ago. This is a natural, delightful, practical and spiritual evolution that makes us happier and better human beings, bringing more of our best selves to the part of life that we all share.

Speaking as a person who has made it his life's work to support people in understanding themselves and growing into the best they can be, this followed by an equally deep understanding of people who are different from you, I assure you this book is a great help on that path. Savor it, watch for your own self-understanding with in its pages, and then observe the other people in your life who are so important to you, yet can be so challenging. Learn, grow. This book is indeed profound enough to alter your life for the better.

Scott Savage MA PC
Principal, Scott Savage Consulting and Coaching
Spring Green, Wisconsin
April 2022

Introduction

IT IS BOTH EXCITING and challenging to live life when you have a good understanding of yourself. For more than 50 years we have been providing psychotherapy, instruction, and mentoring to people who have come to our offices seeking relief from their psychological distresses. In our attempts to provide relief to these people it is our primary goal to help people come to a place of self-awareness and self-acceptance. This capacity to be aware and accepting of oneself is essential so that a person can mature beyond their wounds and arrive at a place of accepting of others. Good therapy, in our minds not only includes healing, but also the passing forward the same healing goodness to others. This doesn't mean that all of our clients need to become therapists, although in these years we are honored to mentor a number of seasoned therapists as well as a handful of upcoming therapists. Rather, passing forward the same healing goodness to others means that when you have found genuine acceptance and clarity of yourself, you find it natural to want to facilitate understanding and acceptance in others. In simple terms, this means when you know yourself, you feel safe enough to know others. This knowing of others means acceptance of what you like and what you don't like, of what you agree with and what you don't agree. Acceptance isn't the same as liking or agreeing with someone, and it doesn't mean that you and other people are the same on all fronts. Understanding and accepting is about giving permission for both similarities and differences. Genuine acceptance and understanding brings about balance. We have always attempted to help people become more self-aware and self-accepting so that they can become more understanding and accepting of others. We believe that self-acceptance and understanding leads to other-acceptance and understanding which in turn, keeps the cycle moving ever forward from person to person from family to family, from community to community and even from culture to culture and nation to nation.

Our orientation towards people is to first see what is *right* about them rather than what is *wrong* with them. We have understood people from this perspective for the collective 100 years that we have been in the business of psychology. Over these years we have encountered many helpful ways of understanding people but the ways that have been most helpful to us, and most helpful to the people we have served, is to see people in a positive light. These positive ways of understanding people are ways to make sense of how and why people think, feel, relate, and act the way they do. We have found that helping a person identify their *temperament*, their most natural life orientation, is the first step towards making sense of how they think, feel, behave and relate to others. With just a brief explanation of a person's temperament things begin to immediately make sense for them. Even within the first session, where we often provide them some indicators of their temperament, it is easier and more profitable to examine their painful circumstances that have usually brought them to our offices.

WHAT IS TEMPERAMENT

Researchers and theoreticians in the social scientific field have been working for centuries on trying to understand humanity in all its forms. To truly understand individuals who come to our offices for assistance in life is to help them *make sense* of things: make sense of what they feel, make sense of what they think, and make sense of what they do. We have found that it makes most sense to identify similarities and differences in the way people see the world, react to the world, and communicate to the world through temperament.

Temperament is just one of many ways of examining personality styles and characteristics. We prefer the word temperament because this term suggests something natural in one's psychological makeup. We suggest that regardless of one's station of life, people can profit from learning and utilizing the concept of temperament in their lives. Furthermore, people can utilize the concept of temperament regardless of their gender, vocation, family, friends, geographical location, or their philosophical orientation to life. Once we help people identify what is their most natural and important element of temperament, it is dramatically easier to assist them in the difficulties they encounter in life. While there are numerous ways of examining and classifying personality styles, we prefer to use a simple four-part temperament system that begins to describe the unique value systems that people have: We identify four different temperaments: *Player, Lover, Analyst* and *Caretaker*. We have found that these terms give people a foundation in understanding how they operate in life, often making the complexities of life somewhat simpler. Each of these four temperaments, as we will examine in the chapters to follow, focus on individual value systems and characteristics:

- *Players* seek and value experience, especially physical experience in order to fully enjoy life.
- *Caretakers* seek and value the care of property in order to bring safety to life.
- *Lovers* seek and value human connections in order to bring human love to life
- *Analysts* seek and value understanding and truth in order to make the world a better place in which to live.

These four temperaments began with Ron in 1982 when he wrote a paper entitled "The Player Personality". Ron found that it was a valuable way of understanding certain people who had the characteristics of a person that he called a "player," namely the way they thought, felt, and acted. Ron was stimulated to use the term "player" by observing our daughter, Krissie, and another friend of ours, Christopher. Ron noticed that Krissie and Christopher shared some very significant characteristics. These characteristics, which we discuss in full in Chapter 1, were enticing, exciting, and wonderful, but they were also occasionally irritating and otherwise challenging. Ron found that when he described the temperament term player to Christopher, Krissie, and some clients he suspected were players, they felt affirmed in being who they were: people who sought experience in order to make life enjoyable. In every case, he heard from the player people in his life, whether friends, clients, or our own daughter, that the term player *made sense* to them. Instead of thinking there was something wrong with them, or worse yet, something wrong with the world around them, the players that Ron encountered found that this term player felt something that was *right* with them.

From this initial discovery that the term player personality was useful to many people, Ron began to examine people with different personality styles, which ultimately led the way people felt, thought, spoke, and otherwise engaged life. With some careful observation of the whole business of personality temperament, and even more careful explaining his thoughts and considerations, Ron came to use the other three temperament terms: caretaker, lover, and analyst. After even more consideration and thought Ron created the Johnson Temperament Indicate (JTI) as a way of identifying one's temperament. We have used the JTI for 40 years and running along with the other measures of understanding people. You might consider taking the JTI that we have included in the appendix as a way of examining what your temperament might be. While not a perfect instrument of personality analysis, as no psychological test is, the JTI, often in conjunction with other measures of personality, has helped us set a foundation for understanding people in order to help them improve their self-understanding and ultimately their self-esteem and social-esteem.

STRENGTH-BASED PSYCHOLOGY

This strength-based approach to understanding people is not new with us. There are many popular ways of understanding people including that of personality differences, intellectual differences, cultural differences, gender differences, and age differences. Carol Gilligan (1982) discussed the differences of personality evidenced in gender differences, which then led to differences in speech and relationships. Howard Gardner (1983) brought us an important aspect of understanding "what is right about people" in his identifying (at least) seven different kinds of intelligence. Buckingham and Clifton (2001) provided a strength-based approach to people in business. Katharine Briggs and her daughter, Isabel, provided perhaps the most profound way of understanding "personality type" by use of the Myers-Briggs Type Indicator (1995) based on Carl Jung's understanding of "psychological type" (1971). David Keirsey used

Myers' personality type terminology to develop a four-part model of "temperament" (1978), which suggested that there were four two-part combinations of the Myers-Briggs system.

The idea that people have different temperaments began at least as far back as the Greek philosopher Galen (2nd century CE), which was actually based on Greek philosophy one thousand years earlier. Galen proposed that there were four principal temperaments based on the four basic elements in the world (fire, water, earth, and air), which then related to the four "fluids" in the body. These fluids then determined one's basic personality (temperament). Several writers since Galen have identified four temperaments including Keirsey noted above. Also originating in early history has been the use of the Enneagram made most popular by Riso in 1987. The Enneagram uses both type and temperament terminology with a design of nine different personalities. Many books have been written, both scientific (Bates and Wachs, 1994) and theoretical (Dabbs, 2000), some oriented towards a temperament system based on psychopathology (Dougherty and West, 2000). An interesting pathology-based system of understanding personality was developed by Alexander Lowen (1958) who "diagnosed" personality and pathology by "body type." Lowen's work was an extension of the earlier work done by Wilhelm Reich (1933), and then expanded to a more positive understanding of personality by our own expert therapist, Dick Olney (1915-1994). Building on the positivity of Dick Olney, we came to appreciate even more the value of assessing people via their strengths before their limits.

DEALING WITH SUFFERING

Over these many years that we have worked with people, we have studied various ways of understanding people including the utilization of standard psychological diagnoses, so many of which are psychopathological, such as depression, anxiety and personality disorders. Certainly, it is important for us as clinicians to know how some of these disorders develop in certain people, how they are manifested, and the dangers that they present. While we know the text book definitions and causes of psychological distresses, limits and illnesses, and we treat them to the best of our abilities, and, certainly, we know firsthand how terribly people suffer, we also know that only looking at what is wrong, just having a diagnosis and treating the symptoms with psychotropic medications will never complete the healing. We believe that most of what ails us emotionally and psychologically can be resolved through the arduous work of self-examination. Self-examination should primarily look at what is right with us so that when we review our limits and weaknesses as well as our traumas, we have a foundational understanding of our basic nature. We believe that if you first know what is right with you and have learned to balance your strengths with the rest of your life, like your personality, intelligence, passion, and background you will be able to utilize these positive elements in facing and conquering the distress in your lives and ultimately do the same for other people. Once we understand clients' basic orientation to life and people, i.e., how they order their lives, we can then help them see how both their strengths and their weaknesses make sense. It is this *making sense* of how people think, feel, and behave through an in-depth understanding of their personalities and other aspects of how people are naturally constructed combined with resolving old traumas that full healing comes about. We do much better work with people who can dare to find, face, and finish old traumas by building a foundation of good self-esteem based on good self-understanding and self-acceptance.

We find that we can much better serve the suffering of our clients when we also know their strengths that are based on the naturalness of their personalities. We believe that each and every human being has strengths, which if understood, valued, and enhanced, can lead to greatness. But when these very strengths, whether of personality, intelligence, or otherwise, are not understood, they can lead to failure in life. Sadly, one's very strengths can be suppressed by oneself or by someone else in their lives, or worse yet people can be shamed for the very strengths that they have. There is also the possibility that these strengths can be indulged, whether by the individuals themselves or by their environment. If, for instance, an individual is gifted in, say, reading or music, it is possible for the person to singularly use these gifts without developing a way to relate in a broader way to the world. Many fine people are extremely good at one aspect of life but have failed to broaden their functioning in order to succeed in life. While we always look to help people find healing in their lives, which often means helping them see the wounds that they have suffered, we begin the process of psychotherapy with a wholly positive view of personality, intelligence, and other gifts that an individual has. You can't start emotional healing with an attitude of fixing the person but rather with an approach of self-understanding and self-acceptance. Self-understanding and acceptance provides a foundation upon which an individual can find balance in life and become a source of good for humanity.

Many of the daily difficulties people experience erupt because they are not aware of their gifts and strengths. It is when we either don't recognize our gifts, or, when we overuse them in compensation that we end up in conflict with other people who have different gifts and strengths. So, the heart of our work with people is to help them understand their strengths first, find ways to enhance these strengths, watch for indulgence of these strengths, and then to relate to people who have different strengths. We do this primarily though mentoring them in self-acceptance and awareness of their personality style or temperament. We know that self-awareness is the not the end of the road, that people must move beyond themselves and "pass it forward', but we all have to start with learning about ourselves so we can then learn about others and share life in a broader way. The best modality we have found in making this happen is by looking at what is right about people, coming to identify their core value systems and learning the language that best speaks those core values and preferences through temperament.

Over the years our four-temperament system continues to be a simple and clear way for people to understand themselves. It has been particularly gratifying that people have found these four temperament terms not only make sense, but have given them building blocks of self-understanding and self-acceptance. Even more gratifying is the fact that when people can identify with one of these four temperaments, they can add to that self-awareness a positive understanding of other people in their lives who have different temperaments. It has been a true joy to us when we have helped people see something positive in their lives that might have been seen as something wrong with them. When, for instance, a player can appreciate her need for experience and excitement in life, she not only can affirm herself and her orientation, but she is better able to see and appreciate, say, her caretaker husband, her analyst daughter, or her lover friend.

In the present volume we have endeavored to glean value from all of our predecessors in the field of personality analysis. Blending with what we have studied over the years we have come to find that our four-part temperament system seems to meet most people not only with a confirmation of their personality characteristics but with their core belief systems. People frequently report that they can readily identify themselves and others using our four-part temperament system. We believe that we have added to the psychological literature, and even more to humanity, a way of self-value that is not only self-affirming as people see that they have potential greatness but also provides a positive view of others with different personality characteristics. The oddity of looking at strengths first is that it leads to a genuine humility because we can't be good at all things but we can improve ourselves and improve our affirmation of other people in the process. Understanding people is the name of the game for us. We hope that our four-temperament system will add to these many ways of understanding ourselves, particularly understanding how we think, feel, act, and relate to the world. All of these ways of understanding contribute to personal value, which then naturally leads to valuing others.

We have devoted two chapters to each of these temperaments, the first being an understanding of the thinking, feeling, and behavior of each of these temperaments, the second being the contentment and acceptance that can come by understanding one's temperament. We then proceed to discuss the challenges (difficulties) that each temperament has. We include a chapter devoted to how people can mature within their own temperament and add to their nature elements of other temperaments. Our final chapter is an examination of the positive connections that can occur between people with these four different temperaments as well as the combinations of temperaments that many people have. While we do not shy away from the challenges that we all have in life, we focus on strengths of temperament in order to foster self-awareness and self-acceptance before tackling the challenges that every temperament finds in life. Our hope and desire in the present volume is to help people understand themselves by seeing their temperament, value temperament, and enhance the expression of this temperament in their work, relationships, and life at large. If people can first value their own temperament, they can then avoid the dangers of indulging their temperamental nature, and they can relate better to people of different natures. We, Deb and Ron, are quite different in temperament as are our two daughters. So, let's start by telling you firsthand how these four temperaments have operated in our own family, hoping to give you a basic first-hand glimpse into this thing we call temperament.

OUR FAMILY OF TEMPERAMENTS

Our own family of four is composed of Ron (husband and dad) who is primarily caretaker, Deb (wife and mother) who is primarily analyst, Krissie (daughter and sister), who was primarily player and lover and Jenny (daughter and sister) who is primarily lover and caretaker. By chance, we represent the four temperaments that we have briefly described and will describe further in this book. When we started writing this book, we didn't realize the fact that we actually had a family composed of four people representing the four temperaments. The more we wrote, the more we became aware that between the four of us, all four of the temperaments are represented in significant ways. No one is singularly only one temperament, something that we will discuss later. Rather, people are usually composed of a primary temperament and a secondary temperament with the third and fourth temperament playing a reduced role in their lives. Our goal would be that everyone we work with become first familiar with their primary and secondary temperaments and then begin to become aquatinted with what is often the lesser developed portions of their temperament. Our two daughters both have substantial characteristics of the lover temperament, but daughter Krissie was more predominantly player and secondarily lover and then a portion of the caretaker while Jenny is primarily lover and secondarily caretaker with some player following in line. In fact, both Deb and Ron have secondary player characteristics, so some of the glue that held our family together was this player part in all of us that went beyond the challenges of life by finding travel and games as a balance from the chores of life. We have loved each other dearly as most people love their families, and we have shared an immense number of experiences together like running out of gas on the Interstate, sharing traditional Swedish Christmas meals, traveling to Italy, spending time at our cabin in northern Wisconsin and simply making beds and doing the dishes and trying to get the homework in on time. We have not enjoyed all these experiences, but some of them remain in our hearts and minds forever and have fused us together for eternity. We have had our challenges, most of which have come from our very profound differences in personality. As we noted, both of our girls were strong lovers and that was the weakest of our temperaments so we failed in comprehending in those early years how those differences played a role in our conflicts. Even so, as we have matured, we have slowly come to realize that our challenging differences in personality have also been a means of learning about each other and people at large.

In giving you a snapshot of our family, we hope to give you a glimpse of what the following chapters are about. We believe that understanding one's individual temperament is an important part of the foundation of much of the rest of life, most importantly how we deal with people who have different temperaments. Our relationships with other people are intractably involved in the interaction of people with different temperaments. These relationships can be those of intimacy, good friendship, extended family, work setting, play setting, and even the casual encounter with the cashier at the grocery store. We think that if you really understand yourself, you will really like yourself, and when that happens, you will be in a position to really understand other people, and even begin to like someone who you have otherwise disliked, or at least, understand them. But before we go too much into how we interact with other people, consider the four people in our own family as representatives of the four temperaments we will describe in this book. It is important for us to note that our daughter, Krissie, died three years prior to our finishing writing this book. Yet she lives in our hearts and our memories as a playful and loving person and clearly displays one of the four temperaments we will present to you. While this book isn't about our family, we want to introduce you to the family of temperaments through our own examples. Here's our family of temperaments:

Player Krissie: Daughter and Sister

Krissie was just four when I (Deb) first met her. I was "clowning" in the local mall and was in the play area where Krissie was playing with some other kids. Krissie didn't recognize me in my clown suit, but I knew who Krissie was because I knew her father. She came up to me without any hesitation and with unabated pomp told me that she had ruffles on her panties and asked if I would like to see them? Before I had a chance to answer her question, she lifted up her little dress and showed me her ruffles. Then she invited me to do summersaults on the floor, which I did. Children show their true natures early in life if allowed to do so. Krissie demonstrated her "player" nature in those moments without hesitation, without embarrassment, and without fear of rejection. She demonstrated how wonderfully delightful a player can be.

Eventually I became a part of Krissie's house and home after this chance meeting in the mall. I then had the opportunity to watch Krissie's player nature in all its glory as she continued to grow up. Krissie would skip around the house; she would sing and dance around with abandon; she would grab your hand in hers and smile and with that smile and hand, invite you to play with her. When she was still a child, i.e., before adolescence, Krissie's play was always physical and always looking for some kind of experience. She had an intense drive to engage the world at full speed, something that didn't change throughout her life. We can now laugh recalling how in early high school she accidently broke her foot because she was jumping around the living room and happened to catch her foot under the base of the couch. The next day when she went to school in a cast, she proudly told her friends she broke her foot learning to ski! Krissie wasn't "lying" she was playing. It was simply more fun and exciting to have broken her foot skiing than knocking it on a boring old couch! Always ready for a hug, or grab on your back, or some kind of complex high-5, she could not be ignored. Her presence was as visible as it was dramatic.

Krissie's player/experiential nature was not only physical. She loved the experience of relationships and the words that are a part of any relationship. She loved to engage people verbally in any way possible, always friendly and always inviting. She would tease anyone at any time, whether friends, family, adults, or children. She would tell stories, listen to stories, and tell friendly lies or profound truths without concern of rejection or offense. She would engage in philosophical conversations espousing her belief system hoping that she would hear someone else's beliefs feeling that this kind of engagement was the way of the world. Her forthcoming and engaging nature drew people into conversations that sometimes led to lasting relationships. She assumed that relationships were based on the experience of openness. Importantly, Krissie loved to laugh and to get others to join in with her. At her celebration of life one of her aunt's spoke of her laughter, and we all nodded knowing that her boisterous laugh was filled with brightness and a genuine joy in experiencing of life.

Krissie's engagement of people included men when she reached adolescence and never stopped until she left us on this earth. She was married twice, divorced twice, and had many men before, after and in between her marriages. She freely introduced us to the men with whom she had found favor always seeking our connection in hopes that we, too, would find the excitement she found in these men. While she always asked for our input and understanding of the men she became interested in, in the end, men were accepted or rejected depending on whether or not they had "spark." For Krissie any relationship was about "spark", it there was no spark, there was no lasting relationship. Krissie had a good deal of the lover temperament characteristics of connecting, which was possibly part of the "spark" that she needed with any boyfriend. Furthermore, it seems that her romances were more about romantic thrill than about lasting relationships.

Players need spark, whether in relationships, work, family, or play. They depend on the immediacy of excitement in the experience. They need some kind of excitement in any event, thought, chore, or person. This excitement, as we have said, is very often physical, but it could just as well be intellectual, deeply personal, or outrageously against social norms. Players *seek* attention for sure, but they can just as easily *render* attention if they are interested in the person, the place, the idea, or the subject. There is usually an entertainment quality of players that could come out with free dancing on the street, a deep philosophical conversation, a genuine full body hug, or "holding court" on some subject that is important to them. Their entertaining nature is a means that allows them to engage and experience, not just perform.

Players know the emotion of joy at an intimate level. They trust joy. They trust fun. They trust laughter. Laughter, fun, and joy blend in perfect harmony for players when they are at their best. We happen to think that now Krissie often dances along Orion's belt, convinced that when we look up at the southern night sky, we can see her playing in the stars. We enjoy speaking to her when we have a clear night, and sometimes it seems she speaks back to us, always with a twinkle and a smile. Certainly, she is now at her best with the freedom that she has always needed.

Lover Jenny: Daughter and Sister

Over the past years since Krissie's passing from this world we have had the opportunity to review how we raised the girls, both who were very tenderhearted, but quite different in most other ways. Upon reflection of our years with our daughters we see that we didn't always give Jenny her due in the household. Jenny, being a gentle and quite person by nature, added to her deep loving nature, was easier to just "let be."

Jenny's nature hasn't changed in the recent years, but we have changed in recognizing her as a lover. As we will explain in great detail throughout this book, we all tend to see people through our own eyes, or our own temperament and in so doing fail to recognize the significant differences in others. Because both of us have a significant player element, we were able to see and engage the player that Krissie was but because neither of us has a strong lover component, we were not as inclined to see and appreciate Jenny in her lover nature. Krissie saw the world as something to be explored and experienced while lover Jenny saw the world as a place to connect, accept, and love people in both simple and profound ways. While our daughters both loved people, their love was substantially different: Krissie could easily abide by the "love the one you're with" song, while Jenny's love for people was more intimate, more personal, and more long-lasting. Such is the case with lovers like Jenny: they love deeply and they love forever. Jenny has always been a "love you forever" person. When she was but an infant and into her toddler years people would stop and comment on her peaceful and calm demeanor. More than once people offered comments such as "there is something special about her" or "you have a very special little girl there." We continue to see that godly characteristic in Jenny which all lovers possess: their deep sense of love and connection with everyone.

Jenny and we recently spent a few days together at the Florida Keys where we saw, better than we have ever seen, her basic nature: Her ease in life and certainly in loving. She is as easy now as she was when she was a child. She lives easy, she plays easy, she works easy, and she loves easy. In fact, she sometimes says of herself that she is "easy peasy." As we sat on our deck of the beach house we rented, we specifically asked her what she might want to do: some excursion, an exhibit, or other outing. She responded that we were doing just what she most liked to do; sit together, hang out, just being with one another. Later on, still sitting on the deck, the three of us continuing to "hang out" she told us again, in her gentle, yet matured manner, that she *simply* enjoyed hanging out with us, and that just being together was all that she ever had wanted. This simplicity of loving and being together is typical of all lovers. Lovers just want to feel connected to the people they love. This easy-peasy nature that Jenny displays is not exactly the same with all lovers but it tends to be a central ingredient as we will discuss in Chapter 4. Lovers' connection is a kind of blending of spirits between two people. The situation, the place, the job, the play are all secondary. Primary is the feeling of connection. Simply put, Jenny is and always has been easy to please largely because she doesn't ask so much of the world as she intends to give love to the world in any way she can.

When Jenny was about six, her paternal grandmother, Margaret, took her to the local dime store to buy her birthday gifts. Grandma put her in the cart and strolled the isles until Jenny saw something she wanted. Margaret related to us that after they put her selection in the cart, and asked her what *else* she wanted, that Jenny replied: "I have *enough*, Grandma." When lovers, as little girls or grown women and men are connected, they have enough. When she was shopping with Grandma, she simply appreciated the element of connection associated with Grandma buying her something. It wasn't the item; it was the connection she had with Grandma in the gift-seeking and gift-buying. Riding in the cart with her beloved Grandmother alongside was what she most wanted and needed. She certainly wouldn't have wanted to disturb Grandma, or anyone in the store for that matter, by asking for too much and running the risk of losing the connection she might have with anyone. This acceptance and easy gratitude blend in with her desire for peace and harmony in connection, something we will explore about lovers in depth later. Jenny always was a peacemaker, and she remains so. Argument is just not in her nature. Arguments disrupt connection.

Not only is Jenny disinclined to conflict and very inclined to connection, she does not hold grudges against people who have offended her. The ability and desire to forgive is an important ingredient of lovers as we shall see in Chapter 4. When a former boyfriend failed to pay on a car loan that Jenny had co-signed for him, ultimately creating a substantial financial burden, we heard no complaints about the boyfriend, just grief that her credit score had been damaged. More importantly, she holds no grudges against us as analyst and caretaker parents for being less of what she would have desired in terms of connections. She holds no grudges with her deceased sister despite the fact that Krissie often bullied Jenny, taking advantage of her sister's easy and quite nature.

An important part of people with a lover temperament is their tendency to be generous. While in the Keys Jenny voiced a specific "thank you" for everything, from an elaborate dinner to a simple coffee. Nothing was taken without a genuine appreciation. She frequently offered to provide for us even though the trip was, in its design, a college graduation gift to her. And just as frequent as her appreciation was her offer to take care of us, be it buying the coffee, providing the tip for a meal, or asking us what we would like to do. She just wanted to share and be generous. For lovers, sharing is connection. We experience her tenderness and appreciation in her emails and texts almost as if we were hearing the quintessential "Ooh's and Aah's" that are so common with lovers. We have come to recognize that these are not just emotional accents; they are genuine felt connections. We yet get real cards, like paper cards mailed with stamps on them, for each and everything we might give to Jenny. Her words and gestures could make for any good Hallmark thank you card. Jenny is human, and in being so, she is imperfect, but in matters of love, she is the demonstration of the Apostle Paul's note that "love is the greatest of gifts." As you consider that you might be a lover, or have a lover friend or family member, consider these generous, easy-going, connection-seeking characteristics before we discuss the joys of lovers in Chapter 4 and their challenges in Chapter 8.

Caretaker Ron: Husband and Dad
Ron is always busy. If he isn't writing this book, some other book, some blog, some email, or some text, working with patients, or writing up neuropsychological reports, he is busy doing something else be it vacuuming the office, filling the cars up with gas or running errands. Shortly before we married, Ron

bought a very unique building in the city of Council Bluffs, where we spent most of our years together as a family. This was the building that formally housed the local YMCA in the city. It is notable that this was a building nearly 100 years old, quite ornate on the outside and quite rough on the inside which made the cost of the building very cheap, at least to start with. We could tell you more about this building's history, like it serving the railroad as a place to stay as well as a rooming house for homeless people as most YMCA buildings did in their earlier days.

The very fact that Ron bought this very old building that was in great disrepair represents how Ron approaches life: just do it. Ron was not brought up in a family where he learned to do expert carpentry, so he was not well-prepared to restore this 5-story building to its former glory, which was his hope along with establishing a holistic health center in the building. Soon, it became obvious that this was much more of a project than we could do together, even though our friends and daughters helped us a great deal. We lived, worked, played, and entertained in this building for 20 years. We learned a lot during those years, including what was possible and what was impossible to do with our limited resources. Over those 20 years Ron learned a bit of all the tradesmen skills like carpentry, plumbing, electrical, and heating…albeit with many mistakes made along the way. We offer this as an example of something that caretakers like Ron do, replete with successes, disappointments, failures, and hopes. Caretakers tend to take such things as repair and maintenance as necessary in life and not to be indulged with complaints and defenses. Caretakers assume that if something needs done, they can do it.

While the 20-year project was the most dramatic example of Ron's doing nature, he has always been a doer. He was the primary person who took care of the property his parents owned on a lake in Wisconsin including building a retaining wall at the waterfront, reworking the septic system, painting the boat every year and other activities that his parents and siblings were less inclined to do. This caretaking and doing nature that Ron continues in our present life where he regularly repairs our old office/barn as needed, cares for much of the rest of the property, and does his share of household duties. In a way, his whole life is about caretaking, very often taking care of people by taking care of property. Even his writing, which is his current primary passion, is a kind of caretaking, or doing, as it is he who does all the first drafts of our books and certainly he who uses his grammatical skills to communicate more accurately.

Ron is a person who is particularly responsive to needs, whether those needs are for property care or repair or for a stranger who displays some other emotional or logistical need. You can see Ron opening doors for people who are behind him at the entry to a store or helping someone carry a piece of furniture to her car. Once, while traveling in the Netherlands, we saw a young woman struggling to balance a wicker loveseat on her bicycle. We chuckled and, as I shook my head, we both immediately knew what he was going to do. So up to this stranger Ron went, paused her, just took the love seat off the bike, hoisted it on his shoulders and asked where she was going. Much to the woman's surprise, relief and chagrin, she led us a few blocks to her flat asking "who are you, why are you helping me?" We simply assured her we were silly Americans visiting her homeland. All she could do was shake her head and laugh. Why would a stranger do this? Because he is a care-taker. He does these things easily and without any feeling of obligation, but rather out of love of taking care of things. His primary orientation to our family was taking care of property and people, not so much the experience/player nature of Krissie nor the connection/easy nature of Jenny.

Analyst Deb, Wife, and Mom

Analysts are easy to describe succinctly but they are the hardest of the temperaments for people to understand. We will discuss in Chapter 3 that analysts are always looking to make things better by understanding things so that they can find problems, solve problems and prevent problems. But as we shall see, this problem-orientation frequently causes offense, which we will discuss in Chapter 7. Deb is an analyst and she wouldn't want to be anything else even though it has been a challenge in her life, not only in our family but with extended family and friendships. Having an analyst for a wife is one thing, but having an analyst as a mom is a challenge especially for two girls who shared so much of the lover temperament. What is the challenge? Her very nature: understanding based on problem-seeking and problem-solving, which as we will discuss in detail, is about as far from being lover as you can get.

What does it mean to say that Deb is a problem-oriented person? It means that Deb is constantly looking to make things *better*, whether the things are physical projects, the clients in her office, the rest of her family, or the world at large. In order to be a problem-solver, you have to see things, you have to read things, you have to listen, and you have to connect the dots between things. In order to do problem-solving and the other activities that analysts do Deb has to know things. She knows many things, most by close and intimate observation and other ways of gathering information, but she also knows things by her intuitional ability. However, before she even knows things, she has to gather information. So, this is what Deb does most of the time: listen, watch, read, study, and muse. We can dare to say that when it comes to knowing how the world operates, whether with things practical, philosophical, theological, or otherwise theoretical, Deb knows things. Had she grown up in a family that had encouraged her analytical skills and natural scientific examination, she might have been a research psychologist instead of a clinical psychologist.

This passion for problem-solving that is based on a passion for analysis, which in turn is based on information, makes Deb a person who is curious. There is nothing that escapes her inquisitive nature, whether the process of things in her garden and greenhouse, the clients in her office, or how quantum theory really explains things. The curious nature that Deb has leads not only to gathering information and examining information but also to formulating ideas or theories about how things work. Again: these "things" might be property and machines or people and their relationships. Her passion for understanding that leads to ideas is the groundwork of her professional work. Her greatest pleasure is to have a client say, "Well, that makes sense." when she has offered an analysis as a way of helping the client understand how something didn't work or could work better. As there is no end to inquiry, there is no end to Deb's passion for learning, analyzing, and problem-solving to make the world a better place to live.

Deb's place in our family and contribution she made to the family lies in and around both her information-based curiosity as well as her player excitement orientation. Early in the marriage she initiated Ron and the girls to travel, camping, hiking, and other elements of nature. It was she who thought we should go to Disneyland and then cross over to Mexico for a few days. It was she that said we should go to the Outer Banks of North Carolina, the wild rivers of western Canada, the Head Waters of the Mississippi, to say nothing of going to Italy with both girls when they were adults. In fact, though this might sound inappropriate to some, but exciting certainly to the players, it was she who suggested we "open" a nude deserted beach on the Outer Banks, just the four of us. And then, to the delight and somewhat relief to us all, realized that a couple who saw us took the plunge and joined in the freedom from clothes, albeit a little down the shore. It was she, in fact, who said, "Yes, apply. Let's go!" when Ron found an opportunity to work in St. John's Newfoundland, Canada, a move that proved to be one of the most important decisions of the family, the marriage, and the direction we took in our private practice of psychology. It is this initiative of Deb the analyst however, that often ends in instruction at best and criticism at worst.

Somewhat because she is an analyst, but also because her secondary temperament is that of a player, she experiences most everything through all five of her senses. Ron alleges that she has eight or nine senses including intuition. Deb uses her senses to collect information. She smells, sees, tastes, hears and touches as if she were a living antenna. And then she passes this information on to anyone who is willing to listen. In fact, if you are willing to listen, and perhaps wade through all the information, all the analysis, and all the musings, you will most certainly learn something. It is almost impossible for an analyst like Deb to contain what she knows, perhaps because her "cup overflows" with knowledge and analysis. And if you take her advice…always given with the best of intention to help you be a better person…you will, indeed profit from it. Knowledge for an analyst is like connection for a lover, movement for a player, or doing for a caretaker.

A FAMILY OF TEMPERAMENTS: A SUMMARY

We provide you with three major sections in this book. First, we look carefully at each of the four temperaments in Chapters 1-4 identifying the primary characteristics. We will unpack the experience-seeking of players, the property-care of caretakers, the connection-orientation of lovers, and the problem-solving of analysts. In the second section, Chapters 5-8, we will discuss the challenges that the four temperaments have as well as suggestions for successful relationships with each of the four temperaments. In Chapter 9 we discuss how we can mature in life, first by understanding our own temperaments together with the joys and sorrows that we all have. Then, we discuss how we can add to our basic temperamental orientations the characteristics of the other temperaments. Finally, in Chapter 10 we give numerous examples of how people with two different primary temperaments both engage and how they communicate. In these examples of people who have matured their temperaments, you will find both assurance of your own temperament and encouragement to mature the other temperaments into your daily life.

As we look more closely at all four temperaments, be reminded that everyone has some elements of all four: player, caretaker, lover, and analyst. As you read these chapters, consider how your nature might approximately fall into one or two of these temperaments as your primary strengths while becoming more aware of how to develop the lesser portions into full maturity. As we begin a more in-depth analysis of the four temperaments, allow us to give you a snapshot of what is to follow:

Basic Nature of the Four Temperaments

Players:	Experience
Caretaker:	Care of Property
Lovers:	Human Connection
Analysts:	Meaning and Understanding

Relational Characteristic of the Four Temperaments

Players:	Engage
Caretakers:	Provide and Protect
Lovers:	Sacrifice and Blend
Analysts:	Analyze and Improve

"Spiritual" Orientation for the Four Temperaments

Players:	Excitement
Caretakers:	Property
Lovers:	People
Analysts:	Truth

Now that we have hopefully given you a provocative snapshot for what is to come, we invite you to engage, provide, blend, and analyze what we present. We need to advise you that no one is only one thing, whether one temperament or one personality type. We are all wonderfully made and we are all different. In the chapters to follow, you may find yourself identifying primarily with one of the four temperaments as we describe them, pieces of two or more temperaments. Furthermore, you may see yourself as having some of the characteristics on one temperament but not all of what we suggest typifies these temperaments. We offer this temperament analysis to help you understand yourself, certainly not to put you in some kind of psychological box. Read on, enjoy, challenge, learn, and find a way to use what we have come to learn is one way of true self-understanding that always leads to a better understanding of other people.

Chapter 1

The Player Personality

PLAYERS NEED TO EXPERIENCE life. As much of life as possible. They can't just watch life; they have to jump right into it. If players had life the way they think life should be, they would bounce from mountain-top to mountain-top, figuratively or literally. Players thrive on excitement. Excitement comes from experience, especially experience that is new and different. For players life is either exciting or boring, and there is little in between. When they are at their best, they are fully involved with all areas of their lives. This near-constant excitement-seeking is done first in mind, then in body, and then in relationships. One of the ways you can spot player*s* when they are at their best is by their *eyes*: curious, excited, inviting, and "wide-eyed." This wide-eyed nature of players reflects their openness to adventure and discovery, whether this is a new idea, a new person, or a new physical experience. Players will settle for nothing less than experience, adventure, and excitement.

Players are the most outstanding of the four temperaments, which means that: they *stand out*. They are wonderful people. In fact, they are quite "full of wonder." Wonder and all that goes with it is one of their primary hallmarks. Players want to explore, discover and engage. Because of their innate curiosity players seek to find fun, excitement, and play in all matters of life, whether with property, words, physical activity, or with people. Reflect on Shakespeare's Puck in *A Midsummer's Night Dream*, and you will find a brilliant representation of a player and begin to grasp the nature of this temperament. Puck is full of spunk, activity, and curiosity. He is a jester at heart. He teases, he cajoles, he excites, and he entertains. It is the dream of most players to be a Puck-like person in the world bringing joy, fun, and excitement to all who know them.

We have known many players in our life, and we admit that each of us has a good dose of player in our individual natures. Ron's primary nature is caretaker and Deb's primary nature is analyst but we both have secondary player natures. We can both look back at our childhood days where we explored, experienced, and engaged whatever we did with player-like vigor and enthusiasm. Doubtless, either of us could have been diagnosed with a host of currently popular mental health conditions, but the deeper reality is that we were intent on experiencing the physical world to the fullest extent. Ron heard the stories of his maternal grandmother saying to his mother, "You're never going to raise that child!" or when his maternal aunt went chasing toddler "Ronny" down the street when he was stark naked. Deb remembers the experience exploring the fields of Indiana for hours without any kind of supervision, uninhibited with her eyes wide open to every tree to climb and river bank to splash through pretending to be Lewis and Clark. Ron played table games, backyard games, and sports games, usually with people, while Deb more often played alone due to her introverted nature as she explored the universes of reality and fantasy. Note that we were both "players" by temperament but also that we were quite different in other aspects of our psychological functioning, something that we shall explore later. No two people are perfectly alike, and no two players are alike. Yet, there are many similarities among players that help us understand this temperament. Our older daughter, Krissie, as we noted in the introduction had a large player piece to her personality. Like Ron, Krissie was also very extraverted. She would engage just about anyone she met with both genuine interest in connecting with them as well as an excitement to simply engage and see what play might come about. She was always looking for excitement whether this excitement was with a new person, a new place, or a new experience. Krissie was the consummate player who challenged many traditional rules and often paid the price, like a broken foot, a broken glass, or a broken heart. But when she was at her best, she was simply exhilarating.

We call these folks "players" because they *play* with life, whether ideas, people, or physical experience. It is a bit too easy to say that players are interested in "play," however true that might be, because play sounds frivolous. Play is anything but frivolous to players. They take their play very seriously and it is very important to them. Players have the *gift* of playing. All humans play in some way in order to enjoy the world, and most animals play to learn how to engage the world during their maturing years. Players play because they are compelled to play, and it is their best gift to the world. This gift of playing can bring a certain knowledge of the world, knowledge of oneself, and a knowledge of potential limitlessness of life. Players give the world joy. As with all four of the temperaments, players' basic nature is profoundly good. To understand players, we first need to understand how they see the world, how they evaluate the world, and to understand their basic value system.

In a way, players have a kind of childlike view of the world, a kind of innocent belief that they can say anything or do anything in order to experience all that is possible to experience in the world. During the first year of life infants ideally get everything that they want, but they really don't want much. In fact, infants' wants and needs are nearly simultaneous. Infants just need to be fed, comforted, and nurtured. But when they reach toddlerhood, things change dramatically because now they can walk and talk as well as run, scream, and throw things as they begin to discover more of life. There is nothing wrong with toddlers wanting to explore the world as it is wonderful to watch this exploration and challenging of boundaries. There is more learning going on during the toddler years than any other time of life. Players seem to retain this view that the world is a place to explore, challenge, and otherwise engage because it is interesting and exciting. Even though these characteristics are common to all players, not all players are alike.

TYPES OF PLAYERS

Free Players
Children require "free play" in order to develop and to enhance their creativity and independent thinking. A child's free play is spontaneous activity that engages property, people, and the physical and imaginary environment

without direction. You see children engaging in free play with the physical environment when they do something that *seems* to have no purpose, like swinging their arms, spontaneously dancing, running, climbing, or twirling themselves around. Yesterday, we had the opportunity of watching two young boys playing at the seaside with their parents watching. One of the boys was just running into the water and then out on the sand making circles and flapping his arms as he ran. Asked by his dad what he was doing, this young man innocently replied, "Just playing." We were privileged to be raised at a time, largely in the 1950's where most children were instructed to "go and out play" possibly followed by "dinner is at 6." We often see our neighbors' sons free-playing with the ropes and swings that their dad has constructed for them.

For many players free play is essentially physical but free play can be more personal than physical, which means that the player person, child or adult, gets lost in a myriad of thoughts. Such a person might be seen staring off as if seeing an apparition. That same person might then spontaneously laugh, scream, or cry for no apparent reason. Likely, she has been so lost in thoughts, dreams, and visions that she was free-playing…all by herself. While free play in children looks like it has no purpose, it is a way that they are mastering the world and their own engagement in the world, both the external world and their own internal world.

Free play, regardless of temperament, allows a child to learn to navigate the physical world first, the personal world second, and eventually the interpersonal world, in order to find safety and pleasure. Free play helps a child experience the excitement of exploration, and then discover the limits that are implicit in all things. A child who climbs up on the bed is playing with the bed and playing with her body as she explores the possibility of such climbing. This same child also finds that it is possible to fall off the bed and bump her head on the dresser. She learns that it is possible to find the excitement of jumping on the bed while also learning the limits of such an activity. Free play helps children learn the possibilities and the limits of the physical world and the limits of their physical bodies. Free play is so much about discovering and creating a connection with the environment.

People that we call *free players* are particularly oriented towards the exploration, engagement, and excitement of doing something or saying something that is completely spontaneous, sometimes without regard for the consequences of their words or action. Like free-playing children, adult free players may walk into your office and pick up a letter opener from your desk and in one fell swoop shift into a forward knee stance, extend the letter opener towards your belly and exclaim "on guard!", then just as quickly withdraw the letter opener, return it to your desk and chuckle with a shrug of their shoulders and sit down to work. That brief playful moment is indicative of players' need for immediate excitement and filling that need with a common object transformed with a flash of imagination. Adult players have retained the childlike spirit of exploration and challenge, and they can be found in all walks of life, all professions, and in all relationships. They do not need to be professional athletes, musicians, or actors in order to do something physical, musical, or dramatic. They do not need a piano, a stage, or a basketball court in order to play. They can find simple spontaneous play in any medium. There is always something to play with and there is always someone to play with. We call these folks "free players" because their play is freely displayed at any time, at any place, and with anyone. Free players are satisfied with the random opportunity to play and go with the flow of it, letting one moment lead them to the next moment. Spontaneous engagement is the name of the game for these folks. Some players go the distance in training and discipline in order to hone a specific area of play, but most free players just play all the time, or try to play all the time. Individuals who engage in extreme sports may be free players who have honed their skills, but this is a small minority of free players. Most free players do not require great distance, expense, and skill to enjoy their free play nature. They don't even need the opportunity for play because they make their own opportunities. Free players can find play in any environment if they have enough freedom to do so. Ron frequently free plays with some random person at the grocery store, like yesterday when he wanted to "be assured that these donuts were sugar-free, fat-free, and gluten-free". Deb plays best in her garden house often talking to plants and flowers without hesitation and embarrassment. Jenny free plays when she texts us, always with a flurry of emoticons. Krissie was always ready to free play with anyone, at any time, and with anything. You cannot trust players to be cautious, or even "appropriate" in their free playing because their intent is to engage the world in play as much as possible.

A few years ago, we spent a week in Iceland with our good friend, Tim. All three of us have strong player elements in our natures, which frequently showed up. Several times while hiking in Iceland, we would all go in different directions and find our way back together after an hour or two. On one occasion, Deb and Tim were hiking together and I took a different route and got ahead of them. So, I climbed up a little knoll, waited for the pair of them to pass by, and carefully threw rocks in their hiking path while I kept hidden for a few moments and chuckled quietly while they looked up for dangerous rock falls only to eventually see me grinning unmercifully. Two or three days later, when Deb and I were together enjoying a bit of privacy under a beautiful waterfall, it was Tim who had scrambled up the backside of the falls and plopped a couple of large rocks into the water. We reflexively started to bolt but just happened to look up and of course, there was our player friend returning the favor I had previously bestowed on him.

Tim had the remarkable opportunity to use his player side in his profession as Outdoor Recreation Director at the University of Colorado. Most players do not have such privilege. Now retired, Tim tells us sometimes he gets on his horse and "just rides" to see where he might go and what he might find. Other free players might do this kind of exploration in writing, singing, playing guitar, hiking, playing volleyball, driving, reading, or day-dreaming. Free players can sit and dream for an hour or more and enjoy their travels to various parts of the universe. Our grandson, Gavin, can sit on the dock at our cabin in northern Wisconsin for hours, evidently just dreaming. Video games can be a great way for free players to find free play, which many free players find enticing and exciting, just like some people get lost in the characters of books they read.

There are many opportunities for free play depending on one's particular inclination and the opportunity that one's environment provides. Deb had the fun experience of "dancing" with Matt Harding a number of years ago when he came to Madison. Matt, a self-described "non-dancer" initially created the opportunity of traveling the world in sponsorship of chewing gum and then became his own international sensation doing his funny little jig. Deb's reflection of Matt is that he was a "free player" who found a way to enjoy his passion for traveling and get paid for it by people who sponsored him. Robin Williams found free play in drama and stand-up comedy. We know of a lawyer who free-plays in his work, albeit with a certain amount of discretion. We know of several therapists who are great at "play therapy" with children because they tap into their own player natures. More than once, Ron has been called "Dr. Marbles" because he often plays marbles with young patients as a way of engaging them. A child whom a parent has described as incorrigible can sit on the floor with Ron shooting marbles, listening to instruction, taking turns, and being fully engaged, things the parent reports never happen, possibly because the experience is new, different, physical, and interactive. While teaching children floor games Ron has the opportunity of observation of their demeanor and interactional capacity by tapping into that player part of himself.

Free players who have found fame, fortune, and freedom are rare. Most free players are not as concerned with the professionalism of their play as they are the adventure of their play even though they may easily have a natural talent towards such. They don't want to put the work into developing a professional play skill like sports, music, or drama. They might fantasize being on Broadway, playing guitar to a large audience, or being in the Final Four basketball tournament, but rarely would they do what is necessary to achieve such success. A free player who likes acting might simply enjoy his dramatic flair in spontaneous moments just as a free-player sports person can be fully satisfied in a local pick-up game. More typically, free players just want to play at any time and with anyone. Ron recently saw a child brought into the office by his father who is concerned that his son displays no interest, much less passion, for academics. Ron asked this young man what he might like to do if he "could be great at something." His immediate...and his only...answer to the question was that he wanted to "'play."

Free players who are more introverted by nature might engage in quiet games of chess with friends, or perhaps doing some kind of artistic endeavor with paint, pencil, or clay. But the largest majority of players don't even seek these structured and organized times to play. They would rather just play with whatever is in front of them and whoever is in front of them. They find more joy in poking a friend in the butt, making some kind of spontaneous word play, or finding a way to use an old bathtub as a part of a garden. The key word for free players is *free*. But not all players are of the free type, doing spontaneous fun things. Some are quite serious in their play.

Professional Players

Many players have found a way to play for a living. Professional players get paid for playing, usually in one of the professions that uses the word *play*, like flute *players*, Shakespearean *players*, or volleyball *players*. People who are outstanding or particularly successful in a play-based profession have refined their orientation to play towards one area and developed their skill to be able to sell their skills. These folks have focused their play with structure and discipline as a means of finding excellence in their chosen profession. Professional players can be found in almost any profession including the traditional play-based professions of music, athletics, and drama as well as such widely diverse occupations as chess, computer programming, politicking, photography, and the military. The Army, which has an inordinate number of players in it, employs video game players who orchestrate drone attacks on the enemy. Those people have found a way to play for a living but have added to their basic play orientation discipline and practice, something that free players tend to see as boring. Professional players have trusted their passion and then engaged a discipline that allows them to "play" for a living.

Some of the very best professional players become quite famous possibly because they combine the player-like element in their professions together with the work that it takes to become truly great in a field. We think it is the unexpected, unrehearsed, spontaneous element that is so typical of players that might contribute to some professionals who reach greatness. Consider the musicians James Galway on the flute, Yehudi Menuhin on the violin, or even Elvis Presley on the guitar…plus a certain hip movement that may have been player-made. There are many actors that come to mind when we think of players but none as outstanding as Robin Williams who often was given a loose script from which he could improvise his lines like he did in "Good Morning Vietnam." Many more athletes come to mind including the likes of several boxers, like Muhammad Ali who most certainly "played" while he boxed. Look at your favorite actor, musician, or athlete and see if you can see the person displaying player characteristics.

It behooves us to note that everyone who plays pro hockey, performs on the big screen, or sculpts marvelous figurines out of marble and sells them for thousands of dollars does not necessarily have a player personality. People of other temperaments can be very successful in these play-based occupations, but they approach their work from a different perspective and purpose. A typical complement for some athletes is that they are "workers," which we might suggest is a term we assign to caretakers. While a few chess masters might be players, the bulk of them are probably *analysts*. Player nurses might find a way to play in their work but majority of nurses are caretakers or lovers. We will study caretakers, analysts, and lovers in later chapters. Free players and professional players share interest in the new and exciting, but extreme players take playing to a whole different level.

Extreme Players

People we call extreme players engage in some athletic discipline that affords them the opportunity to include significant risk in the sport as well as the highest level of discipline. I have two of these women in my current practice, both doing half-iron marathons. One of the women speaks of her desire to work hard and do her best, to press herself. She conditions relentlessly and with a drive that supersedes everything else in her life. The other woman speaks of the intense spiritual connection she finds with the environment as she swims, bikes and runs as well as the intensity of a felt sense of connection with the other participants. In my recent session with her she was preparing to leave town the next day for an event out of state. She was buoyant with happiness and excitement. As we dialoged about it, she mentioned the spiritual connection we just noted, and added that when she was in her event she felt "whole, one with herself." While this particular woman plays to master her own discipline, her play of engagement with the environment and her comrades supersedes the will to win. I believe that this woman is a close combination of player then lover, wanting the trill of excitement in racing yet requiring an intense connection with the other contestants. Whenever we watch the Olympics, we can't help but admire the absolute determination of the participants to give their all, to play fully and compete for the gold. Other extreme players speak only of the exhilaration of the moment. Andy, our "adopted" son from Sweden who spent his senior year of high school with us, enjoys such sports. When he was here recently showing us a video of his recent base jump off a mountain in Norway, we could feel the adrenalin with him as he described his own sensations when he took that leap. We sat around the table and as he showed us the video he giggled, and it was my sense he was reliving that absolute thrill of playing the dare to fly. As a professional pilot, he also engages his player nature but with more reserve, of course.

"Just Players"

Most players do not fall cleanly into free playing, professional playing or extreme playing: they *just play* whenever possible. Whether free playing, professional playing, or just playing, players have the natural gift of play that may be focused on one area or in several areas. What all these players have in common is bodies and minds that are oriented towards the excitement and joy that comes from curiosity and engagement: the weekend hiker who plays at spotting the owl's nest or stop to watch an ant tow his load, or the local actress who may be skilled enough to be on Broadway but isn't interested in giving her whole life to just one realm of play. Many people play out of personal passion, a hobby, or simple retreat from their daily routine. Some players, probably extraverts, want an audience, while others, probably introverts, would prefer to play alone or in a select environment.

Most players are not expert in what they do for a living and do not need a stage, a ball field, or an instrument. These player people are the normal folks who go about their daily lives, their work, and their relationships with a play orientation. The primary focus of this chapter is on common people who have common abilities, minds, and bodies, but with an uncommon need for excitement that comes from experience. Vendors at art fairs just might be starving artists who enjoy their creations more than their sales. Gardeners, Deb among them, most certainly play with plants and flowers. Players who are in sales might find it fun and playful to engage customers and sell their wares and services. A patient of mine talked about his father, evidently a consummate salesman, who while driving with his family on vacation, once spotted a mall and exclaimed that he wished he could just go into the mall and "sell something." Players of this sort will be heard saying things like, "it's just fun, I just enjoy it", "I'm just playing at it" or "it's just play time for me." Bartenders, real estate agents, flight attendants, hair stylists, and many, many more speak of their work as play.

CHARACTERISTICS OF PLAYERS

Players' primary characteristics revolve around *experience*: engaging the world in ways that make life exciting. They bring to the world a high level of energy that shows itself in curiosity and adventure. They also have an internal sense of potential *greatness* that often leads to their desire to entertain. Yet players are more than their characteristics: they are people with the passion and purpose to enjoy life and want to make life enjoyable for everyone they meet. Players as we understand them are experiential, physical, entertaining, low boundary, and have a "felt greatness" in their nature.

1. **Experiential**

The experiential orientation of players includes curiosity, exploration, adventure, and newness. All of these experiences are exciting to players. The heart of players' experience-seeking is exploration. Prevent players from opportunities for experience, and you will prevent them from their natural zest for living. Players' lives start with being curious.

Curiosity

All people are born with some innate curiosity about the world. To be curious is to be excited about potential discovery. This multi-pronged attribute is natural for all young children but for players it remains a constant ingredient throughout their lives. The player needs to uncover the unknown and discover the hidden treasures beneath the surface to spark her curiosity. The player's curiosity is based on her basic belief that under every stone there is a diamond, under every leaf there is a remarkable insect, under every inanimate object there is something dynamic. Furthermore, the player believes that under every word, there are more words, under every feeling, there are more feelings, under every thought, there are more thoughts. There is always something exciting *underneath*. For the player, there "just has to be something more."

I fondly remember seeing our grandson, Gavin, being first capable of getting around on his own when he was about two. He would find a bug in our yard and become immediately fascinated with it. He would pick up the bug and just examine it as if he were looking through some portal into life itself. He would set the bug down (or more times than not, squish it) and then toddle on to something else that became his complete universe for a moment or a minute or more. This is a good representation of the naturalness of a child's curiosity that players maintain as they grow up. We watched the PBS series *The Durrells in Corfu* not long ago. If you are familiar with the series, recall the youngest son, Gerald, a naturalist who not only becomes curious of every creature he encounters, but in his own way, merges with these animals. Gerald is a picture of a young player at his best. He is fully involved with the curiosity he has for animals. Not all players are naturalists, but all players are curious about the vast areas of the world, and perhaps for the few players who enter the field of astronomy and cosmology, or oceanography this interest stretches from the depths of the sea to the outer reaches of the universe.

Exploration and Discovery

Exploration, and its cousin discovery, erupt from curiosity. Curiosity is often just for its own purpose: to go, to think, to see, to hear, and to experience something for its own sake. When you add exploration and discovery to the mix, the object of interest expands into a new adventure of potential discovery. Each exploration leads the player into a new thought, a new idea, or a new opportunity for further exploration. A gardener might leisurely walk through a path and then immediately stop to look at a budding yellow rose, but a player-gardener might poke her finger into the bud to see if the bud will stay open after she removes her finger. If it does, it is okay for her; if it doesn't, it is equally okay. She is just exploring and discovering. She might do the same poking and discovering with the geranium or the calendula that is just budding. A caretaker-gardener might spend more time caring for a plant than exploring it or understanding its nature. An analyst-gardener might do the same but for a very different purpose: understanding. Understanding is not the player's primary purpose in exploring, but it is often a byproduct of the exploration. Players don't necessarily have to *do* anything with what they explore and discover, they just want the *experience* of discovery. Perhaps you can begin to see the potential for conflict between a player's exploration and discovery compared to people of other temperaments, which we will discuss in Chapter 5.

Exploration and discovery can occur in many forms, both formal and informal:

- The geologist or anthropologist digging through rubble
    - Or the guy digging through the dumpster parked across the street from his house
- The professional bow hunter seeing how a new stabilizer works
    - Or the kid seeing how far up in the air he can shoot an arrow
- The professional guitar player putting together a new series of cords on his electric guitar
    - Or the amateur guitar player seeing how long he can hold a chord
    - Or the guy with no real musical talent who is great on the air guitar
- The swimmer working on a new technique with her butterfly stroke
    - Or the girl who tries to swim for two minutes underwater to "play dead"

Curiosity leads players to exploration, exploration leads to discovery, and discovery leads to adventure.

Adventure

Adventure combines the best of exploration and discovery but adds the important component of physical movement. This "movement" could actually be engaging the next chapter in an exciting book or another episode of *Star Trek* (we are Trekkers) but most of the time, adventure is about engaging exploration through physical movement. We will discuss the need for physical activity with players in more depth shortly, but for this short discussion, keep in mind that adventure for a player blends the exploration with something new, and the new is something that involves physical movement and activity.

An adventure for players is anything that takes them to where no one has been before. Adventure by its own definition implies a new experience.

Helen Keller once said that "Life is either a daring adventure or nothing". Very often adventure is about pressing the limits in some physical form. We were in Scandinavia a few years ago, among other things hiking glaciers. It was a beautiful sunny day and the adventure guide, our "Ice Troll", was gracious to extend the season for one day as we scurried to make this ice adventure happen. Once we had learned the ropes, literally, and how to "cowboy down" and "heel up" in our crampons across the glacier's ridges, we were ready to repel down into a moulin, functionally an abyss formed out of melting ice tunneling down through and under the glacier, from which, by the way, there is no return. You need to be careful around moulins. You fall in a moulin unsecured, you die. The whole day had already been a remarkable adventure for both of us. But by midafternoon while we sipped on hot chocolate and our guide was securing three different safety ropes into the ice in preparation for our descents into the moulin, Deb decided to get some close-up pictures of the moulin. She boldly exclaimed to us guys that "this might not be very pretty, but it will work" and promptly got down on her belly and started scooching towards the rim of the moulin. Within a second on her bellying down, our guide shouted at her to "toe in" meaning, dig her toe crampons into the ice. Then he firmly commanded her to carefully back up. Once Deb was in her original location, our guide shook his head and said "Your metal crampons adhere to the ice; your body melts the ice." Deb apologized and immediately recognized that while activating the player part of her personality, she had definitely pressed the limits too far. She was just exploring and seeking the adventure of a photograph of the moulin up close, but needed the professional reminder that it would take but one slip at the edge of the moulin, and she could have endangered all of us. We will discuss the dangers implicit in players' adventure-seeking later in Chapter 5 as well as other dangers in players' behavior.

Newness
Adventure is often about exploring something new. Newness is attractive to players because of the unknown element implicit in anything new. This could be through mental play with a new book, a new person, a new event, a new sheet of music, a new car, a new teacher, a new movie, or a new location. Many players spend a good deal of their money on new things, which we might

roughly call "toys." These toys can be specialty cars, perhaps car models, real cars, or even trading cards with pictures of cars on them. Players interested in video games might buy the newest version of some car-racing game, while other players might be compelled to have the newest laptop, cell phone or the most recent hybrid hydrangea or the newest fashion in sports gear. Newest doesn't necessarily mean best, much less the best buy for the buck. Newness means an opportunity to explore and experience the new "toy".

Newness doesn't necessarily have to be with physical objects. Player musicians might be good at playing popular tunes, but their real interest is in creating a new sound, a new music mix, or a new instrument with which to play a familiar tune. Ron remembers a time when he had become reasonably skilled at waterskiing and looked for different ways to play behind the motorboat. He tried to ride a table turned upside-down with modest success; he tried riding a log with complete failure, and finally then turned to more dangerous activities like putting the ski rope around his foot while skiing. He survived but not without some bruising and gulping of water. Ron's dad once drove Ron and some of his cousins the wrong way down a one-way street in Minneapolis which thoroughly entertained Ron and his player cousin, Chuck. Did his father want to endanger the kids? No, he just wanted to play.

Newness can also come with social engagement. Players are a rare commodity in typical group gatherings like church or service groups. But they might be fascinated with a new neighbor next door, a new person at church, or a new co-worker. Furthermore, players can be interested in something new that could come along with an old friend. Maybe a new conversation about an old topic. Maybe a new conversation about a topic never explored. Maybe an experience with a friend that neither had ever tried before. I don't have to be explicit to suggest that players like the new and different in their sexual lives. This leads us to the second primary element in players: physicality.

2. Physical

Players are intrinsically physical. Their physicality shows itself in the elements of physical movement, body awareness, and high-level activity level. Players see their bodies as vehicles to explore the world, and they do it with abandon. But their physicality is more than movement. It is an awareness of every part their physical bodies as well as an intrinsic sense of the physical world around them. Their movement is very much entwined with their desire to experience things physically. Players use physical movement to engage the physical world, the social world, and perhaps their own understanding of the spiritual world. In all this engagement players are seeking to find excitement, create excitement, and use excitement in a positive way.

Movement

We noted that players have a certain "wide-eyed" nature, using that term both symbolically and physically: their eyes move…almost constantly. A good friend of ours who lives in Newfoundland, Canada, where we lived for four years, has a good deal of player in her nature. While she is extraverted by nature, she often looks away from you when you are having a conversation, as if she is watching all the world around her as she is simultaneously engaged in conversation with you. This looking away is not out of boredom but because our player friend needs to see the whole world while simultaneously listening to someone who is talking to her. This looking around that players do while in a conversation can be disconcerting if you are intent on saying something that is important to you, but it is the way a player engages the world: *see everything, listen to everything, and be prepared to engage everything all the time.* Additionally, players use their olfactory, gustatory, and kinesthetic senses as much as possible, much like a developing child explores their environment. Players often want to taste everything, perhaps your coffee or glass of wine, with or without your permission. They might want to taste a bud off a tree or some of the beach sand. Recently, a mother mentioned that she was concerned about her son because he "just had to touch everything." Deb was visiting one of our neighbors and their little girl kept going up to Deb and touched her various body parts much to the mother's dismay and multiple corrections. Ron has had several player kids as patients who wanted to smell everything, which can be a challenge socially. If you pick a book off the shelf, they may take the book out of your hand and sniff it. "Oh, that's interesting", they might say, and "that smells like my aunt Rita." All of the five senses incline players to some kind of engagement, usually towards something that is new and different even if it is a momentary experience. Consider what it might be like for you to have all five of your senses operating all the time. We might mistakenly say that players are *distracted* by one or more of the things in the world that come into their senses, but more accurately they are *attracted* to everything in the physical world.

Players don't actually need anything that is external to their bodies to entice them. They find a great deal of stimulation within their own bodies. Physical movement that you might see with players is often in their facial gestures. We have already mentioned how "wide-eyed" they can be. They might lick their lips, almost as if they want to lick every bit of life out of the air. The boy I just mentioned who "touches everything" also likes to "chew on electrical cords." Diagnosis: player. Dangerous: potentially. Challenging: certainly. A player I have known for many years always chewed on something, very often paper. Many players constantly fuss with their hair twirling it about or even pulling it. They can be hyper-aware of physical changes in their bodies. While all humans are grounded in their physical nature, players' movement and gesturing suggests that they are particularly aware of their physicality.

A particularly common element with players is their hand movements. You have all seen the unofficial trademark hands of a player: the simultaneous rhythmic moving of both hands with thumbs and little fingers extended in a fashion that suggests they are "ready to boogie." It can't be by coincidence that this particular hand movement, shaking the hand while the little finger and thumb is extended in opposite directions with the three middle fingers pressed into the palm, is very similar to the ASL (American Sign Language) sign for play! Deb learned the basics of ASL *overnight* because of her natural physicality. Even in folks who are not predominantly players, you can see the abbreviated form of this hand moment in just one or two fingers. Spot a player passing you on the highway (often speeding), and you might note her little finger raised up from the steering wheel as if to lead the rest of the body down the road. It is as if, that one little finger "knows" that excitement must be engaged even if the rest of the body must be constrained. Other player-like hand movements include the "let's par-dee" movement of both hands in the air as an invitation to drop what you are doing and play. I suspect that the use of high fives, various culture-driven handshakes, and fist bumps might have been invented by players as they sought to have a spontaneous way of connecting to another person just with their hands.

In addition to the frequent use of their five senses to engage the physical world, players often engage in various forms of full body movement. There are many forms of this kind of physical movement but the basic element is that the player's whole body is somehow involved. There can be some kind of full torso undulation, a combination of rocking and rotating, or dancing in place. Yesterday, I (Ron) was with a teenager who I was asked to evaluate for a prospective adoption. Julie didn't even sit down in my office. She preferred to stand, move, and very often dance. Then she told me that she liked to dance. What kind? Hip hop and ballet. Hip hop and ballet? I thought: how different her interests in these dances. Then, in a second breath she told me she also liked ballroom, tap, and square dance. No doubt Julie has a lot of player in her nature, not just because she liked to dance, but because her body was in constant joyful movement.

What can look to a non-player as a lot of wasted physical effort might be the player's way of engaging the world with as much of his body as he can. At his best, this player movement is an expression of an inner source of joy and satisfaction. There are times when players seem to experience a certain anxiety demonstrated in a kind of agitation, mostly because nothing is immediately interesting or exciting. They might even say that they "gotta move." More often, their body undulation is a sense of self-satisfaction and engagement with the world around them as if they are gathering all the energy possible in their physical space. Players live for the thrill of life and express the anticipation of thrill through their bodies.

As we already suggested, some of the most successful players are professional athletes. Sports players in particular are some of the most easily recognized players who utilize play through their bodies. When you watch a professional athlete be fully bodily involved, you are watching a player who has mastered the art of being player in his or her sport of choice. The athlete who is fully athletic and fully player is the one who not only makes the touchdown, but who embellishes the touchdown by doing hand stands, belly dancing, and elaborate and multiple "high fives" after the touchdown. I remember Michael Jordan, the former great Chicago Bulls professional basketball player, enjoying his success at "going to the hoop" or "dishing" the ball off to a teammate in the last second or switching hands from right to left seemingly "just for the fun of it."

Stage performers, too, who are often players by temperament, physically metamorphose into the character they play. The best stage performers not only engage their character, they become the character and in so doing engage the rest of the cast, the props, and the audience as part of their play. Deb very much enjoyed playing in her local community theater. She was very good and was recognized as very good but would frustrate some of the less engaged cast because as soon as she showed up for rehearsal or performance, she physically entered her character and would not break from it. Even back stage while between scenes, she worked to keep her character alive in all respects. Some of the cast would try their best to shake her but it didn't work. She symbolized what Shakespeare said, "all of life is a stage" and she was the player. Robin Williams used his body and facial expressions as spontaneously as his words. A less outrageous but equally dramatic actor, Meryl Streep, might be a player because she can play any character at an Oscar level by defining her characters so often with the most subtle hand and facial gestures. Drama is but one artistic form that players gravitate to. Music is another.

Musical

The physicality of players is related to their musicality. It is rare to find a player who was not taken by music, playing music, listening to music, moving to music, singing, humming, or whistling to music. Most players have at least tried music in some form and many professional musicians are players. At the very least, players are always in accompaniment of their I-pods, radios, or the imaginary music going through their brains. We think that music is in players' souls—as well as in their bodies. We suspect that players' interest in music is much broader than exists in other people possibly because of some kind of unique inner rhythm. This inner musical element, as well as their general movement inclination, might suggest that players have a well-developed "right brain". Roughly speaking, the right brain is the primary housing for music as well as many other things, like emotion, visual input, and auditory input all of which lead to players' kinesthetic output.

Some players take their inner musical nature into voice and instrumentation. The musician-player is one who physically, emotionally and musically feels the music she plays. Many player musicians are compelled to engage their whole bodies when playing, singing and even when composing. Ron recalls seeing his math teacher, who also tutored the flute, instructing a fellow student in how to move with the music while she was playing the flute. We understand that many composers first hear their music internally and then go about externally reconstructing that which was born inside of them. It isn't surprising that many of these musicians when reconstructing their inner sounds move their hands and bodies in great detail, especially facially and with their breath as if directing the music into being while they transpose their inner music to the staff paper, the keyboard, the guitar or as they improv on the saxophone. Musician-players don't just become their music; they are their music. It seems necessary for virtuoso Yo-Yo Ma to grimace constantly as he plays his cello, and even off stage his facial vibrancy is demonstrated in what I suspect is a player nature. Many years ago, we went to a Yanni performance where he highlighted a pair of dueling violinists. These two gifted musician players not only *dueled* their instruments, they dueled their bodies as they bowed their violins daringly close to the other and then with what seemed to be a playful smile, turned heels and returned to their individual play. It was spectacular to both hear their masterful capacity as well as to watch them pair their music with their bodies in a physical challenge. This same masterful body synchronization can be seen when watching folk musicians such as fiddlers, bodhran players and other percussionists. These people are not just playing their music, their music is playing them.

The importance of music for players is not limited to professional musicians. Music has always been a modality for most people to engage emotion, meaning, and self-expression. For players, music adds another dimension: players' movement itself is a conduit for joy and music serves as a player's conduit for physical movement. While the player listens to music, she might be playing her air guitar, directing her invisible orchestra, dancing, or just moving her body to the music. Her body just moves—whether or not she wants it to. The former American Olympian skier Peekaboo Street "played" her air guitar before one of her downhill runs. She had her radio headset on; she was singing the words to the song, and her body was in constant movement-head bobbing, knees bouncing. She was totally enjoying her environment at the moment when most Olympians would be in deep concentration about the upcoming ski run. Rachel Marron, the character that Whitney Houston played in the 1992 thriller "Bodyguard" is clearly a player, as I suspect Whitney herself might have been. Houston portrayed the Rachel character not only as a vocalist but also the daring player who sought excitement at every opportunity. The list of examples of professional player musicians is exhaustive.

Players' orientation to music is certainly biological and inherited as are the elements of all the temperaments. It is almost as if music is always roaming around in their bodies just waiting for a place to exit. It is likely that music gets into a player's basic body rhythm more than it gets into other people's early body rhythms. Players have a natural ability to "feel" music, particularly the intensity of music. It would seem that jazz would be players' most natural musical outlet because of its improvisational nature, but that theory has not seemed to pan out in my observation of players' interest in music. There certainly are players doing jazz, but more likely they gravitate towards something with a more consistent beat like rock music. I (Ron) had the privilege of seeing a live concert with the Dave Brubeck Quartet when I was in college. I remember how each member of the quartet yielded to a member who seemed to be in a groove. No words needed to be spoken. Maybe they were all players. The body movement of many musicians, whether rock guitarists or orchestra cello players suggests this inner musical movement. Players *need* to move when they hear music or play music. Sometimes the music they hear is just in their heads.

High Activity Level

Movement for players is a natural energy that drives them, and it often leads them to some kind of dancing, usually very informal and spontaneous in form. Players are undoubtedly the best dancers in the world—if they let themselves go. One player said that when he dances, his body "just won't keep up." Now what does it mean that "his body just won't keep up"? When players come to the dance floor confident, they feel the music around them, the energy inside of them, and their bodies are too limited to express all this energy. Consider King David from the Bible who "danced before the Lord with all his might" through the streets of Jerusalem. By the way, he was naked at the time. When was the last time you went to a wedding dance and observed little folks doing their own personal jig? These little ones evidently feel the music or rhythm inside and it takes over for them. They are uninhibited and free. They may or may not turn out to be players, but the movement points to the naturalness of what players tap into.

With both pleasure and a bit of embarrassment, I (Ron) remember the night after a great time of dancing on a cruise ship when a lovely woman came up to greet my wife and me at breakfast and spontaneously put her big lovely arms around Deb, nearly knocking her down exclaiming "thank you, thank you." Then when she stood back, she exclaimed the joy of having "free danced" with me into the wee hours, now declaring me "a dancing machine!" When I dance, that old player part of me can take over and I simply forget myself. Dancing can be a platform that best energizes my internal drive for movement. As I write these words, Deb and I are soon on our way to a New Year's ballroom dance venue where there will be wonderfully skilled dancers. I will struggle to keep up with the circle of dance and try hard to avoid stepping on another dancer's feet, and all that awareness will take a bit of fun out of my desire to dance with abandon. One of my all-time favorite movies, a classic on dancing players is "Flashdance" (1983). In review, it is not only the phenomenal movement through dance but the lyrics to the hit song by Irene Cara that address this important piece about players. Cara speaks of enlivened passion from an internal rhythm that takes hold of the heart. "I am rhythm," she said.

This musical movement that players demonstrate is undoubtedly rhythm based, but also connects to the overall understanding of the importance of movement with players. Deb says that movement for her is a form of energy that supplies a refreshment, a liberation from repetition or other menial tasks. Deb can sit at her computer and be quite productive, but *needs* to move away from the screen after an hour or so. We have a set of swings right outside our office that were set in place when our grandchildren were born. After 70 minutes tops Deb will get up from her computer, go outside and swing hard with her full body leaning backwards so her head is looking up at the trees behind her. She traces the limbs, she says, and then comes back to work. She occasionally reports that the movement loosened her thoughts and expanded her ideas. Deb also says, as do many intuitive and creative players, that movement "connects her to the universe and God." She says that movement not only energizes her but metaphysically serves as conduit through which she can create more energy, whether in front of the computer or with a patient. This seems to be a combination of Deb's intuitive nature and her player nature working hand in hand as she goes about life and work. This combination works well for her, while I blend my player nature with my predominant caretaker temperament. When we blend combinations of temperaments, we get some interesting results especially in relationships. We will discuss the combinations of temperament orientations later in the book. Before we get there, let us take a step beyond players' movement and experiential interest to entertainment.

3. Entertaining

We have noted that players see potential play anywhere: objects are potential toys, people are potential play-mates, and the world is a potential playground. This all-encompassing play orientation to the world inclines players to make play at any opportunity. We think most of the kids who are "class clowns" (which Deb was voted in HS) may be players trying to create play in the classroom by entertaining their classmates. An important part of professional players, whether by voice, instrument, athletic endeavors, or dance, are trying to entertain us because it is their job to do so. But for players in everyday life there still is a need to entertain whoever is around them. It is as if they see anyone and everyone as a potential audience to be entertained. Many players find it difficult to be *in* a crowd. They want to be the *center* of the crowd, the center of attention, the center of the action whether the crowd is a crowd of one, two, twenty or two hundred. One player whom we both know well wore a t-shirt that classically read, "Let Me Entertain You".

The entertaining that players do actually erupts from a generous spirit and is wholly honorable, if not always generously received by their audience. If players succeed at becoming good entertainers, they can be at their very best because they have learned to hone their entertainment to the audience, knowing when to speak and when to be silent, when to tease and when to comfort. Jack Benny did some of his best work with complete silence, albeit with a facial presence that profoundly communicated, as did Lucille Ball. Benny would rather wait for the right moment when something had been said and look slightly to one side implying that what was said was outrageous. He would do this sly sideways looking entirely silent, which was his trademark. The facial movement with Lucile Ball was quite different with a facial contortion and a kind of a whine that was compelling.

Players do not need to dominate the stage even though they often do. They would gladly share the stage with another player, whether the "stage" is the living room, the farmers' market, or a classroom. Better yet, a player would love to compete with some other entertainer for the audience's acceptance and laughter. The dueling violinists at the Yanni concert may have been playing a rehearsed piece but there is no doubt, that they were in the midst of some of their best play as they musically and physically challenged the other on stage, each vying for the prime light and then, just as happily challenging the other to accept the spotlight. These musicians are brilliant in their trade. Players can appreciate others' play and entertainment as easily as they can entertain. Players often fight for the stage, get the stage and keep it for as long as possible, and then seemingly, without self-regard, relinquish the stage to another performer, just for the *play* of it. Actor Robin Williams once did a spontaneous gig with player-humorists Jonathan Winters and Marty Feldman while sitting on the stage in front of an audience. These three spontaneously went back and forth outdoing one another with plays on words and other humor-entertainment. It was a moment that a player dreams of: having the audience completely in their hands, helping people enjoy themselves, laugh at themselves, and laugh at life. A good entertainer is one who can reach into my space and cause me to laugh, to breathe a breath of pleasure or joy without my expecting him to continue entertaining me for a lifetime.

The player's basic psyche contains the notion that if everyone could laugh, play, explore and engage most of the time, there wouldn't be any problems left in the world. This is the prime philosophy or value that often drives players, especially the drive for entertaining. In the very moment of play nothing else exists for the player. Players are not just interested in laughing and enjoying life; they are more interested in connecting with other people through their entertaining, enjoyment of the moment, and physical movement. One of the quickest ways to connect with people is to make them laugh and enjoy life. There is a good bit of evidence in the psychological literature about the psychological and physical value of laughter. As the old proverb says "a merry heart doeth good like a medicine." What evidently happens when people come to laughter is that body tension is loosened, something that is obviously healthy.

The entertaining nature of players usually starts early in life. Player children are those who spontaneously show off their new summersaults to your dinner guests. They show off their new shoes to the store clerk. They show off their new-found frog to the gas station attendant. Player kids just show off and feel confident in their entertaining. Few people take offense at young children showing off their new panties or spontaneous dancing. This "showing off" is not selfish or self-centered; it is an attempt to entertain and thus bring fun to other people. When parents are confronted with their player children's need for entertaining, they might mistakenly see this as a need for attention. Players only want attention in order to entertain. Their desire for entertainment knows no boundaries.

4. Low Boundary

One of the most distinguishing characteristics of players is being persons that we call "low boundary". The essence of this term is that people with this nature (not all of whom are players) understand that all boundaries are artificial, meaning that someone has made the boundary and he or she has the right to challenge that boundary. A low boundary orientation should be compared and contrasted with high boundary people, who see that boundaries are necessary, or we would have chaos. The truth goes both ways: yes, all boundaries, or at least 99.9% of them are human-made and in a sense "artificial"; and yes, boundaries are necessary or we would have chaos. Low boundary people tend to be spontaneous and love freedom, and as a result tend to be less planful and orderly. Players see boundaries as impediments to engagement, experience, and excitement.

The term *low boundary*, one that we have used for many years, speaks of the in-the-moment nature of players. We do not use this term exclusively in regard to professional or personal boundaries between people as the term is normally used. Players challenge all boundaries, including those of people's physical space. This low boundary orientation is both a summary and a hallmark of players. Time and space for players in many ways does not exist. Free players use the moment to ignite their play in the living room or the on the street, while professional players ignite the moment with their play on the stage or on the playing field. Players take the moment and make it their own. This in-the-moment nature is one of the greatest characteristics of players. They find energy, freedom, excitement, and generosity in the moment.

It is this low-boundary, freedom orientation that facilitates players' other characteristics. The low boundary component ignites his excitement orientation and pushes his curiosity into discovery. His low boundary component challenges him into adventure and thrill seeking, and unleashes his basic physicality into playful and artful movement. This low boundary capacity delves deep into a player's soul and psyche to bring out the best of all people knowing that rules are but guidelines for behavior, not absolutes to be followed mindlessly. This intrinsic knowledge that "all things are lawful but not all are expedient," said by the Apostle Paul, leads the player to personal greatness and stimulates greatness in others.

5. **Felt Greatness and Commitment to Life**

All temperaments possess a felt greatness and commitment to life. Our basic orientation to psychological practice is to help people find their "greatness," which means what initially attracts them, feels natural, and takes practice to be competent in the skill. This idea of "greatness' in not about how people compare themselves to anyone else but how they can like themselves, love themselves, and ultimately improve themselves so as to have a meaningful impact on the world. We think that all persons have a special knowledge of God or a higher resource, however they define God or even if they are agnostic or atheistic. We have come to believe that each human being knows something about God (or the universe at large) that other human beings do not necessarily know, and that each of us can demonstrate this godly element in some way. Players seem to know their "God-ness" element of play more than people with other personality features. It is possible that players just admit to feeling somewhat godlike, whereas people of other temperaments might be reticent to display something that may seem arrogant. This sense of what we call *felt greatness* is quite typical of players, although few of them would be able to articulate their feeling of greatness. Some of the most successful musicians, athletes, and actors seem to be able to admit to their greatness. We are reminded of Muhammad Ali's "I am the greatest" comments that often infuriated many people because they conceived of his felt greatness as arrogance. To feel *great* is not to feel great*er* or *better* than someone else. Greatness is a quantum step above good, better, and best. To feel great, one feels this intrinsic God-ness and simultaneously feels a need to exercise it.

Perhaps the best way to sum up the players' basic life philosophy which represents their felt sense of greatness is their intrinsic sense of the *big-ness* of life. Players want to *live* big, *show* big, and *do* big because they seem to have a deep sense that life is much bigger than we know. Theirs is a very intense commitment to life and its bigness. They want to live large and help others do the same. This is not greed or narcissism that it might seem to be; it is an intimate understanding that life is good and should be engaged as fully and largely as possible. In fact, when a person of any temperament, of any culture, and of any gender feels great, this person feels confidence to engage the world and possibly challenge the world for the better. This confidence-based challenging leads players to challenge rules, but more importantly, it leads them to potentially great things. Then, oddly, it leads to humility because when people see their own greatness, they see other people's greatness. We will see that greatness is not the sole property of players. Caretakers, lovers, and analysts can also be great and help others become great if they can feel great themselves. One player has told me that his basic interest in other people is to enliven them and *free* them from the apparent confines of life, which players see as artificial and unnecessarily restrictive.

Players see greatness, whether in themselves or potentially in other people, as related to experience, excitement, and entertainment. They have an intrinsic understanding that greatness exists potentially in every human being, which is a deep philosophical truth. Some of the truly great men and women of the world like Martin Luther King, Jane Goodall, Mahatma Gandhi, Galileo, and Margaret Mead saw the bigness of the world in ways other than play. These people did not feel superior to others, but they were, indeed, superior human beings who left lasting legacies for the rest of us to treasure. Consider how deeply these great people felt the passions of their trades. Players feel equally deeply.

PLAYERS AND FEELINGS

In *I Want to Tell You How I Feel* we made a distinction between feelings and emotions. Simply stated, we propose that emotions are an important subset of feelings but the concept of feelings is broader than emotions alone and reflects a very basic element of every human being. We suggest that feelings are so important to a person's psychological structure that while they can't be defined, we know they exist and "feel" them in four ways: physically, emotionally, cognitively, and actively. Regardless of one's temperament, gender or any other way of understanding people, every human experiences and expresses feelings in these four ways. Depending on one's temperament people tend to experience and express their feelings predominantly in one of these four ways. Players experience and express their feelings predominantly physically as is presented in the following diagram borrowed from our previous book:

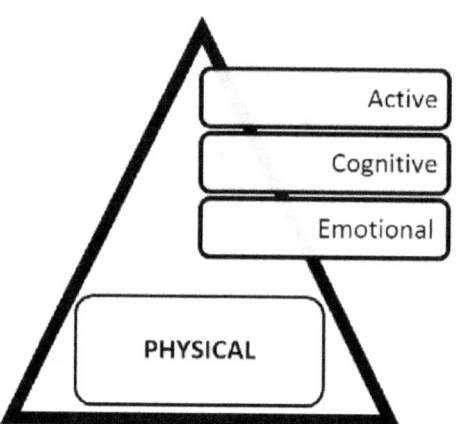

The other three temperaments have different preferences for the experience and expression of feeling.

We see players' *feelings* primarily in their bodies, namely how they stand, how they move, what they do with their arms and legs, and in their facial and vocal expressions. Earlier in this chapter we described how players are physical and active, but it is important to note that while they are often active, their first experience and expression of their feelings is how they engage their bodies. Watch what a player does physically and you will see how he is expressing his feelings. You may not know what he is thinking, you may not know his emotional state, and you may not know what he might do, but you will be seeing his *feelings* in raw form. In fact, he may not be able to tell what he feels emotionally, what he is thinking, or what he might do, but you can be certain that if a player is feeling something, particularly when this something is important to him, he will display this feeling in his body posture, movement, or appearance.

Players are at their best when they feel joy, express joy, and work to instill joy in the people around them. Because joy is an emotion that exists primarily in the present, namely when I presently am enjoying something, players are very much in the present, not so much in the past or the future. We will use this paradigm of *feelings* and *emotions* as we discuss the other three temperaments, but keep in mind that players are first physical in their experience and expression of feelings, and that their distinctly preferred emotion is joy. In the later chapters we will discuss how players' physical experience of feelings and their preference for the experience of joy can be both helpful and hurtful in their relationships, just as feelings and emotions are for all temperaments.

Consider the player temperament, and in this consideration note the people in your life that may demonstrate player characteristics as we have described them. Now, consider the element of your own psychological nature that may be player-like. If you can see players in your world and the player part of your inner world, you are on the way to understanding this central ingredient in life. Now, we will endeavor to suggest three other central ingredients in life starting with what we call the *caretaker* temperament.

Chapter 2

The Caretaker Personality

PLAYERS AND CARETAKERS BOTH like *things*. And they both like to *do* things. But their *liking* and *doing* are quite different. Players see the world as a place to *play*; caretakers see the world as a place to *work*. Players want to *play* in their doing; caretakers want to *produce* in their doing; players want the experience of doing and potentially the *excitement* in their doing. Caretakers want *accomplishment* in their doing. Players want to *use* things; caretakers want to *save* things. Players would agree with the first dictum of the Westminster Articles of Confession: "the chief end of humankind is to glorify God and *enjoy* Him forever." Players want to enjoy God and all of God's creation. Caretakers take to heart the dictum that God gave Adam and Eve in Genesis: "Take care of the world." So, while players might want to play with everything caretakers want to take care of all of God's creation.

Caretakers grasp that they have a mission to take care of the world. Not just people but all of the world: animals, plants, and physical structures. Importantly, caretakers engage in their taking care of such things in the service of humankind because caretakers understand, more than any of the other temperaments, that humans need animals, plants, and physical objects in order to live and to thrive. Players serve the world by creating as much excitement as possible, and we will soon see that lovers and analysts also serve the world in their own unique ways. Understanding how people of all temperaments serve the world will help you understand how you serve the world, perhaps in ways that are quite different from your friends and family.

Caretakers intrinsically understand that all things need care and that all things occasionally need to be fixed, repaired, restored, or cleaned up. If you're not a caretaker yourself, you certainly may see how your caretaker friends engage in protecting and repairing things. However, it is equally possible that you have not actually seen them doing their work of restoration because caretakers can be quite unobtrusive in their caretaking activities. You might see that physical things are cared for, like the kitchen cleaned up, the kids' room put back together after a day's playing, your car washed, or the toilet paper replaced on the dispenser. You might have seen that the kitty litter is changed, the dog is bathed, the lawn is mowed, or the garden is weeded and, that someone stopped to get the milk and eggs. People with the other three temperaments often do such things and may be thoroughly responsible with property. Caretakers see things that need protection and restoration just as players see opportunities for engagement and excitement. This property orientation is a feeling of responsibility for the property itself. Recall that we noted in the Introduction that caretakers view property as spiritual.

Caretakers' need for protection and restoration goes beyond physical property. They also take care of people, albeit in ways that are different from the other temperaments. Their caretaking of people usually takes the form of *taking care of things used by people*. A caretaker can really enjoy seeing a cleaned-up car, but this could be his car, your car, or anyone's car. I have known caretakers who are compelled to turn the lights off in car in some parking lot that belongs to a complete stranger. There is a special kind of love that caretakers have for things so they can be effectively used by people. In the back of the mind of a caretaker is the desire to show their love for people by helping people make effective and productive use of the things in their lives, whether living, like animals and plants, or nonliving as cars, kitchen sinks and office break rooms. Hard as it is for people of other temperaments to understand, caretakers love things, human or animal, living or nonliving.

I (Ron) can speak forthrightly about the love of things because my basic temperament is that of caretaker. I remember being surprised by the activity of a caretaker acquaintance of mine one morning some years ago. I heard the hammering and sawing being done by this man repairing my back steps. My friend, Jim, was getting the job done that I had asked him to do. I hadn't actually expected him to get this job done so soon because I just asked him to look at the steps the day before. Jim is the kind of a guy who tears right into a building project, thinks on his feet, and makes adjustments to the project as he goes along with his work. He doesn't ask a lot of questions, just enough to get him going and keep him busy for the next few hours. Now, many years later I know another caretaker-like carpenter, my neighbor Lonnie, who operates in the same way: examine the project for a few minutes, jump right into the project, and make adjustments as necessary. Jim and Lonnie displayed their love for me, and simultaneously for property by plying their trade on my behalf, but I never heard either of these good men say that they loved me. I didn't need to hear those words because I felt their love in their actions.

Not all carpenters are caretakers, but many successful ones are, as are most successful workers in the other trades. If I hear of someone giving up a building trade, like painting, carpentry, or plumbing, I suspect that he or she was not a caretaker by nature but found their way into the trade because they thought they could make a good living painting, plumbing, or swinging a hammer. But after being in a trade that requires a lot of work, often routine work, players and people of other temperaments are often bored or disappointed in the trades. For the most part the trades are built on people who simply like things and like to take care of things. Players, as we learned in the last chapter, do not generally engage in care taking, nor do analysts and lovers whom we shall study in later chapters. Thank goodness for the caretakers of the world because we would have a very chaotic world if we didn't have them. They build our roads and bridges; they pick up our recyclables; they keep our computers working; they take care of stray animals; they do routine data entry of people's medical needs and help keep them healthy and alive. They manage our portfolios and do our taxes. They take care of the world of people by taking care of the things in the world. Let's look more carefully at the characteristics of caretakers.

CHARACTERISTICS OF CARETAKERS

1. Business

Consider the two ways of pronouncing this word, business: "biz-ness" and "busy-ness." Caretakers are both: business people and busy people. Caretakers are usually quite good at "doing business," like conducting the affairs of a private enterprise, or better yet, working for someone else in conducting corporate business. The basic nature of caretakers lends them to the rudiments and requirements of succeeding in the business community because so much of doing business lies in the arena of taking care of things like money, property, and people. Because they are people who like to get the job done, business owners like them and usually count on them. I have known several "project managers" who might not know how to swing a hammer but they are good at getting people under their direction to do various elements of the project while the caretaker oversees everyone's work, often without criticism. Leave caretaker employees on their own, and you will be able to count on them doing their jobs without further interruption. Leave players on their own with a job to do, and you might return two hours later to find them entertaining their workmates, playing with their workmates, or engaging their workmates in some activity that the player deems good for everyone to do. Caretakers are good at doing things on their own or following directions of someone else who is trying to make business work. You want something done, without play, conversation, or questions, ask a caretaker to do it.

Doing business is only part of caretakers' *business* nature, but caretakers also have a *busy-ness* nature. A caretaker can become completely absorbed in an activity *for activity's sake*. Given that my basic temperament is that of caretaker, I can speak about this characteristic quite personally. I am almost always busy at something. The "being busy at something" all the time brings us caretakers great pleasure. Our view of the world is that it needs to be cared for. It also needs to be protected, repaired, and organized. All of these activities are caretakers' way of taking care of things. There is always something to do in the world for caretakers, and this doing something is what caretakers feel inside of them. Caretakers are often so busy in the work of caretaking that they don't realize that hours have passed, dinnertime has passed, and bedtime has passed. As I am writing this sentence, there is a "doing" nature to it, a busy-with-something nature. I have just finished with a patient and I am waiting for my next patient who happens to be a few minutes late. There is something enticing, perhaps even exciting about finishing one project and then jumping right into another one. Consider how different players' excitement is from caretakers' excitement. The difference is between the producing of a caretaker and the experiencing of a player.

The busyness nature of caretakers inclines them to have several projects in the making all the time. There are usually lists of things to do, people to see, and places to go. When the caretaker finishes one project, however small or large, she will usually move right on to the next project with hardly a breath. Mary is such a person. When I see Mary in her natural state, she is usually in the midst of completing a list of things to do. One such list included these items: "bank: cash check, get cash; store: milk, return cans; check on daughter Mindy's school performance; give Marge the committee minutes; pick up grill at Joey's friend's house; start grill at 6 P.M." It is likely that this list was not even inclusive, meaning that caretaker Mary had several other things to do among the listed items, but she kept them in her head. It is also likely that she expected too much of herself, and that the charcoal wouldn't be successfully started at 6 P.M. as she had hoped. She might be a bit disappointed at her not being able to fulfill all her self-defined goals for the afternoon on this list, but she would enjoy her busyness. Not all caretakers have Mary's written lists, but they always have lists in their heads which keep them pleasantly occupied with performing tasks and accomplishing things. As a caretaker myself I always have a list of "do's" on "my" side of the kitchen counter, another one on my office desk, and a vague list in my head.

The enjoyment that caretakers experience in their busyness is hard for people of other temperaments to understand. The fact that caretakers enjoy their busyness mystifies players who require that any activity needs to be exciting and playful because they don't realize that busyness *is* exciting and playful for the caretaker. I have often been on the receiving end of compassion from friends because they saw me as overtaxed. I have heard things like, "I am so sorry that you have to work so hard, Ron." But friends who render such compassion miss the point of my busyness and do not understand my enjoyment in being busy. Working hard gives caretakers great pleasure, as does finishing one project and jumping right into another project. The joy that caretakers experience in doing something is the same feeling of joy that players experience in playing. Keep in mind that caretakers, players, lovers, and analysts *enjoy* different things. Caretakers enjoy work.

I am quite sure that temperament is an inherited trait just as many other personality characteristics, like introversion and extraversion. I did well by my father because he was a caretaker, usually working, usually busy, and usually looking at property as needing routine repair. Dad taught me many things over the years I was a child, especially the care for property, but I didn't need his instruction for me to love caretaking. It came to me naturally. I never remember dreading work set out for me to do. I never remember having *nothing to do* like so many people often express. I never remember being bored. I always had my desk ordered and clean when I was in school. My desk is not always free of papers but it is never messy or cluttered. Nobody ever told me that I should do these things. It just came naturally to take care of things, whether my things or other people's things. I am compelled to take care of things that are in some kind of disrepair or disarray. Do you know someone in your life who insists on shoveling one inch of snow even though it's supposed to be 50 degrees tomorrow? Are you a person who has to cut the lawn even though it might rain any minute? To truly understand a person with a caretaker nature you must grasp this core value that caretakers have: take care of the world: property, animals, plants, and physical objects, and in so doing, take care of people. Caretakers go beyond taking care of things: they need to produce things.

2. Production

Players get bored often and easily, while caretakers never get bored. The basic difference between players and caretakers is in how they approach activity. Players see activity as a form of *experience* but caretakers see activity as a form of *production*. Caretakers can play at their work like players do; they can find meaning in their work like analysts do; and they enjoy being with people like lovers do. But beyond play, meaning, and people, caretakers need to get something *done*. It doesn't much matter to them what they do, as long as they have opportunity to do something, produce something, or repair something.

The business community loves caretakers because bosses can count on their caretaker employees to finish the jobs given to them. In fact, sometimes bosses have to tell their caretaker employees to go home instead of staying at work until the job is done. I know many caretakers who struggle to use up their vacation days even if they lose them after a year. Our office manager/secretary, Cheri, is certainly primarily a caretaker, and we have had to remind her that it is time to call it a day on occasion because she "just had one more chore" to do. Leaving work with unfinished tasks is hard for caretakers, especially if they are in the midst of completing a task that isn't quite done. Caretakers are notoriously last to leave work, come home late from work, and bring work home, as our dear secretary Cheri has done many times. This tendency to produce is true of caretakers at every level of employment: secretaries working on office work after hours; lawyers working until midnight on cases; and nurses checking on one of their patients even after they have clocked out. The productive nature in the caretaker temperament is shown in a variety of visual elements: a clean desk; bills paid on time or early; car fixed and running smoothly; house cleaned thoroughly even though company isn't coming over; back yard manicured. One of the best hallmarks of caretakers is that they do more than is expected of them.

All caretakers have the same values in doing, producing, and repairing, but the things they do may differ. All caretakers value property, but they do not all value the same property. Lonnie the carpenter values his tools and the five cars he is restoring, while Cheri values an orderly desk and all insurance claims properly made. Some caretakers value caring for people and do such things as changing diapers for adults in a care facility. Some caretakers want a meticulous lawn, while others might want to tear a car apart and then put it back together just for the doing of it. All caretakers like the sense of accomplishment: looking back on what has been accomplished in the previous hours or days. I often find myself simply enjoying the accomplishment of my production: having seen eight patients, having written 40 pages of a manuscript, having finished remodeling the kitchen, or even having finished putting away all my books and files.

American culture rewards production, regardless of quality. Because of this valuing of producing, it is easier for caretakers to adjust to American society than all the other temperaments. The Japanese culture also values production, but has added to this value a deeper concern for quality that is not always present in American production. This quality-based caretaking of the Japanese was quite evident in the 1980's when their cars surpassed American cars in quality. Originally, American car production was rewarded for quantity of cars beginning with the mass production of the first Fords in the early twentieth century. American cars dominated the world for more than 60 years before the Germans and Japanese began to produce cars with more quality. It took 20 years for the American car culture to accommodate to the market's demand for better quality in automobiles. Yet, there is still much reward for quantity over quality in America. It is the busy mother who is seen as motherly, the busy businessman who is seen as successful, the busy teacher who is seen as most helpful, and the busy pastor who is seen as properly pastoral.

Caretakers are always production oriented, but some people with this temperament add a dimension of quality to their drive for quantity. The dual drives for quantity *and* quality can make life very exhausting. A young man recently came to my office because he had had some kind of mental collapse. His father, an acquaintance of mine, was gravely concerned because his son had seemingly become entirely overwhelmed at work and displayed symptoms that suggested some kind of emotional disturbance. I learned originally from the father that Craig had been working some 100 hours a week at his summer "business internship" program that was part of his college curriculum. Dad also noted that his son had been sleeping less, working more, and losing a substantial amount of weight. In my first visit with Craig, I quickly recognized that he was a person of caretaker temperament but that he wanted both quality and quantity in his work. He had hired some of his friends to do his lawn care and maintenance business. He quickly learned, however, that his friends had neither the drive for production, nor the passion for quality that he possessed, yet he was the one that had recruited the business from his customers, and he felt obligated to get the job done and get it done right. So, he spent time checking up on the work of his employee friends and repairing or redoing the work they had done. If he were to be successful in having people working for him, he would need to be a manger, but he had no idea of how to do that. He knew how to *do* things but he didn't know how to *direct* people to do things.

With great grief, as well as financial loss, he gave up this project and began to look heartily on how he could find a place in life where he can do both quality and quantity. It will be no easy task. His first thought is that he needs to have a small business without employees that he can manage. Successful work for him will most likely be about doing rather than directing. This is an important characteristic of caretakers. Generally, they aren't the supervisors or the project managers, but rather the go-to people.

The producing and doing nature of caretakers engenders appreciation and reward from the world around them, but it is not the external rewards that caretakers seek. Rather, caretakers find internal rewards from doing and producing. The second-grade student who always keeps her desk clean and efficient is probably a young caretaker, and enjoys keeping her desk clean because it gives her personal satisfaction. That same student is likely to be the one who really enjoys doing 2 plus 2 a hundred times for the fun of it, while that repetitive activity would bore a player and seem senseless to an analyst. Fortunately for caretakers, most traditional school activity suits caretakers well because it is usually production-oriented.

3. Talking

Caretakers tend to talk a lot, mostly about what things they have done or need to do because their view of the world is about doing things. This could be the things that your friend did yesterday, or just as likely the things that someone else did yesterday. If you have an important person in your life, perhaps a good friend or a member of your family, who is a caretaker by nature, you know about this person's tendency to talk about doings. If your friend is talking about what he did, note the great amount of detail about what he did, when he did it, the successes he had, the failures he had, and the intentions he has to do it better next time. Note also that this same caretaker friend will be inclined to tell you the same story over again, perhaps with just as much energy and vibrancy when he tells you the story a second or third time. Caretakers who are introverted by nature will tend to talk about such things with one person, while extraverted caretakers will talk to almost anyone. My dad, consummate caretaker as well as extraverted, was able to strike up a conversation with a cashier at the store or the man pumping gas in the next lane, all without any semblance of real connection. He just needed to talk about what he was doing or what he has done. I remember a time when he actually started talking to a guy who was at the next gas pump and told this total stranger something about how he used to be in medical school and had forgotten most of what he learned. This combination of talking and engaging served Dad well in sales because he could engage anyone at any time. More introverted individuals will likely find an audience with you that they haven't found with someone else and tell you about their latest projects. These projects could be of great significance, like recently getting engaged or just as likely tell you how he had folded the sheets before he came to work.

Caretakers not only talk about what they have done themselves, they can also talk about what someone else has done. This kind of talking can be just as vibrant and animated, but it is always about some activity. People who have a primary temperament of caretaker and a secondary temperament of lover will likely be the ones who talk to you about their children or grandchildren and even what the neighbor's children have been engaged in. Consider the time you heard your friend tell you about her granddaughter's birthday party or recent success at forensics in school. Talking about something that someone else did doesn't even have to be in the recent past. Caretaker/lover people can be vivacious in telling you something that they experienced 20 years ago.

People who might be listening to a caretaker talk about their doings might not understand the caretaker's need to talk, especially when they are repetitive. I recall being at a couple's house when their phone rang. The wife immediately answered the phone and began telling her friend the various things that she had done and what others had done. Then after hanging up the phone, she immediately called another friend and said the very same things with just as much animation and elation. Then, after she had finished with these two conversations, she returned to the living room where I had been talking with her husband, and proceeded to tell us what we had both heard her tell her friends. We have a friend who will seemingly take every opportunity to tell us about each and every activity of his various family members, many of whom I have never met, much less have any interest in. It doesn't matter to Guy that I don't know his grandmother who has cancer or if I have met his second cousin who just bought a motorcycle. He enjoys telling us about such things because he thinks something that is interesting to him is also interesting to everyone else.

It might seem that this talking is selfish, i.e., that the caretaker is looking for attention for herself, but such is not the case. The talking that caretakers do is a way of their loving people and seeking some kind of connection. Deb is especially kind to me when I leave my office for the day to let me tell her a summary of every client I saw that day. Interestingly, I might then ask Deb about her clients and I will simply get a conclusion of her day but certainly not a rundown of every client she saw. My telling Deb about every client gives me the opportunity to not only re-experience my day, but to also hold to account my production for the day, that is, my caring for each of my clients. When a caretaker is telling you about the things they have done, they are trusting you will listen and understand them better, perhaps love them better. More importantly, they are doing what they think is the best way to love you: talk about what is most important to them: providing.

4. Providing

A good portion of the doing that we see with caretakers is related to providing something to the people in their lives or even to the world at large. This "providing" takes several forms including providing material *things* but they might also provide a *place* to have a cup of coffee or a place to sleep. We believe that this providing is one of the best ways caretakers actively *love* people. Because they are so good at taking care of property, caretakers will see what needs to be done and go about providing what they think people need or might need to bake a cake, help paint a friend's old barn, clean up the dishes after the meal or see to it that your travel arrangements are all in place. Think of that friend whom you occasionally visit in Colorado who always has bath towels on your bed, and extra toothbrush in the spare bathroom, or always provides the fresh coffee in the morning. This friend may not actually be primarily a caretaker by temperament but she has learned how to do caretaking from someone who was. I truly enjoy a dinner out where the maître d, the wine steward, or the server really enjoys providing for their customers. We had a favorite restaurant a number of years ago in downtown Madison where the wine steward came to our table where Ron asked him for a recommendation of wine for our meal. To our complete surprise, the wine steward reminded us of the wine we had chosen on our last visit to the restaurant *a year previously*, and then asked if we would like that wine or try something new. He remembered what wine we had because of his caretaker nature. He loved us by caring enough to remember what wine we drank. We can similarly feel cared for and provided for by a cashier who takes his or her job as an opportunity to serve the people on the other side of the counter, like a recent matron at a restaurant, Betsy, whom we had met at her "other job" the night before where she was equally taking care of us in a different way. These are people who render love with physical provisions.

Not only do caretakers look for the physical needs of people and the care of property to meet those physical needs, they may also provide for the emotional needs of the people around them. When we discuss the Lover temperament in Chapter 4, we will examine how lovers enjoy connections with people more than anything else. Caretaking people will provide for the emotional needs of people by more practical ways, like providing a place for you to be by yourself if you need to be alone, or taking a walk with you if you need a companion in a particularly difficult time of your life. When our daughter, Krissie, died, we were well cared for by many people in many ways, but I recall our friend Bud, caretaker by nature but not a person who routinely gives hugs, who managed and looked after many little chores at Krissie's celebration of life including taking pictures. He may have said that he was sorry for our loss but I don't remember it, nor do I remember him ever telling me that he loved me. He doesn't have to. I remember his love for us in practical ways, which is exactly what he did.

Some professions, like nursing and teaching, require many caretaking duties and are best suited for people with a caretaker temperament, but any profession could be one where a caretaker enjoys the process of providing for people. I knew a family practitioner who has a caretaker temperament evidenced by the extended amount of time he spent with patients. I have heard from more than one person I have referred to him who are amazed that he has spent so much time with them, not the typical 5-minute assessment and script writing that is more typical of doctors. People who enter the medical field with a caretaker temperament might look forward to providing for patients' basic needs but find that they need to spend an inordinate amount of time charting and caring for so many patients on the floor that they can't do the basic providing that they would like to do.

The providing nature of caretakers is not limited to the helping professions. Caretaking is an essential characteristic of early parenting and much of the whole of parenting. Parenting of infants and toddlers requires the repetitive nature that is natural to caretakers. While no one likes being awakened at 3 in the morning by a screaming infant, caretaker parents take these events in stride. It is the caretaker who easily gets out of bed for the third time in one night to *provide* for his infant's basic needs of feeding and diaper changing. I remember many such semi-sleepless nights. When I was aroused by one of my children's hunger cries, I did not feel the *urgency* of my daughter's needs for sustenance or comfort as much as I felt the *necessity* of getting out of bed and going about the business of warming the bottle and getting the dry diaper ready. Very often, I didn't even think about whether I wanted to get out of bed; rather, I just got out of bed and did the necessary. I know the parents of a child who required almost 24/7 care due to a unique abnormality in his breathing. These parents never had a complete night of sleep for the first three years of their daughter's life. Their daughter, now in her 20's, has no idea of the nearly constant care her parents rendered to her.

The pastor of a church I used to attend was a caretaker. She had five children, all within about eight years and once said she wished she could care for another five. As a pastor, she served the church caring for the flock, cared for her husband and attended to some to his professional work, and cared for her mother who lived with her family. She also rendered a good deal of care to her extended family. She never seemed hurried or hassled. She was seldom intrusive although she preached with confidence and displayed great self-assurance. She even preached once about a conflict in her family of origin, an experience that she took as instructive in how to manage life's difficulties. After this difficult sermon and greeting her parishioners, she went about the business of caring for her children, teaching Sunday school class, going home to fix dinner, all while continuing to provide for her young children and her husband. This good lady was an idol to many of the people in the church and seemed to epitomize what it means to be a caretaker in the role of pastor.

5. Property-oriented

Caretakers are particularly good with management of property. Sometimes we refer to caretakers as "groundskeepers" because they take care of the "grounds," which could be the hospital ward, the kitchen, the infant's room, or the actual grounds of the house. Caretakers see the grounds of the world in the larger sense of grounds, i.e., taking care of the world. As a result of their tendency to take care of things, they tend to own a lot of property, partly because they rarely throw anything away that could be of use in the unknown future. As with all the characteristics that we identify as typically character-like, people of the other three temperaments might also have one or more of these characteristics.

Charles is a friend of mine who has a player temperament. He hates to work on his lawn. For him it is tedious, yet every spring he belatedly and half-heartedly spreads pre-emergent weed killer on his lawn and does the other necessities of lawn care as the summer wears on, but he hates every minute of lawn care. He cuts his lawn every two weeks unless he absolutely has to cut it more often. Charles' neighbor, on the other hand, spends countless hours on his lawn meticulously caring for every blade of grass. He has a lawn service care for his lawn, but after the service has left for the day, this man goes out and does more work on his lawn. Not all people who like a nice lawn are caretakers, but most are. In fact, I know of a man with a player temperament who runs a lawn service, but really isn't interested in lawn care at all. He just does the lawn service for a living because it is something that generated him some good income in his early years, and he could never get away from it. I know of two tree surgeons, one who is a caretaker, and one who is a player. The caretaker likes doing the tree surgery, whereas the player likes the thrill of being up in the trees.

The way caretakers manage property is only the behavioral evidence of their basic personality structure. These folks seem to fuse their personalities with property, and then they feel emotionally connected to property. For instance, books might be valued for themselves rather than for the information they contain or for the pleasure they give in their reading. Sam has a library of books, but he admits that he will never read most of them. His books are very important to him, and he has them all ordered, visible, and available for use if necessary, however improbable that may be. I borrowed a book from him some time ago, read a few chapters and put the book aside. My friend has asked about the whereabouts of his book several times, and I finally felt compelled to return his book half-read. Sam is not so interested in getting the book immediately back because he would gladly allow me to have the book for years if necessary; he just wants to know that the book is alright. He wants to know where his stuff is. As a caretaker myself, I can't blame him. I want to know where my stuff is too. You would rarely, if ever, hear a caretaker say "oh, it doesn't matter, it is just a book" or "that isn't important, it is just something that I had around". Stuff is always important.

There is something about having "stuff" that is very basic to caretakers. Caretaker children often have physical things that are important to them, like security blankets, special cups, and clothes. Having stuff looks materialistic to most people, but it is not the valuing of material things that brings caretakers problems. Materialistic people seek to acquire material goods to such an extent that they need more and more. Such is not the case with caretakers. They do not necessarily seek to *acquire* property as to *protect* it. Caretakers save property for future use, although they might admit that most of the stuff they have saved and protected might never be used. I used to enjoy going to auctions. Once, there was a box full of multiple line phones going up for auction. Seeing those phones prompted me to consider that there might be a time when I could need them so I bought them. They sat in the box in the garage for a long time before I could bear to let go of potentially good usable phone even though I didn't need them. Caretaker's garages, basements, and attics are full of such boxes.

Potential use is not the only thing that caretakers value about property. They also value the actual use of property, namely for the purpose it was intended. A dish is never meant to be used as a Frisbee the way a player might see it. A hat is always a hat, and usually used to protect one's head from sun or snow, never "just a hat" that can be tossed aside rather than hung on the hook. Caretakers get irritated when property is not used properly, and see playful use of property or neglect of property as "abuse." A caretaker may not use the air conditioning on an 80-degree day because she is saving it for a really hot day, whereas a player turns air conditioning on because it is there to use regardless of whether it is 70 degrees or 100 degrees. A wealthy person that I know walks up his hallway stairs to the bedroom on the side of the stairway so as to protect the carpet in the middle…for future use. This 65-year-old is protecting the carpet in his house from what most people would consider to be normal wear. I have my unique habits, sometimes silly habits of protecting property. Certainly, most of the property I have kept and protected will never be used again, but I don't know which items might be used and which might not be used, so I tend to protect and preserve it all. Not all property is valued the same by different caretakers, but when they value property, it is almost *sacred*.

6. Spiritual Nature

Caretakers consider property to have intrinsic *spiritual* value. They can value property over people's feelings, or over people altogether, not so much because they are selfish but because they see their sacred responsibility to save and protect property, ultimately for human use. In this sense caretakers can be very generous with property. They just want their property cared for responsibly. A caretaker girl could easily loan her favorite toy car to her player brother erroneously thinking that her brother has the same value for the toy car, only to be gravely disappointed to find the car ignored, lost, or broken because it was, indeed, a "toy" to the player brother. When that toy is lost or damaged, the caretaker child might be truly grieved. The toy was sacred to her, but *simply* a toy to her brother. I remember giving my collection of toy cars to a neighbor friend of mine because I had outlived an interest in such things. Some days later I asked my friend how he was enjoying the cars. To my great disappointment he simply said that his younger brother had lost them. It didn't matter to him because he was not a caretaker. It mattered a great deal to me. The toy cars were simple but they were sacred to me.

7. Simplicity

There is an attractive simplicity about caretakers. Their view of life is so much about what is, that they are very good at seeing the facts and saying the facts. I wonder if the boy who saw that the "Emperor had no clothes" was simply stating the obvious. He was not trying to understand why the emperor had no clothes. He just saw that he was naked. Seeing what is, more than seeing what could be, is the heart of the simplicity of caretakers. They do not by nature look under the surface. They look at the surface. They do not ask how and why; they ask who, what, when, and where. Yes, caretakers can be simplistic, but for the most part they just look to understand things in as simple a manner as possible.

Caretaker's simplicity is related to their *doing* nature. They can truly be satisfied doing almost anything. As we noted, they rarely get bored, probably because there is always something to do. Their activity can be intense or it can be easy; it can be intricate, like fixing a computer, it can be delicate, like a jeweler repairing a diamond ring, or it can be repetitive, like the man on the assembly line. Simple doesn't have to be trivial. The most successful IT people are not those who ask *why* the computer isn't working; they ask *what* isn't working, what was happening when it stopped working, and what was happening in the room when it stopped working. The true scientist may be a genius but he can also be a person who can do 200 trials to find the exact combination of chemicals that does the job he wants done. When we think of scientists, we tend to think of the Einsteins of the world, but most scientists do much more mundane things that developing theories like $E = MC^2$.

CARETAKERS AND FEELINGS

Recall from the last chapter our discussion that everyone experiences their feelings through their physical sensations, their emotions, their thoughts, and through their activity. We know that when we "feel" something, we first have a physical experience, that followed by an emotional experience, eventually a cognitive experience, and then an experience of some kind of activity. Caretakers, like everyone else, experience all of these elements of feelings, but tend to *experience and express* their feelings primarily in activity, just as players express their feelings primarily in physicality. Caretakers experience the world feelings in physical, emotional, and cognitive ways but their predominant means of expressing these feelings is in some kind of activity. This diagram is our conception of how activity is the central modality of feeling expression for caretakers:

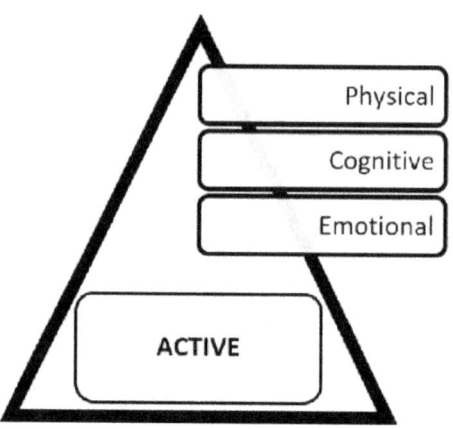

Note that caretakers experience all four elements of feelings but their preferred expression of feelings is in what they do. Again, as we noted with players, the other three expressions are a matter of preference and may not be in the same order for every caretaker. Some caretakers, for example, will be inclined to use physical expression in addition to their strength of activity if they also have player inclinations. If, for example, a caretaker has some analyst characteristics, then they may rely on their cognitive expression in addition to their active expression. In this chapter we have been studying about the property orientation and the activity of caretakers. We propose that all their activity is a reflection of what we call a "feeling" deep in their souls. Watch a player feeling something, and you will see her move her body in some way. Watch a caretaker feeling something, and you will watch him *do* something. Note how these two experiences of feelings both involve some kind of body action, but they are quite different: the player wants to experience the feeling while the caretaker wants to produce something as an expression of her feeling. Both players and caretakers feel emotion, just as much as the other temperaments, but emotion is not their primary expression of their feelings.

While we note that emotion is not the primary expression of caretakers, they certainly experience all four of the basic emotions: joy, sadness, fear, and anger. Notably, caretakers can have all of these emotions while they are expressing their feelings in the work that they do. You have seen that a caretaker friend of yours will be happy when he has succeeded in some property management exercise, like repairing his car or writing a book. Likewise, you can see the sadness displayed in his disappointment when he has not been successful in fixing the car or writing his book, or anger when he doesn't have the right wrench or find the right word. You might not see the emotion of fear, but fear is a very important aspect of caretakers' psychological functioning, which we will describe in Chapter 6. So, caretakers display the emotional experience of joy even though their joy comes from very different experiences: players are joyful when they have some kind of new experience compared to caretakers who experience joy when they have succeeded in some kind of activity.

The world needs caretakers, just like it needs people of all temperaments. The world is a better place because of caretakers' immense amount of activity in the care of property, but keep in mind that property is sacred to them just like experience is to a player. We can say that caretakers love property and providing, while players love experience. Now we shall examine how some people love meaning and other people love human connections.

Chapter 3

The Analyst Personality

ANALYSTS ARE UNIQUE. THEY are quite different from people with the other three temperaments. We have learned that players think that everybody should be playing all the time, and caretakers think that everyone should be working all the time. In the next chapter we will see that lovers think that everyone should be connecting to people all the time. Analysts are a bit different: they don't necessarily think that people should be like them. They know that all people all different, and they know that they are quite different from most people. They find that people are interesting and they want to *understand* people, especially people who are different from them. They don't necessarily want to change people, but rather they want to help people go about life in a better way. They are particularly interested in *why* people do what they do. Like all people, analysts would like be understood, but they care much less about being understood compared to people with the other three temperaments. In fact, many analysts have had so many experiences of not being understood that they do not expect to be understood, which is what makes this temperament so unique.

Analysts' interest in understanding reaches beyond people. They want to understand how everything works: how machines work, how some sports teams succeed and some fail, how grass grows, how a moon eclipse happens, how ideas are formed, and how ideas are abandoned. The key word for caretakers is *what* because caretakers are primarily interested in property. The key word for players is *when* because they want to engage in some activity. We shall see in the next chapter that the key word for lovers is *who* because they are principally interested in connections with people. The key words for analysts are *how* and *why*. "How does it work and why does it work?" Or, "Why doesn't it work?" Or, "Why did she do that?" Or, "How does he do that?"

Analysts are fascinated with discovery of *causes*, i.e., where things started, where they originated, so, when they hear someone's thought, they immediately want to know the origin of that person's thought. Likewise, when they see someone do something, they want to know why that person did what he or she did. The inquiring of analysts always seeks to see more and understand more. Analysts ask questions of people, and then ask more questions like, Why people do what they do, Why people believe what they believe, and How do people's beliefs square with what they do in life. Their interest in origins leads analysts to be intrinsically interested in people's motivations. Their interest in their own motivations is equally important, but they usually keep these thoughts to themselves.

Because they are so interested in other people, and ask so many questions, they are much less inclined to speak of themselves and their own motivations. As a result of this tendency to understand other people, analysts are the least understood of the four temperaments. The world profits greatly from analysts' analysis because they work diligently at this business of understanding. They are the scientists of the world, the examiners, the problem-solvers, and the architects. Without them we would not have safe buildings, operating computers, medical specialists, and good psychologists. Every element of life has been examined, to one degree or another, by analysts so that the world can work more efficiently. The world truly needs analysts.

CHARACTERISTICS OF ANALYSTS

As we discuss the characteristics of analysts, we remind you that these are not entirely unique to analysts. We wish to highlight how these characteristics tend to be typical of analysts while some analysts may not have all of them while some non-analysts may have one or more of them.

1. Looking for Causes

In their wanting to understand things analysts try to figure out *how* things work and *how* people work. The heart of this analytical seeking to understand people and things is looking for *why* things happen and *why* people act the way they do. Caretakers ask the question, "*What*" (What is it, what color is it, what does it cost, what I can do with it, and what is she doing?) Analysts ask the question, "*Why*" (Why is it that color, why does it cost that much, why was it made in that way, and why is she doing that?) Analysts are fascinated with causes and origins. Why did Sally turn out to be such a difficult person? Why did Sam turn out to be such a successful person? Why did that doorbell fail to work? Why did that candidate get elected? The primary way analysts look for causes is to ask questions, and most of these questions start with the word why. Sometimes their questions start with the words *who, how* or *what*, but analysts are still really looking for *why*. How does that machine work? What made it stop working? How could that problem be fixed?

Analyst people believe that things should *make sense*. This also applies to what people say, think, or do. They are not satisfied with just seeing something and accepting something the way caretakers see the world. They are not particularly interested in experiencing things the way players go about life. Analysts' play is in theorizing how things work and how people behave in the ways that they do. They think that there are answers to everything, and their duty in life is to find these answers. When they encounter a new person, they are immediately inquisitive and interested. Their first thought is something like, "Who this person is, what makes him tick, and how he is different from other people?"

While analysts are interested in why things *do work*, they are more interested in why they *don't work*, whether human or non-human. If an analyst is trying to understand another person, she will look for what might be problematic in the other person's life and what might have caused this problem. She thinks that she can be helpful by identifying the probable causes of a person's difficulty by first identifying the difficulty, and then searching for some kind of cause for the difficulty. Analysts think that if they can find the cause for the difficulty, the cure of the problem will be forthcoming. In this analysis of what is wrong with someone, the analyst is seeking to be of help to the individual. An analyst would ask the same question of nonliving things: Why is this machine not working? What is wrong with the engine design or functioning? What can be done about it to get it running properly? Questions are at the heart of an analyst, so analysts think that if they ask enough questions, they will find all the answers to why things and people work—and why they don't work.

Analysts don't always ask these questions out loud. They may be content to simply observe, muse, and consider why a person acts in a certain way or why a machine works in a certain way. A woman analyst that I know always meets new people with questions in her mind. She is introverted, as many analysts are, so she often keeps her questions to herself, but her basic approach to meeting someone, whether for the first time, or for the tenth time, is to ask questions about that person. Many times, she has met someone new and been entirely silent, true to her introverted nature, but anyone watching her could tell that she was thinking, musing, considering, evaluating, and intuitively gathering information about the new person.

The seeking for causes and reasons for people's behavior and words is a thoroughly good thing to do. This search for origins is a kind of cosmological approach to the world and all that is in it. Some analysts are theists and some are atheists, but they all look for origins and causes. This endeavor should be honestly identified as "spiritual," but not necessarily theological in essence. Currently, popular atheists now speak of "spiritual atheism," which seems an odd combination of words. These folks seek to know what it means to be a person and how personhood has developed. Analysts are searchers and seekers after truth, be it theistic or atheistic. In their searching they are quite content to be uncertain. Uncertainty just spurs their inquisitive nature. They can be quite content to spend hours searching, examining, and theorizing about a problem without the demand that caretakers tend to have to fix the problem as quickly as possible. Searching for origins is tantamount to searching for truth. Truth comes in many forms, and sometimes truth is quite paradoxical.

2. **Finding Paradoxes**
When someone looks for truth, especially if this truth is profound, like the existence or nonexistence of God, such a person is a searcher or a seeker. Searching and seeking for truth is always incomplete, and it is often paradoxical. Albert

Einstein, certainly an analyst by temperament, discovered that time is not constant, that time slows down the faster one travels to the point that time stops at the speed of light. It is paradoxical to think that time is not constant because it seems so counterintuitive, yet Einstein's theory is generally considered correct. A true scientist can never have a conclusion about something he is researching before he has examined all elements of the phenomenon. All scientists know that their research is incomplete. Furthermore, they know that they will encounter paradoxes: two or more things that seem both to be true but are in apparent opposition to one another. When this happens, the researcher/scientist must accept the fact that he has found a paradox. If an analyst asks enough questions, he will eventually be forced to see that simple answers never answer significant questions. This is well illustrated by the old philosophical paradox: If God exists and is all-powerful, can He create a stone so big that He can't move it? For many people contemplating such a question is just a waste of time, but for an analyst it is fuel for the fire of thought.

Analysts love questions, but they love paradoxes more. Paradoxes stir thought, contemplation, and more questions, but paradoxes rarely lead to absolute and concrete answers. This inquisitive nature of analysts sometimes leads them to talk in paradoxes forcing the listeners to wonder what these analysts have really said. When they talk this way, analysts are not seeking to confuse their audience, but rather to get people to think deeply and to contemplate, but not necessarily to find exact answers. My personal mentor and theology professor, Dr. Vernon Grounds, was a brilliant individual as well as an analyst. Dr. Grounds instructed his students that it was impossible to understand the most important matters of theology without accepting the very basic nature of paradox in theology as well as in daily life. I later learned that his own mentor was the philosopher Soren Kierkegaard who also talked about the centrality of paradoxes in philosophy, theology, and life in general. In perhaps his most important work Kierkegaard discusses the story of God of the Jewish Scriptures asking Abraham to take his (favorite) son, Isaac up a mountain to sacrifice him. Kierkegaard reports that Abraham somehow knew that God was One "who did not seek human sacrifice" and simultaneously trusted Him as a result of his belief about God's nature. But he also took Isaac up the mountain fully expecting to sacrifice him at God's bidding. Trusting someone, even a god, to that extent is certainly paradoxical. Who among us could possibly even consider sacrificing one of our children, or anyone for that matter, to a god who seemingly wants human sacrifice? In a different volume Kierkegaard suggested that people need to pray mostly when they *don't believe that God exists.* How could one pray to a god in whom you don't believe? Analyst theologians are able to consider such paradoxes as not only enticing, but also necessary to really understand how God might act, how people might act, or how the world works.

A former patient of mine who was genuinely agnostic loved honest inquiry, including a particular fascination with paradoxes and conundrums. William loved to find stories, whether fictional or factual, that portrayed the complexity of life, particularly the things that could not be understood. Paradoxes, themselves are not complete truths but rather pieces of truth that lead to a greater understanding of truth. Truth is something beyond paradox. It is one of those things that is so important that it is not definable, like time, distance, and mass are undefinable. William, in his very honest agnosticism about God, also became honestly agnostic about everything, love included. Did he really love his wife? Did he love his children? Did he love life? Everyone asks what love is and wonder if they love someone, but people with the other three temperaments are usually content to "just feel it" (lovers), "just experience it" (players), or "just do it" (caretakers). There is no "just" with analysts seeking to engage in this thing we call love. They are compelled to understand what love is, what it comes from, why it occurs at all, and whether there even is a thing called love. The deep searching for truth, which naturally leads to paradoxical truth is part of how William and other analysts find meaning in life. Analysts know that the search for ultimate truth does not have an exact end, and they are best equipped to reside in the nebulous as they continue their search. The search for truth is a journey filled with increasing truth bolstered by continued questioning and searching. Analysts do this searching well because they can live with uncertainties.

3. Accepting Uncertainties

Analysts' looking for causes and love of paradoxes are related to their liking of uncertainties. The operative statement that analysts frequently say is, "I don't know..." usually followed by, "...but I think there are many possibilities," which Kierkegaard wrote some 150 years ago. An analyst seems happiest when nothing is for certain because then anything is possible. The known universe is filled with uncertainties as scientists continue to remind us. Astronomers and quantum physicists seek out the extent of the universe and how it actually works, while atomic physicists seek to find smaller and smaller subatomic particles that might explain how and why matter exists. Most scientists would agree that there is much more unknown than there is known, whether it would be in the expanse of the universe or subatomic structure. While not all scientists are analysts, and not all analysts are scientific, scientific inquiry is built on the notion of uncertainties. When I read scientific articles, whether in my own field of psychology, or in other scientific arenas, I frequently find a similar statement at the end of the scientific article, "The entire function of this process is *not well understood*."

Because analysts take an inquiring scientific orientation towards all things, they are familiar with living with the unknown. In fact, *analysts often prefer the unknown* to the known. Quite the opposite with caretakers who truly like the known and avoid the unknown as much as possible. Ask a caretaker a question, and you will probably get an answer. The caretaker will like the book or he won't like the book; she will vote for candidate A and not for candidate B... and may not even be able to tell you why she voted that way; she will fix the apple pie the same way she has fixed it for 30 years, and very possibly the way her grandmother fixed it 50 years before that. Not so with the analyst. Ask a question of an analyst, and you will hear something like, "I don't know... but maybe it was this way or that way." Analysts love uncertainty, whether of what they are going to do, what they are studying, or what they are thinking because uncertainly breeds possibilities and inquiry.

There is something truly central about this business of "not knowing" that analysts like. If an analyst already knows something, she is not likely to restudy the matter or reanalyze the matter. She will just go on to something that is truly uncertain so she can enjoy the process of discovery. She will be looking for the truth. She will be theorizing while she is looking for facts. However, once she has found some truth and some of the facts, she will be much less interested in it. She has enjoyed the seeking, not necessarily the finding. Analysts have much more fun looking at the possible than the real. They might look at several possibilities and enjoy figuring out which of them is true, but when they find the truth and the facts, they are on to finding another truth. Finding the truth within another truth is much like wooden nesting dolls all hidden one within another.

Accepting uncertainties and enjoying paradoxes are not the sole property of analysts, but they are the stuff of how many people go through their days and their lives. Boris is a Jungian psychoanalyst and a longtime friend. Boris and I (Ron) have shared breakfast on Thursday mornings for nearly two decades. His fondest and most exciting times are those when he has found some element of uncertainty or paradox in his readings, which are usually Jungian in nature. He once said to me that it was most exciting for him to encounter some kind of paradox with a patient he was seeing because he could understand the paradox and appreciate the paradox more than his patient, thus being able to assist the person more adroitly. He can easily say that he "loves" something one moment and the very next sentence say that he doesn't like it. As a caretaker by nature, it is a stretch for me to understand Boris but I always come away from our breakfast meetings stirred to thought and contemplation. I look forward to our next shared breakfast. Analysts look forward to everything.

4. **Predicting the Future**

Analysts love to predict the future. It gives an analyst great joy to be able to gather enough information to be able to adequately know what is going to happen in the future. This desire to be able to predict the future is how analysts relate to both people and property. They are interested in being efficient, accurate, and faithful to life, which includes people, property, and truth. To do so means that analysts need to predict potential problems and find ways to prevent these problems before they occur. Analysts like to know as much as possible about what might happen in the future so they can do the right thing. They seek to examine all the data available to them in order to be certain in their action or words. Being able to know what might be going to happen in the future requires that analysts study as much as they can about the present. The analyst requires of herself that she know everything that everyone else knows before she is willing to make a prediction about the future. The analyst's reasoning is this: if I gather all the information about a particular problem, I will be able to know the correct procedure to follow to prevent problems from occurring.

One of the best ways to gather information is to ask other people what they know, what they believe, and why they believe it. Asking questions of people is by far the primary means of planning for the future and predicting the future. Thus, asking questions is analysts' most regularly used method of human interaction. My psychoanalyst friend, Boris, always greets me with questions. He asks me how I have been doing since we last met. But more importantly, he asks me what I think, what I have written, what I have done, and what I am up to. He is interested in my thoughts, my writings, and my doings. He is not terribly interested in my feelings although he certainly is capable of understanding feelings. This question-asking method of conversation is quite typical of analysts as it is their way of engaging other people. Analysts love people by understanding them, particularly why they have done what they have done. Then, the analyst might seek to help his friend by advising him about the future.

When they are at their best, analysts want to prevent harm from coming to anyone. They want their friends to know what the consequences might be if they do this or that. One way an analyst can love a friend is to help his friend understand that his friend's probable future is success or failure. Analysts want to love their friends by being able to predict future results from current behavior. Another of my analyst friends, Dave, is inclined to listen to what I am doing and make suggestions as to what the probable result of my behavior is. If I am seeing a particular patient who is difficult for me to understand, Dave will offer suggestions as to what might happen in the future of this patient's life. If I am writing on a certain topic, Dave will predict how my writing might be accepted by publishers. If I am thinking in a particular way, Dave will predict where my thinking may end up. He will help me by predicting the probable end result of my behavior.

Analysts like to analyze people to be able to predict the future, but analysts equally like to analyze impersonal things, like property or information, to see where things will be going in the future. Without a doubt, analysts are the best predictors of the future regarding where things will go. They are the successful people in government and business who look at the stock market, the availability of resources, the business trends, and the way things are happening. They gather as much information as possible and make educated guesses about what will happen in the future. The businesses that have the best analysts usually succeed. It is an analyst's dream to be able to gather all of the available information about a particular matter, like the stock market, and then be able to successfully predict what will happen in the stock market.

Some time ago I had two stock brokers as patients, both of them analysts. Interestingly, neither of them has been particularly successful in the business of stock brokerage. They have not succeeded in the business of stocks because they were more interested in analysis than in sales. Unfortunately for these fellows, as well as for many people in the stock business, developing a successful business in stocks has more to do with sales than it does with analysis of stocks. Neither of my stock broker patients had much real interest in sales, like cold calling prospective investors. Rather, these guys had interest in being able to gather all the information possible about various stocks in specific, and the stock market in general, and make predictions about what various stocks will do in the future. My brother, also an analyst, was an insurance salesman for about a year. During that year he had a guaranteed salary, but then he had to live on the commissions of sales he had made. Bill spent hours examining the data related to insurance, like the percentage one got for an investment in insurance policies. He sold me a policy. He sold *himself* two policies. I don't think he sold another policy over this entire year. He didn't really care about selling insurance policies and making money at it; he wanted to understand the insurance business so he could help people insure themselves appropriately.

There are many professions and businesses where analysts can be at their best. This could include the investment business where they could use their analytical and predictive skills effectively. A good profession for analysts is psychology, but not so much practical psychology and psychotherapy but in analytical psychology and research. Successful analyst therapists are those who have found ways to utilize their strong analytical interests with people who are like-minded, if perhaps less likely with people who want a quick fix to lifelong problems. I have known several very successful analytical therapists who have been in the business of therapy for many years and used their analytical abilities without losing heart over patients' disinterest in psychoanalysis. There are successful analyst people in all manner of business including public relations, engineering, lab technology, detective services and investigative journalism to name a few, but these analysts always need to find a way to enjoy their analytical interests and add a measure of patience with people who are less analytically inclined. One of the stock brokers I noted above found his way into a profession that allowed him to be about half analytical and half productive. While imperfect, it ultimately satisfied his basic temperament together with the necessity of doing something other than pure analysis.

The challenge for analysts in finding appropriate work is for them to be able to know and value their analytical temperament and balance the necessity of the large amount of caretaking that most jobs require. I recently did a psychological evaluation on a person most certainly with an analyst temperament who is entering seminary. He expects to be in the parish ministry sometime in the future, but he is also aware that typical pastoral work is not primarily analytical. It is caretaking. He is hoping that he can be in parish ministry for a few years and then perhaps find his way into higher education teaching. I trust he profits from the caretaking nature of parish ministry so that he can move into a more analytical mode of ministry.

Aside from the well-known and successful analysts that are psychologists, business people, and theologians, most of the analysts of the world are content to examine everyday information, like who make predictions about what will happen tomorrow or the week after next. Most analysts analyze for the fun of it. My brother-in-law is an analyst and now retired from a rather caretaking job at the Post Office. He did his job faithfully for 40 years, but his real interest was always in analyzing things and people. It can be enjoyable to be with Dennis when we are watching a ball game because he loves to analyze what might happen, what could have been done, or what should be done by the coaches and the players. His analysis is usually correct.

5. Internal

Analysts, by their nature, are "internal." Internality, sometimes called "interiority," is a psychological functioning that figuratively takes information in, digests it, and analyzes it. This "information" could be something seen or heard, by the other three senses, or perhaps even an intuition that the person has felt. Analysts operate in this "internal world" most of the time because they are always observing the external world and analyzing it. Internality includes possibilities, imagination, and musing. This internal world is one of subjectivity and possibilities more than the external world of objectivity and visible reality. Analysts who are introverted by nature are even more internal than analysts who are extraverted by nature. Extraverted analysts spend more time examining the concrete and visible things in life, like statistics and maps, while introverted analysts prefer to consider what statistics or maps might mean or what they might represent to the readers. Extraverted analysts are also more likely to share their analyses openly, while introverted analysts might be satisfied to just know something. While some analysts are more internal and intuitive than others, all analysts remain persons who first like to consider things privately within themselves. This internal process of consideration, musing, and evaluation is what makes analysts so distinct from the other three temperaments. No one thinks as deeply as an analyst. As might be expected, the internality of analysts often leads to their being misunderstood as we have noted.

I am not certain that analysts dream more than non-analysts, but certainly analysts are inclined to remember their dreams and think about them. My wife, wonderful analyst that she is, hardly ever has a night without vivid and elaborate dreams. Deb has these incredible dreams that not only are elaborate and long, but her dreams are much more important to her than my dreams are to me. Deb finds great personal meaning in her dreams, and the substance of her dreams gives her understanding of her life and occasionally gives her direction. More often, however, Deb's dreams are simply interesting to her and something to be analyzed. My psychoanalyst friend Boris loves dreams more than any other part of psychotherapy. Dreams enliven him as he sees in them possibilities of understanding, analysis and problem-solving. The more complex the dream, the better because the dream can lead to in-depth analysis. In fact, I recently had a dream that was somewhat disturbing and certainly thought-provoking. I talked to Deb about it, and I might talk to Boris about it to possibly gain some insight into my own internal psychology, although as a caretaker, it is not very important to me as it would be to Boris and Deb.

I suspect that the brain functioning of analytical types is much more complex than it is for the rest of us. It may be that analysts need to dream to make use of their complex brain power. Clearly, dreams are a psychologically internal part of human life. There are, for instance, some people who seem to have the ability to dream about what might happen in the future or, as my wife has attested, dream to *finish problems* they haven't yet found solutions for in their waking state. Religious literature frequently speaks of the value of predictive dreams. In cultures where dreams are seen as predictive or instructive, shamans interpret dreams to the dreamer. Likely, such people are analysts.

While dreaming is certainly an internal process and interesting to analysts, thinking is even more important to them. Analysts' first reaction to any new situation, new person, new book, new feeling, or new idea or dream is to think about these things. Deb almost always thinks about something when she first sees it or hears it. Her first reaction to almost any situation is to ask questions and to search for reasons. Our daughter, Jenny, primarily a lover who has matured her analytical part has always had a way of thinking about life that keeps her musing on the how's and why's of the world. On the rare occasions when I was visibly angry at Jenny as a child, she always listened, contemplated, and internalized. I almost never knew how she felt because quiet people, like many analysts usually internalize their assessment processes. Some of Jenny's greatest personal success has come from her privately observing someone else's behaviors, most specifically their mistakes, and apply what she observed in her own life so she might avoid those mistakes she noticed in others.

Analysts are people of deep feelings, but analysts' first response does not necessarily display their depth of feeling. While analysts are motivated first by feelings, like all human beings are, they examine their feelings analytically. If they speak at all about feelings, it will be what they *think* of their feelings. Their feelings, while not usually displayed, run along the line of passion for truth-seeking, theorizing, and making the world a better place. They are much less inclined to express feelings of hurt, sadness, or anger, much less fear. They might feel afraid for a moment but quickly transfer that feeling into a question of why they were afraid. Caretakers usually act first, think second. Players engage first, feel second, and think third. Lovers, as we shall see in the next chapter, feel first, act second, and think third. The nature and ability analysts have for thought makes them much more fair-minded by nature, more predictable in action, and more contemplative of the four temperaments. They are probably also more honest in their dealings with people in the sense of speaking what they think, but they are not necessary "honest" or open with their emotions. Analysts seek truth, particularly as it is found in theoretical analysis but emotions for analysts, while real and important to people with other temperaments, are not necessarily the stuff of truth for analysts.

6. Truth-Seeking and Truth-Speaking

Truth-seeking is the central ingredient of analysts. There are many varieties that this truth-seeking can take. For instance, there are analyst theologians for whom God is the center of truth, and there are atheistic philosophers who hold truth be the core of human existence. Most analysts are neither philosophers nor theologians, but rather people who are always in the pursuit of truth as they go through their days of work, play, and relationships. This truth-seeking includes the many elements that we have already discussed, like looking for causes, accepting paradoxes, and accepting uncertainties. If you can grasp this intense desire for truth that is so central to analysts, you will have a grasp of how they see their purpose in life: to find truth. When analysts speak, they usually have put a lot of thought behind what they say. Although it is sometimes hard to get analysts to verbally commit to something, when they do agree to do something or be somewhere, they will usually keep their promises. Analysts like to keep their word because they want their words to be a reflection of what they think. And what they think is a reflection of their internal personhood.

Not only are analysts truth-seeking, they are truth-speakers. One of the reasons that analysts tend to hedge when they express an opinion is that they always have in mind possibilities that can clutter a clear and definitive answer to any question. They tend to respond with more hedging when asked questions than when they speak spontaneously. Analysts may not be the most tactful people, but they are more willing to call a spade a spade without undue regard as to how their words are received. If you want really want to know if you look fat in that dress, ask an analyst. You want to know where he stands politically, be prepared for a dissertation that might not fit your thoughts, opinions, or feelings.

7. Possibilities and Ideas

Most people have waking dreams and hopes for the future. Analysts are very interested in the future. Related to this future-orientation is their desire to do something meaningful, something unique, and perhaps something great. In order to possibly do something great analysts must consider possibilities and options. For every one thing that an analyst does, he thinks about doing another hundred. An analyst is always considering options, things to be done, books to be read, sentences to be constructed, ideas to be contemplated, stories to be concocted, math puzzles to be solved, or cars to be made. His is the desire to create the ultimate invention, like the perpetual motion machine, and figure out a way to construct it. Note please, that analysts have much less interest in doing the actual construction of the perpetual motion machine than in considering how it *might* be constructed. It is the *idea* of creating something meaningful and great that stirs the analyst's mind. He or she is fascinated by the *possibility* of creating something like the perpetual motion machine more than in the real possibility of such a thing. Analysts consume ideas. They breathe ideas. They live on ideas.

Many analyst types are misunderstood because of their nature of dreaming and considering options and new ways of doing things. Robert is an important figure in the novel, *The Immigrants*, written by the Swedish author Moberg about a Swedish immigrant family coming to America in the nineteenth century. Robert is much different from his caretaker older brother, Karl-Oskar who is always doing something. Robert is always thinking, considering options, conceiving the impossible, and imagining. Sometimes, Robert mixes imaginations with reality, but such distinctions are not so important to him. His brother Karl-Oskar finds Robert's dreaming to be a nuisance at best, or lying at worst. But Robert is portrayed in Moberg's book as the first to conceive of the Nilsson family coming to America, the first to learn English, and the first to make his fortune (which he subsequently lost because fortune didn't mean much to him). Both his successes and failures were the result of his dreams and imagining. The character that Robert represents is an analyst: he always has great ideas and dreams. He probably had 100 dreams to every one dream he accomplished. Not long after the Nilsson family came to America, Robert was bored and needed a new adventure. This going from one dream to another is typical of analysts. Most of the time analysts go from one idea/dream to another and to another without doing much about any of them. But sometimes they find the means to execute one of their dreams. As with most people analysts succeed in executing one of their dreams about one-third of the time. More often than not, caretakers dream once and then act on it, while players dream and act at the same time. If analysts succeed at a dream, they might get bored with the actual production, sales, or management that comes along with success, and then feel the need to find another dream. Somewhat like players needing new experiences analysts need new ideas. Ideas for an analyst are like adventures for a player or projects for a caretaker. Ideas and dreams are energy producing for an analyst. One idea leads to another and like tumblers in a lock, one insight leads to another until understanding is obtained and some puzzle is solved. Generally, the disappointments in failure and the rewards in success don't seem to mean as much to analysts as they would to others because they know there is more to discover and understand. They just love to dream, consider possibilities and explore their ideas.

How many dreams or ideas did Einstein have before he conceived of the great theory of relativity and challenge Newtonian physics? How many failures did Ben Franklin have before he discovered electricity? How many failures did Alexander Graham Bell have before he successfully invented his telephone? And how many of Bell's several hundred other inventions were really successful? Mahatma Gandhi, the great statesman of India and leader of India's independence from Great Britain was certainly a dreamer-analyst. He dreamed of racial equality on all levels, and he dreamed of an India independent of Great Britain. But Gandhi's life was filled with failures. He failed to bring about racial equality in his original home of South Africa, and he "failed," if we call it that, for 20 years in India of gaining her independence. And then he garnered together 600 million Indians to form their own nation based on his dream of an independent India. Dreaming is usually not successful, but then dreams do not have to succeed. For the analyst dreams and imaginings are a way of life that will eventually lead to something great. Greatness for analysts is much different than greatness for people with the player temperament who need to have active engagement for their enlivenment, or for caretakers, who need appreciation for their accomplishments. Despite the fact that many analysts accomplish a lot of things, they are not the doers that caretakers are. They can more easily be satisfied with establishing a platform upon which their dream might be built. Analysts' greatness is in the creation of something unique, useful, efficient, and meaningful for the world, and all they need is a little understanding knowing that what they have come to understand is the beginning of a greater understanding yet to be discovered.

Dreams, ideas and possibilities don't have to be about doing something great. Rather, they are vehicles through which analysts examine even the day-to-day world. Today as Deb, the consummate analyst, and I, the consummate caretaker, were returning home from a brief weekend at our getaway cabin up north, I asked Deb if she needed to stop at her favorite garden center before we continued homeward. Deb mused about stopping, not stopping, why she might want to stop, and why she might not want to stop, what she might purchase or just want to view all within a matter of a few statements and a few questions. I did what I often do when I hear Deb's musings: I kept silent while listening to her out loud thoughts and possibilities. I have learned to do so over our 40-odd years together, and my silence usually serves her. So, after a few moments of silence, she said, "Let's just get home." In our earlier years, I would try to answer her questions, comment on my own feelings, or worse yet, debate with her about stopping or not stopping. Today, I did neither, and we were both better off for it.

ANALYSTS AND FEELINGS

Of the four expressions of feelings that we have described in the previous two chapters analysts distinctly prefer a cognitive expression. Indeed, they experience all four expressions of feelings, as all temperaments do, but they express their feelings in what they think compared to players who are physical in feeling expression and caretakers being productive in their expression of feelings. This diagram represents the centrality of thought in how analysts express feelings. Note that they have all the other three experiences of feelings (physical, emotional, and active) while preferring cognition:

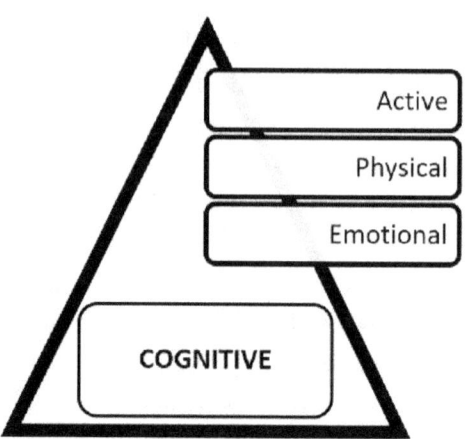

It is particularly important to note that analysts express *feelings* even if these "feelings" are not noticeably emotional. Analysts are deeply passionate about many things in life, particularly truth-seeking and truth-speaking. It is not always obvious that analysts are speaking of their deep feelings because people so easily confuse emotions with feelings. You can remember that feelings are the deeper part of our souls whereas emotions are but one way to express these feelings. Analysts are often perceived and judged as being "unemotional," but they are far from unemotional. Rather, they prefer to express their feelings through cognition in all that it means to be cognitive. They have a certain similarity to players in the realm of feelings because analysts often experience a deep physical reaction to something but then quickly pass by the emotional element of feelings and express themselves cognitively. Inevitably, if you ask analysts how they feel they will respond with "I think…."

We have noted that while there are four expressions of feelings, there are also four expressions of emotions, namely joy, sadness, fear, and anger. We have previously noted that both players and caretakers express the primary feeling of joy in the present. Analysts tend to express the primary feeling of sadness in the present. Recall that both sadness and joy have to do with love, namely that joy is the emotion we feel when we have something that we love, while sadness is the emotion accompanied with the loss of something that we love. With analysts in particular, we need to make a careful distinction between the emotion of sadness and the psychological state of depression because sadness is not depression although depressed people sound sad and look sad. As we will point out in chapter 7, analysts can easily be misinterpreted as depressed when in fact, they are often sad. The fact that analysts are so frequently sad is not a negative reflection on their character, much less a diagnosis of depression. Because analysts love truth to such an extent, they are frequently confronted with the paucity of truth in the world. They see how people shade the truth, deny the truth, convolute the truth, and otherwise put truth in second place to the other elements of life. Simply stated, analysts are more truthful in their lives, both in what they say and in what they do and when they encounter lack of truth in others it is sad. It is understandable that analysts see the lack of truth in so much of life, especially in what people say and what they believe, that they are grieved by the lack of truth. Analysts' primary love is for truth, just as players' primary love is for experience, caretakers' primary love is for production, and lovers' primary love is for human connection.

The world is a better place because of the presence of analysts. They look for truth, and in so doing they examine many possibilities. They look for problems in order to prevent them or solve them. Theirs is a wonderful gift to the world, and we would still be in the Stone Age if it were not for analysts who discovered the wheel and figured out how to write and who introduced the world to the industrial age through invention.

Chapter 4

The Lover Personality

NOW WE COME TO the fourth and last temperament: the lover. We are tempted to say that we have left the best for the last, and in many ways, this is true, but we heartily believe that all four of the temperaments are the best. The best part of lovers, as is evident from the very name we have chosen to use for these folks is *love*. Quite importantly, this love is for *people*, not for *experience* like it is with players, *work* as it is with caretakers, or even *truth* as it is with analysts. Lovers love people with a depth of passion that defies good description, but it is safe to say that they would easily give their lives for the people they love, and perhaps even for the animals that they love.

When we do an Intake Evaluation for a new patient, we always ask, "What is important to you?" With very few exceptions lovers answer with, "family" often followed by, "friends." Family and friends are so central in most lover's lives that they don't even think much about anything else that might be important. The word "family" flows easily out of people's mouths when we ask them what is important, but upon further inspection we actually discern that caretakers, players, and analysts really value things other than family. Some people will be able to identify a special person, like a grandmother or an uncle, or even a stepparent who is particularly important to them. When we phrase the question about what is important a bit differently, however, we might ask, "What is your value system?" This is a much harder question for lovers to answer because they often have not thought what their value system might be beyond family. The lover's expectation is that all value is associated with loving people. Ask this question of value system to caretakers, and they will talk of work and responsibility, players will talk of physical experience and excitement or discovery, and analysts will speak of truth-seeking and understanding. But lovers stick with the word "family" because for lovers the word *value means love*. They may not even be able to define the word love, but lovers know that love is central in life, life is all about love, and nothing whatsoever is more important than love. Lovers love family. Lovers love people. Lovers love. Period.

When caretakers love property, analysts love truth, and players love experience, they still want people in their lives, yet these three temperaments do not really place people first the way lovers do. A caretaker might work all day and night on the house and say that his working "is for the family," but he actually loves the work more than the family. Likewise, analysts might say that their seeking of truth is for helping people, and players could say that they want to bring joy to people, but these three temperaments don't value people the way lovers do. It is certainly not wrong for caretakers, analysts, and players to love the way they do. These three temperaments love people *through* work, analysis, and experience. But in the mind of a lover, it is definitely *wrong* to love anything more than people. For them love is primarily about people, and sometimes singularly about people. All else is secondary: property, play, and truth. In fact, lovers often sacrifice property, play, and truth for their love of people.

Lovers assume that they will always have someone to love, and they assume people will love them. It is just their way. It is something like, "Love is the center of life, so we *can* all love everyone and we *should* love everyone." Lovers will love you without your asking for it. Likewise, they assume that you will love them. This assumption isn't about reciprocity; they don't love you in order that you will love them; they just assume that because they love you, you will love them. It is their nature. They don't try to define love; they don't have to define it because they know what it is.

Love creates purpose and meaning in life, and most people look for a life filled with as much love as possible. Many volumes have been written about love, most songs are about love, many poems speak of its centrality in life, and yet love remains an undefinable to all of us, however central it is in our lives. Love is so important that it is—and must—remain undefinable. We know what love is but there is no definition that does it justice, and so we must be content with talking about something that we can't really define. Sacred literature is replete with references to love. The Apostle Paul identified love as "the greatest of gifts" and Jesus gave us the "great commandment" to love others and to love God as we love ourselves. Jesus actually was quoting the Hebrew Scriptures (the "Old Testament") when he suggested that the greatest commandment was to love. Properly understood, Buddhist theology is also based on love, albeit very differently from a westernized understanding of love, which is centralized around people. Buddhism has at least four kinds of love roughly interpreted as the love of kindness and understanding, the love of compassion, the love of joy and happiness, and the love based on freedom rather than neediness or fear. The basic theology of Islam is much more about reverence to God and service to humankind in general than it is about love of specific people. As we understand Islamic love, it is about the duty to love and do good things. In fact, these Eastern religions focus quite a bit on love of people as well as other things.

We know how important love is to almost everyone, but people with the lover temperament know the most about loving people and focus their lives around loving people…and being loved by people. Lovers are better at loving people and almost always quicker to love people than those of us with the other three temperaments. While we can't exactly define love, we can see the words of love, the actions of love, and the fruits of love. What we see with lovers is beyond words and actions. Lovers display the essence of love at a very deep psychological and spiritual level. We can learn about love by watching lovers and seeing the words and ways that they love.

CHARACTERISTICS OF LOVERS

1. Connecting

Here we are going to use one undefined word (love) with another undefined word: *connecting*. Although lovers can't exactly define the word connecting, they know what it means: love is something that connects one person to another. Lovers strive heartily to create those connections. "Connecting" includes *feeling the same thing that another person feels*, but it is more than that. This *connection* to another person is the essence of what love means to a person with a lover temperament. Connecting is a shared feeling, shared insight, shared belief, shared joy, shared sorrow, shared hope, shared expectation, or shared experience. The key to the connecting that lovers seek is this *sharing* something. It brings them great joy. Sharing also brings them great sorrow. Joy and sorrow are always born of love: if I have something that I love, I will feel joy; if I lose something that I love, I will feel sorrow. Lovers feel both joy and sorrow frequently.

This connection experience is so central to lovers. Lovers thrive in connection. The connection does not have to be permanent but when it is present it is all inclusive in the moment or experience. Our daughter Jenny treasures connection. She loves to scour ancestry sites for distant family members. When she finds a second or third cousin, she will reach out to them in hopes of a "connection". Sometimes her reaching out is returned and when that happens, she is simply joyful to be united with someone who shares her lineage. Many of these connections are brief but some have lasted into in-depth conversations and sharing of history and life events. Regardless, what matters to Jenny is the connection when it is experienced.

Connection at large has at least three basic elements: (1) *sharing* of the same feeling as someone else, (2) *blending* of boundaries between another person and oneself, and (3) a shared sense of *physical attraction*. Frequently, these three elements of connection occur at the same time. Sharing the same feeling with someone else includes all feelings, but predominantly joy and sorrow. A lover is at his best when he can feel these two love-based emotions with a friend or relative. This shared feeling can be the joy of seeing a wondrous seascape, the first breath of a newborn child, or the shared sorrow at the loss of a job or a person. To stand together with a friend as she sees the beauty in these experiences brings immense joy to a lover, but equally important is a lover's sympathy at losses that their friends have experienced. For a lover, in times of great joy or great loss, they do not distinguish between what you feel and what they feel.

Beyond the shared feeling, the second ingredient of the connection that lovers seek is the blending of boundaries between two people. This phenomenon is harder to describe, but it is central to the nature of lovers. When a lover is at her best, she loses a sense of herself separate from the other person and finds a deep connection with that other person. When this happens, there is what we should call a new creation, a *unity of souls*. We often describe lovers as "we, you, and I" persons. The implicit value system of lovers is: *we* first, *you* second, and *I* third. They think of the "we" part as most important and something they seek all the time. Their next operation is the "you" part, meaning understanding the other person, and the last thing lovers do is examine what they think or feel. While lovers certainly feel deeply and love deeply, their focus is so much on the "we" part and the "you" part of a relationship that they are not always aware of the "I" part. Caretakers, players, and analysts are much more aware of the "I" part of themselves. Lovers' hope is to first seek the "we" part believing that the other two parts will follow naturally. In fact, lovers often use the pronouns *us* and *we* instead of *I* and *me*. The underlying philosophy that lovers have is something like, "We are all in life together. We just have to find ways to succeed in life together." Sometimes, lovers even go further believing, "We should all feel the same things, think the same things, and like the same things."

We have many symbols of this kind of blending in the physical world, like the exact intersection of two roads, the mixture of oxygen and hydrogen to form water, and the development of groups of people with a common cause and purpose. We can see this joyful blending when a sports team accomplishes some kind of joint achievement, or when two people work together on a project finding that two minds are better than one. This blending of souls for lovers is deeper than shared experience: it is a gracious loss of self for something greater that occurs when one finds a true connection with another person. Lovers call this greater something a "relationship" but it is more than that. True blending is almost like the creation of a new person composed of elements of each of the people who are blended. We have all had these experiences to some degree or another, but blending is what lovers seek all the time.

The third connection of experience, physical attraction, is not unique to lovers, but it is certainly prolific with lovers. They know at first sight that the physical attraction they have for another person includes a sense of a deep love attraction. This could be the "love at first sight" phenomenon that people often report. Caretakers might love someone because they enjoy doing things together; analysts most naturally love someone who is also of like mind, often in truth-seeking; and players connect best in shared physical experience. All of these other temperaments love deeply and love truly, but they don't have the immediate physical attraction that lovers have for people. Importantly, this physical attraction is not limited to sexual attraction. Note how the lovers you know immediately "ooh" and "aah" when they see an infant, a new kitten or someone who is perfectly dressed.

I (Ron) have known many persons who have had lover temperaments, but certain ones stand out as vividly loving. In each case, my friends and relatives who are lovers seek to connect with the people around them. John, who now works with troubled children, had a long series of unsuccessful jobs and college experiences which always left him unfulfilled. He was a shoe salesman for a while, and perhaps had brief opportunity to engage people and share with his customers as he helped them find shoes. Then he was a carpenter's helper, a job that lasted a matter of weeks because of the lack of meaningful people contact. He was in and out of college a few times trying to find some people element. He couldn't seem to really *connect* with anything in college or work that was human enough to satisfy him. Then many years ago he happened into his present job working with troubled youth. Within months he had established himself not only as one who could easily and effectively connect with children, but someone who could also connect effectively with other staff members, parents, effectively helping everyone. John has succeeded in this professional job even though he did not have a professional degree. He just had the natural gift of loving, connecting, and sharing that is the essential ingredient necessary to do his people-based job well.

Unfortunately, most lovers seem to be less lucky than John in finding work that satisfies their need to love people by means of connection and sharing. I know of three salesmen, each of them having the lover temperament, who have no business trying to sell things when they would rather be loving in more meaningful ways. I know of a bank president who is probably nearly a millionaire who is unhappy in his job (and wealth) because he doesn't have daily experience of connecting. In fact, he would like to connect with the customers who are the least likely candidates for loans. A 65-year-old man I have been seeing for a while was recently fired because of his wanting to connect to his clients. His job looked like a connect-to-people job, but it turned out to be more sales than connecting. Human service jobs, which would seem to be best for lover types, often turn out to be more paperwork and politics than connecting and loving. I can't tell you the number of clients who, working in HR departments, come in to my office dissatisfied with work. They come in exclaiming that they thought being in HR would mean loving and helping people by listening and encouraging only to have discovered that it is more about documenting arguments and form filling. Likewise, many would-be social workers become discouraged because much social work is less social than it is logistical.

Lovers who have succeeded in finding happiness in life have found ways to connect and otherwise love people despite their life situations, despite their jobs, and sometimes despite their family connections. Janet is a person of many talents, including food preparation, interior design and decorating, and other creative and artistic work, but Janet's greatest gift is in her ability to connect with other people. She is able to ingratiate people without ever trying because of her giving and loving nature. When Janet is in my presence, she is immediately and honestly interested in knowing what I am doing and feeling. Her first and foremost interest in life is the emotional welfare of those in her immediate presence, and she finds it hard to engage in much else but trying to find out how people feel regardless of their circumstances. She connects with people at her business attending to customers, with her family members, with friends, or with someone she happens to meet on the street. She is always looking to see how others feel, finding ways to share their feelings, and experience life with them in an emotional way. When Janet is around, you will feel her presence and her love.

As we have noted, both of our daughters have this lover temperament, and both seek connections, but our younger daughter, Jenny, is perhaps more of a true lover, while Krissie's player temperament was blended with her lover temperament. When we talk, text, Facebook, or visit, Jenny is always the one who seeks connection with us. Certainly, hugs are first when we actually meet, but after those moments she is looking to connect with what we feel, what we think, and what we have done. She is looking for connections across the board. She is looking at a way to find us so she can find a way to blend with us. We wonder how these two girls turned out so good in life with one parent a caretaker and the other an analyst. It seems that we all muddled through their childhood together doing our best to love each other. Lovers do it best.

2. Harmonious

Lovers seek harmony. Lovers do best with other lovers in this seeking harmony because both people are willing to make the necessary adjustments in life so that they can live together and love together in harmonious fashion. A lover wants to connect with another person in such a way that the two friends can both express themselves and agree on all things. The harmony that lovers seek with people is something like the musical harmony between, say, the soprano singing the melody and the baritone singing the harmony. In the musical genre these two blend together for something greater than either of them could do alone, but the musical analogy is not a perfect reflection that lovers want in a relationship. Indeed, lovers seek something better than being two different people, but "something better" is not two people saying different things or doing different things but two people doing the same thing or saying the same thing. In fact, lovers want the other person to *see* the same thing and have the same reaction to what they see, feel the same thing, and think the same thing as they do. The connection that lovers want in life is where there is no distinction between two people. Lovers almost always seek a blending. When it is rightly constructed, this person-to-person harmony is godly and joyous, and it is safe. The safety implicit in emotional harmony is the absence of conflict and the presence of agreement. Lovers seek harmony for the sake of connection. We are both old enough to fondly remember Coke's "Hill Top" ad, a commercial that was popular in the early seventies, based on The Seekers' song, "I Want to Teach the World to Sing." The Coke rendition was phenomenal in capturing what lovers are like and what lovers want: everyone standing hand in hand happily singing, "I'd like to teach the world to sing in perfect harmony, I'd like to hold it in my arms and keep it company." Lovers, more than any other temperament are passionate about coming together, being together, sharing together and loving each other.

When lovers find harmony with other people, these people are usually lovers themselves, making it is easier to connect and find common ground. People with the lover temperament can meet and resonate so quickly that they feel they have been friends or family for years. Without knowing it, lover people who happen to meet can feel the connection that is made between them, often without words. They may see the lover eyes, the lover smile, the lover grace, or even the simple hand-to shoulder touch that makes some kind of a connection. I think of lovers as having a set of antennae that are always searching for someone with whom to connect. When a lover connects with another lover, this connection can be across the table or across the room. It might even be across the miles as when lovers find each other on social media and end up talking for hours without ever seeing each other. We both know several lover people who have "fallen in love at first sight" or from across the room. Lovers may or may or may not literally "fall in love" across the room, but they can certainly they feel connected quickly and be inclined to maximize that connection by moving across the room. This sense of connection is almost uncanny. When this quick initial connection is made, lovers quickly work to cement the connection by finding commonalities in experience, thought and spiritual or philosophical beliefs. Certainly, it is the lover who knows that there is a connection "at first sight."

Lovers are good at finding natural connections, say with other lovers, but more often, lovers need to *create* harmony rather than find it. A mature lover will listen intently to the other person seeking to understand what he is thinking and what his value system is. Most lovers, however, will think about what the other person *might be feeling* and try to identify with it. As a result of this trying to connect with other people, lovers aren't always the first to speak. Rather, they listen, watch, and "feel" what the other person is feeling. Sometimes they ask questions so they can find ways to connect. This activity is a kind of intuition. When lovers are at their best, they actually know what the other person is feeling. They may see it in his eyes or body posture, but their intuition is deeper than physical appearance. They are not naturally seeking to agree or disagree but to feel the essence of the other person. If they can connect to the other person, lovers can find similarities and common feelings that create harmony.

When a lover finds something in common with someone, she will then try to harmonize with that person, which means that she will work to find commonalities with that person. She might carefully state her own thoughts, feelings, or experiences while trying to find similarities between them. Lovers often "harmonize" with their bodies almost as a kind of physical mimicking the posture of the other person. Lovers can be the best of friends as they seek to carefully express themselves, hopefully in concert with what they have heard, seen, and felt with their friends. They try their best to be unobtrusive when they speak, so when they speak, they are quite unlike players' excitement-seeking, caretakers' property-maintenance, or analysts' truth-seeking. They find excitement, care of property, and truth best in the harmony that they create *with* the other person.

The lovers that we have mentioned above all have this characteristic of seeking harmony. Daughter Jenny rarely displays any kind of anger or displeasure. Rarely are lovers easily angered, especially at the beginning of a relationship. Instead, these people spend hours and hours seeking to connect with people and find similarities that make for human harmony. Lovers seem to have a way to successfully avoid unnecessary anger and conflict because their focus is on agreement more than disagreement. You might hear something like, "Don't we agree that Bob is…," but rarely, "I think that Bob is…."

When you find yourself in the company of a lover, you will usually feel his or her subtle presence. It is remarkable gift that lovers have the ability to find other people's feelings and find ways to blend with their emotions. This blending may come in the form of simple listening; other times lovers will engage in friendly conversation that calls me out of myself. Laurence is at his best when he is in the presence of someone who is honestly speaking the language of feelings that he understands and that he can relate to. I have a mental picture of Laurence from many years ago intently listening to someone express his feelings about something that is important, trying to find a way to harmonize with the other person, i.e., *feel* with the other person. Then, Laurence might add something about his feelings and thoughts so that he and the other person can feel something that is better than either of them alone. An old friend of mine once told me that he awakes each day to discover with whom he can "connect," which means with whom he could harmonize.

3. Dreaming

All people like to dream of the future and people of all temperaments dream to some degree. Analysts dream about helping the world find truth; caretakers dream about fixing things in the world; players dream of playing together with people. The dreaming that players, analysts, and caretakers do is substantially different from the dreaming that lovers do. Simply put, lovers' dreams are more emotional and more interpersonal. Dreaming for a lover is much more of a free-floating process where their minds drift into possibilities and opportunities for human connections. Lovers' dreaming is always people-centered rather than things-centered, idea-centered, or play-centered. They don't think much about *why* something has happened the way analysts do, *what* has happened like caretakers, or *when* things can really be exciting as players do. Lovers dream about *how* they could be connected with other people. They might dream about having a perfect relationship, or dream about improving their current relationship, or they might dream of having a relationship with some unknown person where everything is about connection and harmony. Lovers may just dream of "sailing into the sunset."

Lovers often prefer literature that is about connections including romance and western novels, but they can be fascinated with biographies where people struggled with how to engage life with the unavoidable losses and tragedies that occur with everyone. They are sometimes attracted to poetry, especially when the poetry is about relationships. Lovers also like TV and videos that are about relationships. They might tolerate high action or science fiction, but they would rather watch a so-called "sad" movie, which is really a movie about how people worked at some kind of relationship that eventually ended in forgiveness or restoration. It is not so much about the success or failure that intrigues them as it is about how two people find ways to connect…and disconnect. I recall how our daughter, Krissie, was bothered at the end of a movie because the two main characters couldn't find a way to get together. Krissie just didn't like that "people can't follow their love" despite the complications. We could say that lovers' dreaming is impractical and unrealistic but that would be a bit unfair. Their kind of dreaming, often about fantastic and wondrous relationships is good for them. It grounds them by connecting with their spiritual core.

Lovers can dream about places, ideas, and possibilities but these dreams always involve people. I have made the mistake of misunderstanding the dreaming nature of lovers when they talk about doing something or going somewhere. I recall a woman client from many years ago who saw the movie "Out of Africa" and immediately talked about going to Africa. Since the movie "Out of Africa" was so much about a relationship, she saw Africa as a place to meet people, find connection, and make harmony. She even started saving her nickels and dimes to be able to afford such a trip. Sometime afterward I asked this woman about her possibly going to Africa and discovered that she didn't remember her dream about going to Africa. Imagining going there was about finding the relationship personified in the movie. She didn't need to go to Africa; rather, she needed to dream about going to Africa and meeting someone there. I learned something in this encounter: lovers can be satisfied with dreaming without doing.

4. Touching

It is almost impossible for lovers to keep from touching people. Yesterday, Deb and I did therapy with a couple. I have been working with the man for many months, and Deb has been working with the woman. This man and wife have come to a very difficult place in their life together and they needed us to help them sort things out. After an intensive two-plus hours with this couple, and after many tears, we ended the session. After we all stood up, the wife reached out her hand for a handshake, which I accepted, and then, almost as if she had said, "I need more than this," she reached out to me for a hug. It was one of those full body hugs that lovers give where two bodies are close enough to feel one another's heartbeats. It wasn't one of those hugs that I call "A-frame" where two people only touch at head level, nor was it a "C-frame" hug that is typical of men where the two men stand facing in the same direction each with only one arm around the other guy. This was a great big bear hug. It was real, and it was absolutely necessary for her. We had had this intensive connection during our therapeutic hour, not all of which was pleasant, so she needed to feel this physical connection before she left my office.

Lovers need to touch people. They always hug their friends and family members when they see them. They touch the person they have just met, perhaps just on the arm or the back. They touch friends of friends. Touching is natural to lovers, like the woman we saw yesterday. During that session she talked mostly about her relationships and connections, or the lack thereof, including that with her husband, each of her three children, her sister and other members of her family of origin, and her friends. Her view of life was connection-based, and part of the difficulty she was experiencing was the lack of physical contact with all of these people, perhaps most importantly with her husband, who is, by the way, analyst and caretaker by nature.

Lovers' tendency to touch people is clearest when they touch another person who is in pain of some kind. The affectionate touch rendered to someone in pain that is fairly natural for all of us is perhaps more of a wonderful compulsion for lovers: they are compelled to touch a person in pain, whether that pain is physical or emotional. Their touch is very likely healing in a way that lies beyond exact science. There are professional healers, many of whom may well be lovers by temperament, utilize "healing touch" as a principal part of their work. Healing touch is quite simply the healer placing his or her hand on the part of the body of the patient that is in some kind of pain. There is a good bit of research that suggests that physical touch is beneficial to healing pain. Massage therapists perhaps know more about the healing nature of physical touch, but it is also a part of physical therapy, chiropractic, nursing care, Reiki, and other more non-traditional medical practices.

Many nontraditional healing practitioners talk of a healing "energy" that occurs when two people touch one another. There has been some scientific research that suggests physical touch can relieve physical pain, or even enhance repair of tissue damage, but that information lies outside of the purview of our current discussion. However, this so-called energy is also something that teachers of martial arts talk about in their work, especially in Tai Chi. Children are perhaps most susceptible for the effective use of healing touch. I have had more than one experience of helping in the process of emotional healing by holding or otherwise touching people in emotional pain. I have also had the very unique experience of helping my own children through healing touch when they were suffering physically, something many parents have also experienced. While many parents have experienced the healing value of touch, and some people are professional in healing touch, lovers seem to have more of this natural ability to heal by touching.

Not only do lovers touch other human beings, they also touch animals, and are seemingly compelled to do so. While most people are attracted to the beauty of animals, it is the lovers that are drawn to pet the strange dog, and even refer to their own as their "babies". A therapist friend of ours refers to her "girls" in the backyard, which are the chickens she cares for. This affection is not just an expression of fondness, but a genuine sense of connection with the animals. Many people love animals and many use animals as companions, but with lovers there is a deep internal connection with animals that often equates with their connections with people. It seems also true that lovers need to touch physical things that are not even animals, like plants, spices, and in some cases mechanical objects that they love. This could even be the backyard mechanic who loves to run his hand over his Harley, or the finish carpenter who runs his hand over the trim work he has just finished. When lovers touch something, they feel a connection with that thing, whether it is alive or inanimate. The literal physical connection as well as the emotional connection is so important and characteristic of lovers.

Lovers not only need touch in order to be at their best, they need to *be* touched. This need to be touched is not some kind of pathological "neediness", but rather a natural feeling that erupts from their wanting to be connected with people. When we are with Jenny, there is something very special about how easy it is to just hold hands, to hug, to cuddle. It is so natural for Jenny as lover to grace us with touch and to be graceful in receiving our touch. The woman who spent those difficult hours with her husband, Deb, and me, *needed* to be hugged. It was not some sort of problem she had. She was not seeking any kind of permanent relationship with me. Rather, she had felt connected with Deb and me during our hours together, and she needed to solidify that connection with touch. Lovers often give off the "vibes" of needing to be touched. They can even seem vulnerable, but usually this vulnerability is due to their not having been touched enough. This need to be touched and the connection that it represents, at its core is good, godly, and human. Touch is an essential part of any relationship, but much more so with lovers. Remember Romeo's classic desire for the touch of Juliet: "See how she leans her cheek upon her hand. Oh, that I were a glove upon that hand that I might touch that cheek!"

In conjunction with the need to touch and be touched is the phenomenon of cuddling. Lovers love to cuddle. Compared to the other three temperaments, they use this word "cuddle" with seeming abandon. They know instinctually that humans need to entwine both physically and emotionally, which of course, is just what cuddling is. We recognized the significance of this when our daughter Krissie, in some of her more lonely years just preceding her death, somewhat sheepishly told us that she would spend cuddle time with her good friends, a lesbian couple, who graciously shared their cuddle time with her. For Krissie and her two friends, this was simply a natural thing to do. Krissie needed touch and her girlfriends could share their touch with her. It was simply a need met by others who understood the significance of touch in compassion for others. We find it quite moving that two lovers could willingly share some of their touch with someone who had no partner and in need of physical contact. At Krissie's Celebration of Life we had a chance to mention this in appreciation to "the girls," as Krissie fondly referred to them, and their response was, "of course we would cuddle with Krissie." It is natural for everyone to want to touch and be touched but it is central for lovers to offer touch so freely.

5. Generous

Lovers truly enjoy giving. Giving for lovers is a way of self-extending. Giving and sharing demonstrates their felt sense of connection with someone. They like to give hugs, and greeting cards and thank-you notes. They like to bake goodies, bring flowers, pick up ice cream treats, or bring sandwiches for people working on the roof. This kind of giving is not specific only to lovers but everything they give usually comes with intentional thought of what someone might enjoy. Gifts from lovers often represent both themselves as a giver as well as their sense of connection with you as the recipient. It is this depth of thoughtfulness that is indicative of lovers. Analysts might generously give you a copy of a Stephen King book because he remembered the authors you like. A lover doesn't have to figure it out what someone might want or need; they "just know." They have a sense of what someone might need or want, and then follow that knowing in their giving. Caretakers can generously do something practical, and players might generously play some new game with you. Lovers give out of a felt sense of connection with you and out of the specialness they recognize in you.

Lovers' generosity can be in the forms of property, truth-speaking, or playful engaging the way caretakers, analysts, and players are generous, but more often they are generous with their emotional support. They listen. They listen carefully. They feel. They feel genuinely. They cry with those who cry, laugh with those who laugh, tease with those who tease, and join in with friends who are angry at their ex-spouses. They actually *want* to hear about their friend's emotional or relational difficulties. They are the best of "bearing one another's burdens" as the Apostle Paul suggests. They can be up all-night listening, crying, and laughing. They can be on the phone for hours talking and listening without ever thinking about the time. You need some kind of emotional support? Look for the lover in your life and he will be right with you. The only thing that would keep him from coming to your emotional aid is the fact that he is serving someone else.

Giving emotional support can come in concert with the giving of property, ideas, or play the way other temperaments give, but the essence of lovers' giving is always in concert with the emotional connection that they have with someone in need. We have known lovers who have actually stolen things so they could give these things to someone who seemed to be in some kind of need. Stealing from one person to serve another would never be something caretakers or analysts would do, and players might do it "just for fun." For lovers, however, being a Robin Hood-like person is wholly godly and "honest" because they feel sadness with someone when they are in distress and joy when they are happy.

6. Forgiving

Lovers are equally good at sharing joys and sorrows, but their ability to share the sorrow that comes out of pain can be quite astounding. If a lover is around someone that is hurting in some way, whether from physical, emotional, or relational matters, the lover will feel immediate compassion and a desire to give something to the hurting person. Lovers can even show genuine affection for someone who is in pain even though the very same person may have brought them pain in the past. In such cases lovers may actually forget that the person they are comforting has hurt them in the past.

When at their best, lovers not only do not expect anything in return for their gifts of love, they are more forgiving of people who are not as loving as they are. Lovers are more forgiving than people of other temperaments. It is simply easier for lovers to forgive offenses and mistakes in other people. They seem able to understand that much offense and many mistakes are not intentional, but rather due to misunderstanding or misjudgment. When they are secure with themselves, lovers can forget about bad things that have been done to them. They can be on the receiving end of vicious attacks, physical or verbal, and they will return the next day, even the next hour, with a spontaneous and genuine felt concern for their attackers if the attacker displays regret and makes an apology. Lovers seem not to even remember offensive things that were said or done to them. Forgiveness for lovers can come easily and naturally, especially if the offending party shows some kind of contrition. We are frequently impressed with the lovers who come to our office because of their sacrificial and forgiving nature. Lovers seem to be able to forgive the simplest of hurts that they have suffered from people to say nothing of the most heinous of crimes that have been perpetrated on them. Lovers actually profit from their forgiving nature as Shakespeare wrote, "The quality of mercy is not strained. It is twice blest. It blesses him that gives and him that takes." ("Merchant of Venice") Lovers are blessed by giving, sacrificing, and forgiving.

Many well-meaning counselors are nonplused at lovers' ability to stay with partners who are continually hurtful, offensive or even harmful. Lovers' staying with someone who is hurtful is not coming from something wrong with the lover. They are not necessarily "co-dependent" or "insecure." Rather, like all the temperaments, lovers can "love to a fault" and subsequently "forgive" to a fault, something we will examine in Chapter 8, but it is most important to recognize that a lover person goes well beyond the expected when it comes to loving in the form of giving.

7. Sharing

Lovers' generous and forgiving nature is related to their desire to *share*. They want to share everything they have with the people they love. They will share money or property, but most importantly, lovers want to share feelings. Giving, forgiving, and sharing are all a part of lovers' desire for connection. You will not be able to distinguish these things when you are in the company of a lover friend because a lover does not distinguish what is hers and what you might need. My sister, "Cookie," is a lover by nature. She insists that I take some kind of present with me when I leave her house, and when she comes to our house, her car trunk is full of presents for us. The sharing that lover's do is about enjoying your company, being with you, having an experience with you, bonding with you. Remember we mentioned that we had recently had time with Jenny on the beach and that she simply and kindly reminded us that being together, sharing time together was all she wanted. When a lover talks about wanting to share with you, she wants to share some experience with you much more than sharing property, ideas, or play. A lover is one who enters your house and immediately attends to your dog saying, "Oh, how cute," or immediately gives you a hug, or immediately connects with you about your house. If the lover is unable to sense a sharing of the experience, she will be temporarily at a loss as to how to relate to you, and will search for some similarity between her and you, something that you and she have in common to establish this bonding that is so central to the nature of lovers.

In the work setting it is essential that lovers have some significant people contact, i.e., some regular time when they can relate to other people by sharing things in common. Most of the chatter that goes on in offices is among lover types seeking to connect and share with one another while they go about their work. Often, this office chatter is of no real significance in content, but rather serves exclusively to give what might be called meaning to the lover while he goes about his office duties. Some lovers have the luxury and opportunity of having jobs where they can connect and share with people as part of their basic job duties. Unfortunately, many of the social professions are more professional than social, and do not serve lovers' need for sharing of love and life. Lovers can be very good social workers, clergy, nurses, and human resource workers, but what they do best with their work is truly sharing with their clients more than any kind of administrative work. Interestingly, one of the best work settings for lovers is the front office person, the person who greets and meets customers and clients, or the inside sales person who meets and greets new customers.

Sandy, our secretary of many years, was principally lover by nature, perhaps secondarily caretaker, and she served us as well as our clientele superbly. She was the kind of person that people were drawn to because she had a way of meeting people when they came to the front office window. Furthermore, many clients and many of my friends thoroughly enjoyed visiting with Sandy in the office, and she was always gracious in giving of her time and a cup of coffee to friends and patients according to their wants and needs. More than one patient said to me, more than jokingly, that they preferred talking to Sandy than to me. Sandy was able to meet people on any number of ways including ideas, jokes, conversation about clothing or something more personal and intimate.

Some lovers, particularly those with a more analytical second nature, enjoy sharing of ideas and find connections intellectually. These lovers can be the very best of conversationalists. One such person is a long-time friend, Sharon. Sharon was one who was capable of becoming intimate in conversation in a matter of seconds, particularly if the conversation was a bit esoteric. It seems that all one had to do was provide an opportunity for some kind of conversation, and Sharon was ready and willing to join in, contribute, listen intently, and discover some new truth about life. I don't think either one of us has ever engaged such a charming conversationalist as Sharon. Sharon, like many lovers, sought union of idea and commonality of spirit, and as an analyst, found deep passion in dissecting any topic of discussion to discover some new piece of understanding of the universe.

Some of the best sharing lovers do is when there is emotional pain. A lover is at his best when he is able to "feel with" someone else who is experiencing pain. This feeling with someone in pain is a process that defies description because it is essentially a spiritual process that lovers seemingly can tap into more frequently than people with the other three temperaments. Lovers don't wish for others to be in pain so they can share with them, but they possess a sensitivity that is quite profound in this regard. You can see the compassion in their eyes and gestures in their hands as they share you pain; you can hear their compassion in the tenor of their voice; and certainly, you can feel their touch on your shoulder or arms about your neck. It is so real for them that in moments of great pain, like in moments of highest joy, the lover is fully with you. We had many times of tender sharing of feelings after Krissie died. One of the most profound occurred when we were hiking to a waterfall not far from our northern Wisconsin cabin that had been a favorite place for Krissie and her children to visit with us over the years. We were spreading some of Krissie's ashes at the waterfall when a young lady asked us what we were doing. Deb said, "Our daughter died recently and…" but Deb couldn't finish the sentence before this gal called her friend over and said, "Come, Gloria, we're going to pray with these people." So, she and Gloria did just that, no questions asked, nothing expected in return, just these two young strangers embracing us, holding our hands and praying for our comfort. They shared our grief as many people have shared our grief. No one does this better than lovers. These kind lovers "knew" what to do. It was a kind of intuition. Interestingly, we've had many such encounters with "angels unaware" where we were privileged to have some otherwise unknown person share our grief.

8. Intuitive

To be intuitive is to have a "second sense" or a "gut feeling." People of all temperaments have this intuitive ability. It seems, however, that lovers trust their intuition, perhaps more than most people, and may activate it more often. They encounter their intuition as a "just knowing" or "just feeling" experience. It is simply natural for lovers to watch, listen, and intuitively interpret what other people are thinking and feeling—but mostly what they are feeling emotionally. They are particularly aware of feelings of sadness and hurt, feelings that touch them emotionally and stir in them the desire to help, and if possible, to heal. They particularly watch others people's feelings as displayed in their body evidences: eyes, posture, countenance, and even skin tone. This watching that lovers do is usually quite obvious: they look at you, and seem to *feel into you*. Their inclination to intently watch other people can even be intrusive, especially to people who would really rather not be watched, much less have their feelings known. To be on the receiving end of this watching-intuition can feel like being analyzed, or even criticized, but it is neither. Rather, lovers watch to see how to connect, how to feel with others, how to nurture, even to heal other people's emotional wounds. One of my clients, a man who has been happily married to a woman for 32 years recently had an affair with a woman. He describes this affair as "crazy" because his experience with this woman was unlike anything he has previously encountered. He told me that once or twice she "looked into his eyes and saw into his soul." I believe he has found a lover who has "connected" with him more than his trustworthy caretaker wife has done.

Lovers' intuition with people is generally a tapping into their soul, like my client reported, or a "magical" knowing something about you. This knowing generally gives lovers a sense of being connected with you and brings them joy if what they sense is a good thing or a compassion if the knowing is something sad or distressful. Do they really have an ability to know something about you that you don't know? Probably not, but they are more able to "tap into it" and bring it to light, as it were. Analysts also are intuitive but their intuition is based on gathered bits of information that accumulate into a conclusion, like grasping of how something can or does work. Lovers' intuition is based on their depth of feeling experiences that culminate in knowing about a person and their emotional state. Lovers simply trust what they feel about someone else.

Lovers' intuition can be perceived as benign, enlightening, or threatening depending on one's own level of self-awareness. We have known many lovers in our years, and we have generally found them to be benign in their watching and quietly examining of us. Both of our mothers were lovers and they always sought to "know" us regardless if or not we told them what we were feeling. Likewise, our two lover daughters look carefully into our eyes to see how we feel. Lovers who come to see us in our office, hear us give a lecture, or just meet us on the street always look straight into our eyes as if their eyes were spiritual sonar searching for how we feel. Often, such lovers seem less interested in what we are saying or doing as they are in how we are feeling. It is fair to say that their intuitive ability is really about a spiritual awareness of humankind. Many first-time patients who have the lover temperament say they are listening to their intuition in order to know whether we are the right people for them. This primary intuition of lovers is intrinsically connected to their desire for *connection*.

Lovers connect, harmonize, and have intuitions about nonliving things, particularly things of art or beauty, like music, nature, painting, or physical appearance. Asked if they like a picture, lovers will usually be immediately able to answer yes or no, but asked why they like the picture, they will be quite nonplused, and might only answer by saying, "I don't know why I like it." Lovers who are less secure about their gift of intuition are usually more inclined to question people in their environment in order to confirm their intuitions, but this questioning is just a way to confirm what they already believe or know.

9. Love the One You're With

This is, of course, a statement from a song by Crosby, Stills and Nash popularized in the 70's. The phrase "love the one you're with" has been a common expression over the years, but it is the preceding portion of the lyric that makes it so applicable for lovers. "If you can't be with the one you love, love the one you're with". Lovers have this ability like no other temperament. They love like there is no tomorrow, love like there is no one else to love, love deeply, and love "forever." Importantly, though, their understanding of "forever" is an emotional term, or perhaps more accurately, a spiritual term. And "forever" is also situational, meaning that they can feel a kind of forever in a singular moment of time. When a lover loves someone, that love is all that matters, not time, distance, or difference in temperament. When they love someone, they feel that this love will be forever because they don't distinguish the present from the future. This forever is a "feeling," not necessarily a fact. It is remarkable that a lover can love so deeply, feel so deeply connected, feel that someone is the love of their life despite the facts that might seem contrary to this love. While this can sometimes go wrong, something we will examine in Chapter 8, for the most part this is part of the lover's giftedness, just loving whomever they love when they love.

LOVERS AND FEELINGS

If you have known lovers, you have heard their feelings. More accurately, you have heard their *emotions* because lovers express their feelings primarily emotionally. Following the paradigm we proposed earlier, feelings are experienced first physically, then emotionally, then cognitively, and finally in some kind of action. Lovers have all these feeling experiences but their primary expression of feelings is with emotion. They, like the other temperaments can utilize the other three, but their natural preference is for emotional expression.

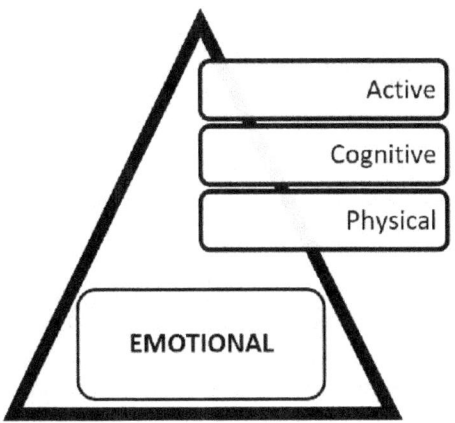

In this chapter we have described how lovers seek human connection first and foremost, and as a result love to be with people. In fact, they so prefer to be with people that they are particularly good at finding people with whom they can live, like, and love. Because human relationships are so profoundly infused with emotion, lovers frequently and easily become emotional. It is a mistake to think that they are "simply emotional" or that they have more emotion than people of other temperaments. They have no corner on the market of having emotion. Rather, they simply value the emotional *expression* of feelings more than physically, cognitively, or productively. They can engage in physical, cognitive, or productive activities, but always their expression of what these things do for them is in some kind of emotional expression. You hear them say such things as, "I just love to work with you," "I just love to philosophize with you," and "I just love to make love to you" and "I just love to be with you." Note all of these expressions are emotional. Whereas people of other temperaments might have these very same emotions, they might not necessarily express the emotion that they have.

Given that lovers have a preference for emotional expression of feelings, it is interesting to note that they share an important emotional ingredient with the analysts we recently studied. We remind our readers that there are four basic emotions, namely sadness, joy, fear, and anger, but importantly the emotions of sadness and joy are always in the present, while fear is an emotion that has to do with the future, and anger has to do with the past. The present emotional experience that lovers have is frequently sadness, the same emotion that analyst tend to have. Why do lovers so frequently feel sad? Because they love so much, love people so much, and so easily connect with people. If they love so easily and frequently and seek connection just as easily, it is reasonable that they will experience more separation. Connect more, and you will separate more because all connections end, some sooner, some later. All connections end, whether after minutes of a conversation or after years of a happy marriage. It is a mistake to think of lovers as "depressed," just as it is equally mistaken to think of analysts as depressed. Depression and sadness are significantly different, but lovers often look depressed and often used the term "depressed" when they actually feel sad. They feel sad frequently because they love more easily and lose more frequently. The underlying mantra of lovers could be: love freely, lose more often, and feel sad more frequently. They do not necessarily despair of these losses and accompanying sadness, but they frequently express these feelings. We will discuss the challenges of feelings with lovers and the other three temperaments in later chapters.

Lovers love. Their love is beyond description as are all the important things of life. Lovers love to connect. Lovers give, give more, and give again. Their generous nature is phenomenal. Lovers know about feelings and how to recognize them in themselves and in others.

We have looked at each of the temperaments by describing their best giftedness. In the next four chapters, we want to review the challenges of each of the four temperaments and how to best engage each temperament. We do not think of these challenges as negative, much less being something wrong with people, but as part of the package of what it means to be a normal human being. Remember that we do not first look at what is wrong with people, but rather look at what is right. In fact, we try hard to never look at what is wrong with anyone while being aware of the limitations that all people have. Each temperament has some limitations and challenges that we will be reviewing in the next four chapters. We offer our apologies to anyone who is offended by what we have suggested is a challenge in your own temperament. Many people do not have these challenges or have found a way to accept them and mature beyond them. If you identify with one of the temperaments we have outlined in the previous four chapters, consider that you may have some of these challenges without thinking there is something wrong with you. You may also see that you have matured over your years of life beyond these challenges.

Chapter 5

Challenges for Players

PLAYERS ARE LOVED OR hated. They will entice you. They will entertain you. They will offend you. They bring much joy and fun to the world, which is their special gift but they can get into more difficulties in life than all the other temperaments combined. The difficulties are sometimes of their own making and sometimes from the negative reaction that they so often get from people who may not want to play all the time. Players, like all the temperaments we have introduced, use their gifts to a fault and that is what gets them into trouble. Our American culture has long neglected players and the play they bring to the world. Worse yet, players have been truly despised because of the offense they bring to people, which is always unintentional. Their cavalier nature leads them to their being judged as irresponsible, disrespectful, or dangerous, but they are none of these things by nature. Male players are seen as playboys who just want to get all they can from people, while female players are seen as wild women who abandon respectability and responsibility. This judgmental attitude toward players has not helped players mature. It has made them defensive. Worse yet, the offense that players so often give has prevented them from successfully giving to the world what it so desperately needs: fun and joy.

The key for success in life for players, which is the same key for the other three temperaments is for them to understand themselves, value themselves, and successfully communicate themselves. Understanding, valuing, and communicating is a challenge for anyone, but it is hardest for players because they don't put much effort into communicating. They just engage experience and excitement assuming that their audience will understand their intention to bring fun to the world. For players, fun and the joy that comes with it is what life is about. It is very difficult for players to learn that much that is important in the world, and much that is valued by many people does not fit into the player mantra, "play whenever you can." It is only through painful maturation that players are able to be themselves and find ways to use their gifts, a maturity that many players fail to find. When players find ways to be themselves while also understanding people of different temperaments, they can be at their best.

In Chapter 1 we laid out the typical characteristics that players have in hopes of people understanding them as well as engendering a self-understanding in players themselves. Players are at their best with matters of experience and excitement, but they are less good at dealing with situations and people who are not so excitement-oriented. In this chapter we will discuss the challenges players find in life.

CHALLENGES FOR PLAYERS

The basic challenge for players is to affirm their experience-seeking nature and their excitement-enhancing nature without going to extremes. The excitement that the player brings to the world is essential for all of us. Without it, life is dull, repetitive, and meaningless. Excitement brings energy to something that might otherwise be a chore. We've told the story before of a matron of a bed and breakfast near Stonehenge we encountered a number of years ago who found a way to cook and serve her guests with her own brand of excitement by dancing and singing while preparing her classic English breakfast. Her jovial nature and procedure initiated a joyful and playful day for her patrons. If players can use their natural talents to enhance others' joy, they will have fulfilled their purpose in life: to make the world happier, a place that is more fun to live in.

The player knows something important that most other people disregard or don't consider: that all boundaries are artificial, meaning that these boundaries have been established by someone and can be challenged. What the player often neglects to consider is that boundaries also provide security in life because a world without boundaries is chaotic and unproductive. In challenging boundaries players tend to scare some people who need rules and procedures for personal security even if these rules are temporary. One of the greatest challenges for players is the constraint they find when confronted with boundaries. Players are not trying to offend when they challenge boundaries; rather, they are trying to stave off the boredom that comes to them when they are constrained by boundaries.

1. The Boredom Challenge

Because of their strong inclination towards excitement, players are very inclined to become bored. They are especially bored with anything that is repetitive, largely because something that is repeated is not new. Since so much of normal life requires people to do things repetitively, it can be difficult for players to simply do much of what we consider to be normal and necessary. Players are at their worst when there is nothing new to a procedure, nothing new to a day, or nothing new in a relationship. A player's mantra is something like, "If I have seen it before, heard it before, or done it before, it is boring to see it, hear it, or do it again."

While players can't tolerate most things that are truly repetitive, they can repeat things that offer some opportunity for change or challenge. Change is a basic part of any musical, athletic, or artistic endeavor, which should make these things attractive to players. Unfortunately, to get good at something, you have to practice, which means doing something over and over again. Furthermore, most work requires that the employee learns to do something until s/he gets good at it, and then does it faster or more efficiently. Players rarely have interest in such a procedure unless it is just for the fun of going faster. They want to play and work at the same time, which is not usually possible in most circumstances in life, like school, work, home life, and relationships. Good coaches and teachers know how to motivate players towards success by helping them try a new soccer kick or a dance routine. Good mentors for players help them learn new ways of playing, more challenging ways of playing, and ultimately more exciting ways of playing. They keep players motivated by helping their students find new and different ways of playing, while subtly improving the player's skills. But coaches and teachers who know how to motivate players' intrinsic play are a rare breed. Those who do well motivating players are likely players themselves.

New and different ways of doing something doesn't have to be athletic or artistic. New and different could be a new way of doing something that has been done before. Deb loves to hike the Utah canyons, something that she has done nearly a dozen times. But when she goes hiking, she will try to find a new canyon or a new trail, possibly with new hiking boots or poles, or God forbid, a new camera lens. Deb goes to the canyons not so much for the newness of them but as a means to escape the routine of daily life. She has honed her player nature by finding the new and different in the same arena. Players who haven't found ways of doing this fall prey to boredom. The danger for players is that they are not helped to see new and different ways to explore the world. An immature player might say something like, "I have already seen that canyon," not realizing that there are new trails to hike, new seasons to hike, and new pictures to take along the way. Players can be "bored" with doing something that might be interesting the first time but not so interesting the second time.

Players want to get things done, but the *things* must be valuable to them and the *doing* must be fun. They can't just "do" as caretakers do. The things that are hard for most players to do are those that are truly repetitive and experienced as mundane: loading and unloading the dishwasher, going to work at the same time every day, driving the same road to work every day, changing the baby's diapers six times a day, paying the same bills every month, going to church at the same time and possibly hearing "another boring" sermon every week, reading the same newspaper every day, or simply vacuuming the same house *again*. Players are not encouraged to find ways of doing such things in ways that are interesting to them. Are there ways of doing the routine maintenance of the household without it becoming a dreaded chore? There might be but it would be a challenge to make vacuuming interesting to a player unless the vacuum somehow becomes a wild animal to be tamed. A player who has found ways to load the dishwasher and change baby's diapers has found a way to play with these activities. I know of a mother with the player temperament who always dances with her baby, despite any crying, when she goes to change the baby's diaper. I know of a man who always cuts his lawn in a different way and trims the hedge a different way every month. These people are playing with their "routine" work so it isn't routine.

Repetition and doing the same thing are not the only thing that players find boring. They can be bored with the same people. Players are always excited about meeting new people who might have new ideas, different experiences, and unique personalities. I recall a time when Deb and I were hiking with a good friend, Elaine, visiting us from Canada. Our friend and I spotted some people speaking in what seemed like a Slavic language. I thought it was Russian given my minimal experience with that language in college. Elaine was fascinated by these unknown people speaking an unknown language and was drawn to introduce herself to them and discover what they were all about. While I was interested in the language, she was interested in the newness of this potential experience. Elaine was immediately interested in "the new and different," namely new people and new language. She didn't know Russian like I did; she didn't have to. She just wanted to experience this new situation and these new people. It was exciting to her. These new, completely unknown people, were exciting because of the unknown they brought to Elaine. I remember her excitement in the parking lot when she heard them speak. She lit up like a Christmas tree and could barely hold herself back from rushing over to them while exclaiming to me "let's go see what they are about!" She might have thought something like, "Maybe these folks have an opinion of Putin, or of Russia, or of America." She wasn't more interested in other people; she wasn't bored with us; she was just interested in *new* people. Imagine, however, how someone else might have taken offense at her interest in these unknown people, seeming to disregard with whom she was hiking.

Players' interest in the new and different isn't a disregard for the "old." It is a need for exploration and adventure, be it with a new person, a new situation, or a new lamp. After 40-some years of relationship Deb knows most of my ways, including my tiresome old jokes, and sometimes simply needs to get away from me. She gets bored with me, our home, our work, and even our play. She needs to get away, which she does, usually to those always interesting Utah canyons. When she buzzes out west, I jokingly tell my basketball cohorts that "my wife left me…again." She always returns, rewarded by her newest experience. These new experiences replenish her and so she can return to the "old" work, house, games shared with me with renewed appreciation and pleasure. If allowed to see the new and different, whether it is people or place, players can avoid the tendency to be bored with what they have. Sadly, most players unfortunately fall into tolerating the routines of work, home, and spouses. Toleration always leads to some kind of, "I need to get out of here" reaction.

We were at a Dane Dance last night, one of the many wonderful opportunities in Madison for summer play. There was a little girl, probably around 10 or 12 who wore a shirt that simply said "This is my summer shirt." The clincher was that the phase was written upside down! I thought, "yup, a player kid!" Maybe it was Dad or Mom who was the player in the family and had the idea of an upside-down writing. Regardless, someone wanted to play with words. Mozart once played the piano while facing outward from the instrument, just to see if he could do it. Players might just learn better upside down or backwards because it is different…not wrong.

There are many historical figures who succeeded in life even though they had player characteristics of the player personality type. We have already suggested that King David of the Jewish Scriptures might have been a player demonstrated by his dancing through the streets half naked upon his coronation. Maybe Alexander the Great was a player given his insatiable need for adventure. Was Cleopatra playing when she got involved with Mark Anthony? How many player carpenters, tradesmen, and artisans have been successful in their trades by multi-focusing and multi-tasking? Previous centuries didn't allow for the quick and easy stimulation we have today, nor did most learning occur in the classroom. Muhammad was illiterate but created the second largest religion in the world. Might he have been a player? Did he really hear the words of the Koran from an angel or did he just trust his intuition? Leonard Shlain, author of *The Alphabet Versus the Goddess*, (1998) suggests that the change of reading and writing from left to right rather than right to left moved western culture away from visual images and emotion into cognitive images. This change may have harmed players' inclination to see, touch, and handle in their seeking opportunities for play, adventure, and exploration that befitted a simpler and freer life than we have today. People in the years of developing culture, language, and reading didn't live vicariously by reading. They lived life primarily by experiencing things visually and kinesthetically. How many sculptors, musicians, and other artists knew how to read 3000 years ago? Probably not many but yet these artisans left visible and vibrant artifacts that tell us much about history, perhaps more than words might do. What do we know of Michelangelo from what he wrote compared to what he painted and sculpted? Perhaps players could avoid the boredom of much of school if they could be taught visually and kinesthetically rather than linguistically through words. The way people learned in previous centuries allowed players to learn effectively, sometimes with words, sometimes with experience, but most current academic settings do not do well for players.

2. The Academic Challenge

The academic challenge is huge for players. Not all, but many players find school to be boring...at least traditional school. Traditional school is not designed for players. Nor should it be because if all classes were adventuresome and exciting, it might be good for players, but not necessarily for the rest of the students. Nevertheless, the very nature of sitting in a class for an hour with a teacher lecturing is unnatural for players because it is not experiential and certainly not exciting and adventuresome. Traditional North American education was built on the "three Rs": reading, 'riting and 'rithmetic. These were classically taught through rote, memorization, and under the directive of "do as you are told." Fortunately, American education has made great strides in reconciling educational methodology with variances in personality and learning styles. For example, we now know about "right-brain learners" and "left-brain learners," the former being experiential, emotional, creative, and imaginative, whereas left-brain learners are those who prefer words, abstractions, and math. We also know that there are many ways of learning, specifically by hearing, seeing, and doing. These ways of learning are usually called *auditory* (words), *visual* (seeing), and *kinesthetic* (hands-on). Players are usually right-brained and tend to be in this group of learners who prefer the kinesthetic and visual.

Players are, in general, very intelligent people, often above average, and actually learn quite well and succeed in *demonstrating their learning* if they are given a chance to learn in a manner that is compatible with their personality style. Simply put, they need to see things, touch things, and do things. The more we allow for these ways of learning the better player students will fare.

Not long ago I was doing IQ testing for a young man and found it quite interesting that this player person didn't remember that Lincoln was the President during the Civil War. I learned that he was an avid football player, so I asked him if he remembered any football plays. He could recite numerous different plays by number, like "246 pass" and knew exactly what his assignment was during each of these plays. Not only did he know his assignments, he knew the assignments for the other 10 members of the team for each of these various plays. How and why could he remember the numbers of so many different football plays together with the complexity of the 11 assignments associated with each of those plays but not remember one of the most historically significant American Presidents? This young player boy simply wasn't interested in learning "facts" of history because such facts were "boring" but could remember the complexity of a certain physical activity because it was experiential and exciting to him. It was the tweaks of suspense of which game plays could be used that enticed this teenage player to remember football plays.

A very significant piece of the academic challenge is compounded because of the players' inclination towards boredom with words. Too many players, especially in their early years, come to believe that they are "stupid," because they don't remember or care about the words. I have come to identify "stupid" as "the other S-word" because it is so bad for so many kids. When a player feels stupid, he will look for ways to make himself *feel* smart. A "smart" thing for a player, of course, is to play. Many player students assuage their feelings of "stupid" by playing all the more, which then leads naturally to their being criticized or diagnosed as being disruptive or ADD. Being interruptive and disruptive can be a way of assuaging both feelings of boredom and feeling stupid. If a player child feels stupid, he can make some kind of fuss in class and at least avoid the terror of boredom *and* stupidity, which is a nasty combination. A teacher recently told me that her player student got down on the floor and started snaking his way through the chairs making snakelike hissing sounds. The attention he received, including the laughter from some kids, the sneering from other kids, and the punishment from the teacher all worked together to kill off his boredom and feeling stupid. The disruption in class is what we psychologists call compensation: he is *compensating* for feeling stupid by doing something that might be seen as really stupid by some onlookers.

Player kids, without any intention of harm or disruption, often get punished for their "disruptive" behavior. Inevitably shame follows. Unfortunately, not only do these player kids feel bored, and sometimes stupid, too, soon they begin to feel ashamed of who they are. *They feel ashamed of their player nature.* They conclude that there is something *intrinsically wrong with who they are.* This feeling of shame then leads to even more outlandish behavior or a deep-seated feeling of inadequacy. It is almost like, "If I am going to be stupid, let me show you real stupid! I will create an even greater show of stupidity." While this does no good for his esteem, he at least gains some temporary excitement from it.

Players seem to get the worst of shame and academic labeling. Sometimes shaming comes in the form of rhetorical questions like, "What is *wrong* with you, Charlie?" Sometimes shaming comes with direct assaults like, "You're ruining the opportunity for your classmates to learn, Charlie." Sometimes shaming comes from dismissal like, "I guess you're just not interested in learning, are you, Charlie." Punishment can come with words or action, like being sent to the office, standing in hallway, or worse yet, given more "traditional" assignments such as writing or reading more. In addition to shaming and punishment, far too many educators, administrators and parents are quick to indulge themselves in some kind of diagnosis: Attention Deficit Disorder, Oppositional Defiant Disorder, Autistic Disorder, Anxiety Disorder, or Bipolar Disorder. None of these diagnoses help a player understand her player nature, much less utilize it for learning and achieving.

Ultimately, we need to find ways for player children to play responsibly while learning effectively but also a way for these children to learn by experience rather than with punishment and shaming. We need to find ways to develop a lasting drive for learning in players that will not only prevent disruptive behavior in class, but more importantly foster a drive for *excellence*.

We think there are two very important components of helping the player child in school. The first one is to simply give them permission to wish, to want, to imagine, to pretend without the shame component we noted above. Haim Ginott was a child psychologist many years ago who addressed this quite well. Ginott suggested that when a child states a fantasy like "there are dinosaurs on the playground!" the parent or guardian should simply respond with something like, "Yes, wouldn't it be fun if there were dinosaurs on the playground!" This initial exchange followed by a brief interaction could well satisfy the player's imagination and avert any negative consequence of shame for "knowing better" and criticism for interrupting. This gives the child permission for their imagination and desire for distraction without giving into the distraction. This of course, isn't a cure all but it would set the pace, especially for a young player, to feel accepted for his desire for all things new and adventuresome.

Another important way to help players learn is to allow them to move. This may be the most important aid for player children. It is simply not possible for players to sit in a chair for 55 minutes while listening to a lecture or doing some kind of homework. Players need to move. So, the task for teachers, and parents at home helping with homework, is to integrate some kind of movement while the player is learning. If players can move while listening, they might be better able to retain what she is hearing. What they hear might even seem exciting and interesting if they have the freedom to move at the same time they are listening. How many of us run while listening to books? It is the same concept, movement facilitates reception of information and for the player, all the more. I believe there is a kind of synesthesia with players that is a combination of two or more of the five senses. Deb, now with multiple college degrees, barely passed classes until late in her high school years. Not until college did she learn that she could read well if she read out loud, read while walking, or read while she was signing (American Sign Language). She was liberated by simply having the privilege to roam hallways and city blocks with text books in hand, reading aloud to herself. Player kids need to read a paragraph, get up and look at the leaves falling outside, come back and read another paragraph or two. If they are allowed this privilege of multi-focusing and multi-tasking, they can read the whole chapter and then the whole book. Somehow, Ron was able to learn while playing and moving, evidently nearly constantly as reported by his maternal grandmother with her comment: "You're never going to raise that child." If we could help player children enjoy the learning process with healthful movement, we will begin to meet the challenge they bring to the academic environment.

Some player kids know their preferred arena for play and can more easily be challenged and disciplined or channeled towards what they want, but most player kids do not. Those who do not, need a good deal of trial-and-error opportunities to discover how they can use their player nature productively. With these kids, there needs to be a good amount of patience while they try things out but also withholding great investments in them until there is some surety that their interest will hold. We remember well our older daughter wanting to play the drums one day. Mistakenly, we bought her a drum set before we realized that it was just a passing fancy and not a real interest. While she might have been interested in percussion temporarily, that curiosity didn't translate into genuine interest in music yet alone a lasting passion for playing drums, nor did her intense interest in learning Swedish after hearing me speak some of my heritage tongue to a visiting Swede, nor her desire to fly jet planes when she saw the movie Top Gun. The challenge is for parents and teachers to give players an environment that enhances their ways of learning without indulging their whims and wishes.

This particular challenge for players has been a passion of ours for a long time, perhaps beginning with our own player natures and certainly in the challenge of raising our player daughter, Krissie. We do not have exact answers as to how players can manage the rigors and necessities of school, yet we believe that if parents, school authorities, and player children talk together and cooperated with each other, the academic challenge that players have can be met and mastered. In the meantime, we want to avoid diagnosing players with one or more commonly used diagnoses.

3. The Challenge of Offense

The biggest social problem players face is that they offend people. They offend because they play when others want to work, think, sit quietly, or perhaps just play in a different way. They offend when they talk when others want to be quiet. They touch when others don't want to be touched. They tease when others don't want to be teased. They offend because of their intrusions on other people, albeit without intending to do so. The hardest social task for players who are truly seeking to mature in life is to remember that *everyone doesn't want to play all the time.* Players' tendency to engage people in some kind of play is often experienced as an uninvited intrusion. Players simply want to bring fun to other people. It is very hard on them when they disappoint other people, harder when they hurt other people, and hardest yet when they are criticized for playing. They think something like, "All I want to do is to have fun and bring fun to other people. Why does this offend people?"

Players bring offense without knowing why they have offended, much less what they can do about it. When they are chastised for playing, they don't know how to react. A player child who splashes water all over the sink and fails to clean the soap off the dishes is not trying to offend his parents, but he does offend them. The adult player offends his spouse coming home late because she found herself talking for three hours to an old friend at a coffee shop having unexpectantly met her at the grocery store. The work supervisor is offended when work is not done in a traditional manner even if it is actually done faster. Friends are offended when they don't hear from their player friends for weeks or months. These offenses lead people to judge players as being irresponsible. The essence of the word "responsible" is *respond*. Players initiate more than respond because they are always seeking experience and excitement. Players certainly have an ability to respond, but they are responding to the excitement in their lives favorably or the boredom in their lives unfavorably. They are not "irresponsible" to Mom when they do the dishes in a nontraditional manner, nor are they "disrespecting" a spouse by coming home late, nor when they challenge the rules of work, nor are they being "inappropriate" when they say something outlandish in a strange crowd. All of these things can offend people because people of other temperaments value things other than the excitement of play.

Players can offend people of any temperament. They offend caretakers when they use a car as a toy; they often offend lovers when they disappear after a good night together; they offend analysts because of their disinterest in meaning and understanding. People with these other temperaments are offended because *they feel disrespected*, but players don't purposely disrespect caretakers, lovers, and analysts; *they just don't care about the things* that caretakers hold valuable, the *people* that lovers hold valuable, and the *ideas* that analysts hold valuable. They even offend other players who might be interested in a different kind of play. The social landscape for players is littered with former employers, friends, spouses, and family who have been *hurt* when players have acted in a way that has made someone *feel* disrespected or disregarded.

The most important offense that players bring to people is that of *emotional hurt*. They hurt people when they violate other people's boundaries, whether those boundaries are physical (usually caretakers), relational (usually lovers), or ethical (usually analysts). The teacher's boundaries may simply be to finish his lesson plan, and she is hurt when she is not able to get the lesson done because of the player's interruptions. Friends and partners are hurt by players' seeming lack of concern about their property, time commitments, and predictability. Players hurt bosses and supervisors who may simply have a desire to get work done compared to the player's desire to make work more fun. Player children offend their parents, siblings, and extended family members with frivolous statements or actions meant to be playful and enticing.

Players often offend because they don't know when to stop playing. Because they are not trying to hurt other people, it takes them by surprise when they do hurt people. In their minds, they are just having fun and are helping others to have fun. It is even possible for a player to see that a friend is hurt and then make fun of it, thinking that it would be best to laugh away the hurt. Recall that players are looking for a new experience above all else. It is also beyond their conception that something that is playful and exciting to them might very well be boring, uninteresting or offensive to someone else. It is in the mind of the player that if she just continues to play, the offended person will get over the silly offense and realize the player's good intention to make things fun. This is the "oh, come on, I was just playing" defense that often surfaces in these encounters. When players begin to realize that they frequently hurt people, they are nonplussed, and they become quite unsure as to how to act with people if they can't simply play. This can lead players to actually avoid being with people and playing on their own. They might even try to give up their spontaneous and limitless orientation to life for fear of offending people.

Not only do players hurt people emotionally; they also can hurt them physically, all with the desire to "play." As with the emotional hurt that they cause people, players never intentionally hurt people physically. Players will prod, prick, and pinch their friends just to seek some brief excitement. While playful and spontaneous to the player, this poking and prodding can be offensive to their friends or even cause some real physical harm. One player patient of mine "stabbed" his best friend with a pencil. He said that he was "just playing" and certainly didn't want to harm his friend. His friend was mildly hurt physically but seriously hurt emotionally. In fact, the friendship actually ended because of this incident, which to the player's mind was trivial and playful while being damaging to his friend. Because this young player had no wherewithal to deal with his offense, he underplayed the effects of his playing and ignored the whole incident. His parents brought him to see me quite distraught about his apparent lack of concern about his offense. I did my best to affirm this young man's player nature while gingerly noting that play can be harmful. Another player almost pushed someone off a 5-story building—just playing, and pleaded ignorance of the effect of such "play." I wonder how many people have been stabbed or pushed off buildings by players. I remember an incident where an adult player was encouraged by another player to jump 15 feet onto a hard surface. The jumper ended up with permanent damage to his knee. Almost all the harm that comes to players, or that they bring to others, is minor in itself, but these harms, even though minor, can do great damage in a relationship, especially when it is repeated. It is no easy task to help a player see that playing can bring hurt and harm… all unintentionally.

Players believe that all people should see the world the way they do, enjoy the same things, and have the same value system. Players are not unique in this perspective. Caretakers, lovers, and analysts all think that people should see the world the way they do and have the same value system, as we shall discuss in forthcoming chapters. As they mature, players need to learn the painful fact that people with other temperaments play in very different ways, and often do not want to play at all. This is a hard pill for players to swallow. All of these potential problems and challenges for players *are not intrinsically something wrong with them*. Players need to understand that they can easily hurt someone, a hurt that may be trivial or permanent, while at the same time realize that there is nothing wrong with them. This is a balancing act that is particularly hard for players, but this balance is necessary to prevent players from falling into truly deviant activities.

4. The Deviance Challenge

The word "deviance" comes from the Latin meaning "off track" (from the Latin *de* = off and *via* = road*)*. Players often find themselves off track in the world, whether that is in school, family, friends, work, or even in play.

Certainly, not all players are criminals, but most are deviant in at least some substantive way if we consider "deviance" to be behavior out of the norm. Players tend to buck the norm and get bored with it so they are bound to act defiantly by most social standards. It is deviant to hit someone, even playfully, who doesn't want to be hit, but is it criminal? It is wrong for a player to steal from someone, but is it wrong to borrow something and never return it because the player forgot about it after they got bored with it? The player child who picks up a squirt gun in the department store, and finds great offense at having to put it back: is that deviance, or is it just player-like behavior? It can be a fine line for a player between looking for excitement and slipping into criminality. There are three primary ways that players can get off track: they can get scattered, they get addicted to something, and/or they find themselves in some kind of illegal activity. These are all ways players "play to a fault" and seek experience to a fault.

"Scattered" Deviance

Scattered deviance is not illegal activity but often construed as intentional misbehavior. We touched on this above when we discussed the academic challenge: the tendency for players to be what we choose to call "multi-focused". The tendency players have to easily become bored and focus on everything and everyone around them can lead to the unfortunate diagnosis of Attention Deficit Disorder (ADD) and/or Attention Deficit Hyperactivity Disorder (ADHD). Generally, their multi-focused behavior is considered "distractibility," but we much prefer to call it "atractability," meaning that they are attracted by sights and sounds. So, if the teacher is lecturing, the player can simultaneously hear what the teacher is saying but also hear the whispering behind him, the rain outside the window, and the dog barking a block away. Furthermore, this multi-focusing ability stretches beyond what is heard into what is seen and felt. The player can see interesting things on the whiteboard, the interesting jeans of the kid in the next seat, and the leaves falling outside.

He can also be *attracted* to the hunger pangs in his stomach, the hangnail on his ring finger, and that nasty feeling in his nose that demands attention. This is the kid that we expect to attend *only* to what the teacher is saying. This is just not possible for the player. We think most of the people who have been diagnosed with one form or another ADHD are players. Instead of being "impulsive" and disorderly, we might consider that they are simply seeking experience and excitement.

Players have always been a part of humanity but historically they weren't *diagnosed* as having something wrong with them. Rather, players were challenged, limited and disciplined. If players did engage in criminal behavior, then they were punished. But they were also encouraged to be the adventuresome, excitement-seeking, experience-seeking people that they are. The player phenomenon isn't new, but the disaster of over diagnosis that players often experience in our culture is relatively new. Both of us have strong player qualities in our natural make-up, both of our children have this characteristic as do both of our grandchildren, yet we six people display player characteristics in very different ways. Certainly, both of us would have been diagnosed ADHD had such a diagnosis existed when we were kids in the 50's and 60's, but thankfully, we were not so diagnosed and somehow survived our childhood. Admittedly, we were challenges for our parents and teachers, and just as true we were disciplined and punished for what we now see as player behavior. But we weren't diagnosed. A big difference between the 50's and 60's when we grew up and the current era is the amount of screen time that is available to kids, something that unfortunately enhances their tendency to find vicarious excitement rather than hearing parents say, "go out and play" as we heard regularly.

Criminal Deviance
Deviance, especially "successful" crime can become addictive like any behavioral addiction. Once a player finds the excitement, the "rush" (endorphins) of having stolen, speeded, hit, or raped, it is hard to help that person find better ways of finding excitement. Our prisons are full of such people, who have become attracted to something, developed a habit for doing something, and then became addicted to that behavior. Unfortunately, these people have

not developed character, the hallmark of which is to be aware of one's nature, to utilize one's nature, and to govern one's nature. We see characterological flaws in people of all temperaments, but players may be inclined to a lack of character development more than people of other temperaments because so much of what they seek is excitement which is often at the cost of someone else's value and welfare.

Players can easily be caught in some kind of illegal activity for many reasons including the (hormonal) rush of trying something new. Players don't seek to be deviant, let alone criminal, but they tend to fall prey to these things. At its initial stages, some activity can simply seem exciting or different, but these same activities can easily become deviant, meaning that they challenge cultural norms and become illegal. From that point, it can be but a small step into some kind of activity that is dishonest that leads to truly criminal behavior. Entry into crime often comes without thought or plan. It may not even be an immoral or unethical act at first. I suspect that most criminals are players at heart who found crime "fun" at first, then addictive, then perhaps necessary to finance their addiction. I have met many player criminals in my office including at least two big-time drug dealers (both of whom have served extensive federal prison time). I have also met car thieves, and many small-time criminals who seldom get caught. I see a 20-something player in my office who regularly steals food allegedly because he "can't afford to buy it," but by his own admission he finds the excursions exciting. Racing a car at 90 on a 55 MPH highway might be fun but it is also illegal, and it could bring great harm to other people. How many heart wrenching stories are there of drivers who hurt or kill others on the highways because they have driven not just once, but countless times while under the influence. A serious criminal might have started playing in deviant ways early in life, but never found a way out of excessive playing. Years ago, one of those drug dealers I saw told me, "I can make $10,000 this week selling drugs. I have never "worked" for anyone except when I had to in the "joint." How do you expect me to go to work for McDonald's making seven bucks an hour when I make $10,000 in a week with just three or four hours of dealing?" It was not an easy question to answer.

A 14-year-old player kid I have been seeing told me he felt "bad" of the minor criminal activity that he did, evidently several years prior to my seeing him, having participated in some level of vandalism. Interestingly, Randy told me that he was brought into this activity by the friend he had at the time. In my discussion with him yesterday, he told me that even though he feels bad for what he did, that it really wasn't his fault, that "they forced me to do it." For Randy, "it just seemed to happen." Players often do not actually see that they have chosen to do something and that the resulting consequence rests on them. Rather, they see things "just happened for no reason." Reasoning is not a particular strength of immature players, especially young players because they are looking for opportunities that "just happen" to them and bring excitement and the potential for experience. Likewise, rationalizing often becomes part of a player's defense, such as demonstrated by the drug dealer mentioned above. In short, many players who get caught in the addictive pattern of criminality never mature into comprehending the dire consequences of their addiction.

Addictive Deviance

The danger of addiction for players is psychological, social, cultural, neurological, and neurochemical. It is first psychological because players seek excitement and adventure in life. It is social because players ideally want to play with someone else, and it is cultural because there are so many opportunities to experiment in the world. Most importantly, however, players are inclined to addictions because of their neurological and hormonal nature, which, of course, is related to them being so physical. Excitement is much related to endorphins, which might be simply understood as "happy hormones." The secretion of endorphins is strongly related to all addictions. You can see how players could seek activities that induce the secretion of endorphins and thereby be inclined to become addicted to some chemical substance or some activity. If something is potentially addictive, players have experimented with it.

The charge of endorphins into their blood system is much of the cause of some players' tendency to becoming addicted to certain chemicals. Players usually have experimented with one or more addictive substances, usually settling on one of these chemicals as a drug of choice. Their tendency is to become addicted to substances that are stimulants, like nicotine, caffeine, and cocaine although alcohol can be a kind of stimulant in large doses. The quick fix nature of drugs gives players an easy way out of their life dilemma of how to survive in a non-playing world.

While players often become addicted to chemical substances, they are much more inclined to become addicted to some behavioral activity. Behaviors that are addictive are called *behavioral addictions*. Most typical among these activities is screen time: TV, Internet, Facebook, Facetime, texting, and video-game playing. The addictive nature of screen time is the instantaneous nature of these activities. Those Facebook friends of ours who send pictures of their daily activities every other hour may be addicted to this medium of communication. I have a 20-something patient who once spent 70 hours in one week playing video games. This same man dropped out of college one course short of a degree because "it was boring." Players in the previous generation were more often simply addicted to TV. It is much easier for players to work hard at perfecting a video game than to learn to dance, play the flute, or throw a baseball. It is even easier for players to vicariously experience dancing, playing the flute, or throwing baseballs on television than to practice at these things.

It is possible that players have a biochemical structure that inclines them to need more endorphins and adrenaline to be satisfied and happy, even more likely, however is that they simply have not had opportunities to play and find excitement in a society that values production and routine. Our world now provides such easy entries into endorphin-producing activities and substances that players have usually not had enough experience with the rigors of work and effort it takes to make one's life personally satisfying and productive.

5. The Discipline Challenge

Most people think of discipline as a means of punishment, but the etymological root of the word discipline is *learning*. We get the words disciple (student) discipleship (learning) from the same Latin root. It is helpful to think of discipline as purposeful and active learning done with a certain effort and commitment. We normally think of discipline coming from an authority figure, like a parent, teacher, or coach, but the value of discipline is much more important when it doesn't come from an authority figure. It is important for people, whether players or not, to *discipline themselves* so that they can achieve some success in their lives. Successful professional players, like dancers, athletes, and musicians have *disciplined themselves* to work at their professional play. Discipline is a challenge for young players, and often for players of all ages, because discipline is normally approached from an authority figure and as a means of punishment, not of practicing and learning. Free players, as we identified them in Chapter 1, have a particularly difficult time disciplining themselves in some disciplined activity because they are more interested in the play of the moment rather than in some kind of professional play. Free players, who are the bulk of players in the world, need to find ways to self-discipline so that their play can be more enjoyable, exciting, and ultimately rewarding. The key words here are *ultimately* and *self-discipline,* something that is not naturally a part of free players' view of the world and of play. They want to play now, play easy, and play all the time with little effort into finding a way to play more successfully and purposefully. Their need for immediate stimulation makes discipline very challenging.

For many adult players, particularly the many who are seen in psychologist's offices, discipline has been their greatest nemesis. Many of these people have not had a depth understanding of their player temperament and have made all the mistakes players tend to make in work and in relationships. They have had failed relationships, failed jobs, failed property management, and failed finances. I just finished reading a book about Daniel Boone and learned the two important things about his life: greatness and failure. He was great in exploration, dealing with Native Americans, trapping, shooting, and nature in general. He was a profound failure in most business matters, not because he was dishonest or deceitful but because he didn't care about money, laws, and property. He was most certainly a player. Most Players account for their lack of traditional success in life by saying something like, "my ideas didn't seem to work out," or "I just couldn't seem to stay interested for long with any job or person." The problem that these players have had with life is that the essence of the word *discipline* has had a *limiting* nature to it, not an *enhancing* nature. Daniel Boone was much disciplined in nature and with Native Americans. He understood nature because he had engaged in nature, experimented, and learned how to manage himself in nature. He did the same with Native Americans finding ways to engage the Native culture rather than challenge it. He was often cheated and often ended up in financial trouble because he simply didn't care about legalities and money. He cared about adventure. He was much disciplined in his profession, which was adventure, but not disciplined in areas that he did not value, like money and formal civil agreements.

You know, and I know, many players in life. You may be a player, and if you're a parent, it is likely that one of your children is a player. You may have married a player for all the right reasons: s/he was engaging, attractive, exciting and fun. A patient of mine was close friends with another man, both of whom were good basketball players in high school. My patient, Brad, had the better natural talent in basketball but he also had a player personality with a deeply ingrained low boundary orientation. He floundered in three different high schools, and then in several different colleges, and eventually dropped out sadly finding himself in jail because of an unfortunate moment of "play" that turned out to be illegal. His friend, on the other hand, much less of a player by temperament, played in the NBA. I wonder how many truly potentially great athletes, actors, and musicians are floundering in life instead of finding some kind of success through the discipline of hard work in their play.

Whether in business, school, or relationships, players need discipline, the discipline to do what you don't want to do *now* so you can do what you do want to do *later*. Ideally, the teacher first encourages the player child in his *wanting* to see the dinosaur on the playground giving the child permission to engage imagination with one or two exchanges in that moment. This encouragement of imagination needs to be followed by helping the child go back to the class syllabus. This blend of encouragement and limitation can help the child enjoy the fun of imagination without being scolded for inattention while quickly adding the necessity of returning to the reality of class study. This procedure can help a player child begin to understand that he can imagine and enjoy the imagining while also learning that reality is also important in life. It might even be possible that the next time he wants to see a dinosaur, he can be encouraged to create a class play about it over recess, then to write an essay on it, then to eventually become a researcher or archeologist. Disciple must come out of our desire and our nature towards who and how we have been created. This kind of discipline has to start in childhood or it will be very difficult to find it later in life. If player children are indulged with too much free play, or restricted too much from any play, they will not find the balance of work and play that is essential to success in life. People with a caretaker temperament can work all the time, but this is absolutely not true of players. They may actually be able to accomplish just as much alternating between playing and working, but only when work is interspersed with play.

Ron's temperament, as we discussed earlier, is primarily that of caretaker, but he also has a fair bit of player in him. In fact, if we look at his early childhood, we see that Ron was player first, and caretaker second. Somehow, he learned that life was not all play and that it was not all work. In his current life he has a balance of play, like playing basketball three times a week, random video games in between patients or writing, and occasional hiking or biking. Deb also has this player part to her nature in addition to her analyst nature. Her play includes a good deal of time in her gardens or greenhouse, hiking and biking, and random driving out to the Utah canyons. Deb needs more time alone when she is playing due to her internal nature, like hiking the canyons by herself. We both work hard for three or four weeks and then run "up north" to our cabin for R & R, which means reading, swimming, hiking, and playing Chinese checkers. Krissie operated as a caretaker at work and with her children, but she was really alive when she was playing, usually with other people. Jenny's playing is more like Deb enjoying a bit of social time but truly enjoying her own time of thinking, reading, feeling, and just hanging out. Each of us has this player element to our natures, and each of us has found ways to honor playing while still maintaining busy work schedules. We both know the value and essential nature of working and the discipline it requires, but we have had to find ways of working and playing so as to do both responsibly.

CHALLENGES FOR PLAYERS EXPRESSING FEELINGS

Players express their feelings all the time, but you won't necessarily realize that they are expressing feelings. Recall from Chapter 1 that players express their feelings physically. When you see a player physically gyrating in some way, playing her air guitar, or dancing a jig, you are seeing the player expressing feelings. Indeed, there is emotion within this expression of feelings but players are much more physical than emotional in their feeling expression. Players wear their feelings on their shoulders…or arms…or hands…or eyes, but not always with words. We are reminded of one of the very first people we knew to be a player as he would be almost unable to speak his feelings while at the same time gyrating and moving sometimes with his mouth agape as if he just couldn't find the words for his feelings. Not all players are speechless when they feel something as many have learned to articulate their feelings quite well, but most players have a hard time finding words to go with their feelings. They feel so quickly and so deeply that they often simply can't find the words. Recall that both of us have secondary player temperaments. As both of us have these physical expressions of feelings secondary to our more basic temperament preferences that we will discuss shortly. Ron will express his feelings playing basketball along with some kind of teasing his opponents, or playing Chinese checkers with Deb while Deb will express her player-like feelings in her greenhouse singing and talking to her plants or hiking the hills touching branches or whispering to the leaves how beautiful they are.

The challenge associated with players' physical experience of feeling can be the difficulty they have in restraining their physical engagement. As we previously discussed, players often offend people with their touching, pinching, or poking someone in their attempt to engage the other person in some kind of play experience. The challenge players have is to restrain and contain some of their physical expression of feelings especially when it involves someone else. When Ron is "just playing" with a friend, which could be at someone's house or in church, he has a habit of grabbing someone's butt. People who know Ron's nature usually find it entertaining but there is the occasion when this physical expression truly offends the other person. Another challenge with players' physical expression of feelings is simply in their significant body movement that might disturb someone else. This could be the simple tipping the coffee mug over because of the player's excitement in the moment or the bumping into someone as she is doing her jig around the kitchen. Nothing wrong with this physical expression of feeling, as there is never anything wrong with feelings themselves, because feelings come from deep inside the player. It behooves the player to simply apologize for offense given knowing that she did not intend to offend. We suggest that people of all temperaments learn the necessity of apologizing for offending while not apologizing for the deep feeling that one has.

While the primary expression of feelings with players is in their physicality, their primary emotion is that of joy as we discussed in Chapter 1. You know when a player is feeling something because you will see it physically and often you will hear some kind of vocal expression. They are better at this expression of joy because they are looking for it all the time in their adventure-seeking and other forms of experience-seeking. This having been said, the danger for players with emotion is their tendency to seek the high points and peaks experiences only and not being emotionally mature enough to accept the necessary sorrows, hurts, and disappointments that always follow any kind of joyful experience. When players are not able to go from emotional mountaintop to emotional mountaintop, they can quickly fall into boredom at best and despair at worst. The challenge for players is to accept the centrality of the two primary emotions associated with love: joy and sorrow. This is a painful task for anyone but especially painful for players as they mature emotionally.

As we leave this discussion of the challenges of feelings for players, we wish to emphasize the fact that however godly and perfect feelings are at an unconscious level, when they are experienced and expressed, great social challenges erupt. It is the task of players, as it is the task of all people, to meet these challenges without self-doubt, much less self-criticism. We need to give children, especially very young children, a wide berth for their finding and expression of their feelings and a moderate freedom of emotion, but emotional and social maturity require us to feel our passions and govern our expression of our passions in order to find genuine personal and interpersonal happiness in life.

SUCCESSFUL ENGAGEMENT WITH PLAYERS

1. Enjoy the Player

There is no one like a player who can make you laugh, join in some spontaneous activity, or engage in some other experience that brings joy to you. Players will take you on joy rides like none other: rides of ideas, rides of dance, rides in spontaneous games, rides to different geographical places, and rides of experimentation. They will help you experience elements of life that you did not think were possible where you see things, touch things, think about things, and feel things that make you feel good in the moment and may, indeed, make you feel better in general. You will not forget these rides, whether imaginary of thought, creative with words, or physical in action. If you are able to join in with these rides within the bounds of your own reason, you will be a better person and certainly an enlivened person.

Last night, as it happens, we took a few minutes to play in a way that has been good for the both of us for many years: dance. I learned ballroom dance early from my mother who was an expert, but Deb learned dance from an expert dance instructor. Neither one of us is a particularly good dancer, at least as compared to the teachers and expert dancers we have seen over our years of learning and practicing dancing in various venues. We were the prime movers of establishing USA Dance in Madison where we live some years ago, but we must admit, that we are probably a couple of the least skilled dancers at the monthly USA dance venue. We enjoy participating in more formal ballroom dance there but enjoy much more the other venues of dance that have been a part of our lives. We danced on a river boat cruise once and somehow received a great ovation for what those folks thought was good dancing. We knew better. We have danced at other places and in other countries, always spontaneous whenever a dance calls us to play. Once we danced at a bookstore in Turkey after having toured the geological/cultural sight nearby. We heard what amounted to a tango on the bookstore loudspeaker, looked at each other and dared to dance a very brief tango. A crowd of young people gathered around us, clapped as we danced our poor rendition of the tango. Afterward, several of them came up to us and asked, "What is your secret?" Secret? We didn't know what they were talking about. Eventually, someone said, "Your secret of being happy even though you two are…old?" The answer, among other things: dancing, joyful, playful dancing. Our current dance instructor, who is not only a superb dancer but the perfect instructor for us once gave us a tremendous compliment. He said, "I hope to someday enjoy dancing as much as you do," this statement being made as we stumbled and rumbled across the dance floor. The dancing we did last night, actually several times, was just as spontaneous and just as fun, but it was in our living room, not another soul around, and was only for a few measures of music yet it was joyous. We danced. We played. We were better for it. This joyful dancing is one the best ways we play together even as we make all kinds of "mistakes" in our dancing.

2. Protect Yourself

It is difficult for us to declare that you need to protect yourself with players because it sounds like players are all dangerous and all their play is dangerous. Such is not the case, but much play is dangerous, and many players are dangerous, especially those who have not matured in the ways we have discussed. This idea of protecting yourself is important because you can be brought into a player's world that seems fun at the time only to learn minutes or days later that the fun was short-lived. More importantly, the fun you might have been brought into might have been harmful to you or to someone else. Being aware of the potential danger that players bring to you does not mean you have to keep your distance at all times. It does not mean that you can't trust anything that your player friend says or does. It means that if you are to engage players and truly profit from that engagement, they will most certainly want to take the adventure farther than you want to go. Don't get caught in being enticed to jump off a balcony just because your player friend wants to see what will happen.

While we strongly advise friends and family members of players to protect themselves from the extremes of players, be careful what you say. You don't have to tell your player friends that they are dangerous…even though she might be potentially dangerous. One of the biggest mistakes people make with players is to try to convince them that they are *wrong* in what they are doing. To protect yourself from the danger that is implicit in some playing means that you are aware of the danger. You need to be cautious to avoid being caught in the moment with players because they are always living in the moment. You may be someone who prefers to live in the future, as analysts often do, or you may want to live in taking care of things that caretakers do, or you may seek the connection that lovers do. The key in protecting yourself is to know how you feel when you are invited, encouraged, or enticed by a player to engage in some kind of play. I have had many experiences of drawing people into some kind of play that was not intrinsically good for them only to later feel chagrinned and sad that I had done so. The key to protecting yourself in the face of players' engagement is to *trust what feels good and right for you*. This amounts to trusting yourself. When you trust yourself and protect yourself, you will then be able to truly enjoy your player friend or relative.

3. Bend without Breaking

We said you need to "protect yourself" when you engage a player, and then said that you need to engage a player as much as possible so as to bring joy into your life. These two suggestions are paradoxical, or so it seems, because you need to do both. You need to be cautious and adventurous at the same time. You might not want to dance with some player who grabs your arm when there is a tune being played in a bookstore, but on the other hand, if it feels right, you might with caution, just might take her hand and accept the invitation to dance around the book stacks.

Many years ago, Deb rented an apartment in the same neighborhood as a good friend of mine, a consummate player. While Deb had been introduced to him, she did not really know him. I am told that when my friend saw Deb driving towards him, he pulled right in front of her, stopped, blocking the street, turned his radio on full blast and got out of his car and started to dance. Chagrinned but not worried, Deb stopped her car, put it in park and joined Ricky in a spontaneous dance. From what I heard about the incident, Ricky and Deb seemed to gather a cadre of people in the neighborhood who watched, clapped, and then started to dance themselves. I wonder what would have happened if a cop had seen this melee. Might such an officer of the law arrest everyone or join in with the dancing? Legal? Not really. Harmful? Not really. Joyful? Absolutely. Right for everyone? Absolutely not. Good for Deb and for the spectators? No doubt.

Joining in with a player playing doesn't have to be dancing. It doesn't even have to be physical. Most of the activity that players do is not so outrageous as to stop traffic on a neighborhood street. More often, your player family member will just tease you in some way, which then invites you to tease him back. Here again, you have to be aware of your real limits, not necessarily the limits of society or the rest of the family. You might join in teasing him about the color of his shirt, or how he stumbled over a book on the floor, or some kind of misstatement that he made. He teases you, and you tease him back, but then you find yourself on uncertain ground because you could easily hurt him just as he could easily hurt you. You might even notice that his words do, indeed, hurt you but you are able to return the playful hurt in kind without the intention of inflicting harm. Maybe your player friend uses some kind of blue language as he is just experimenting and engaging you. You might be offended and choose not to engage. You might be enticed to swear back at him. Perhaps each of you goes back and forth finding increasingly vulgar expressions until you reach the end. No harm done…if you have not bent to the point of being broken.

Players bend the rules all the time so you have to give your player friend liberty to bend any rule at any time. This doesn't mean that you approve of bending the rules. You just have to trust your gut as to whether you join in with the rule-breaking play or not. Swearing might be intrinsically bad for you and bring you great offense. You don't have to swear in response to swearing. You might just need to back off a bit and find some solace in allowing the player to play with words that are not playful for you. This means that you have to know when to start playing and when to stop playing.

4. Knowing When to Stop

Trust your feelings. It's that simple. "Trusting your feelings," however, is not always an easy task. We wrote extensively about feelings in our *I Want to Tell You How I Feel*, making note that feelings are experienced first physically, then emotionally, then cognitively, and actively. You might feel jittery in your stomach (physical experience of feeling) when you begin this activity. You might have a bit of anxiety (emotional experience of feeling) when you are in some kind of player-initiated experience but it still "seems" right to continue. You might have a thought (cognitive experience of feeling) that you can go through with this activity even though it looks scary. You might say something (active) that seems out of character for you. These are examples of "trusting the feeling" that it is right for you to continue. On the other hand, you might have physical, emotional, cognitive, or active feelings that suggest you should not engage or stop the engagement.

Trusting your feelings is really important when you are doing something with a player. You need to hone your own preference in how feelings erupt for you and go with your preference. You can give time to a player but you should never give in. You can engage in some player-initiated activity, but then quickly discover that it is simply not good for you to continue. This is the moment you need to stop. It may have been "fun" in the first few moments but then your gut says "Oh, no, this isn't for me." Starting an experience is almost always exciting, and stopping is often sad. These are your feelings, not your player friend's feelings. To engage with players, you need to trust your feelings, not the feelings of the player. If you stop before your player is ready to stop, you will most certainly hurt his feelings. You just need to make a careful exit from the activity with justification of your actions and without criticism of your player's desire to play. As the writer of Ecclesiastes said, "There is a time for all things." There is a time to play and a time to stop playing. When you stop playing, you will then need to return to your nest, return to your own way of life, return to being what is best for you to be. Knowing the challenge of players, a player friend of mine said, "Never get onto a situation without knowing how to get out."

5. Always Return to Being You

If you happen to be as lucky as we are in our marriage to have a player partner, friend, or family member, you will have many times of play together. You will discover, even in these times of joint playing, that one of you will want to stop playing before the other one. You can manage that. However, if you are not a player by nature and have only a part of the player temperament in your nature, you will need to play when you want to, stop playing when you don't want to, and return to the life that suits your temperament. The most important thing for you in life is to be yourself, value yourself, and communicate yourself. You will communicate yourself if you stop playing when it is no longer good for you to play. Your player friend will be disappointed but hopefully she can manage that disappointment by being sad and finish being sad. More importantly, she may come to realize that your differences are important and appreciate that you took the time to play.

We quoted Shakespeare's *Merchant of Venice* in our discussion of the lover temperament. Recall that Shakespeare suggested that the giving of mercy is "twice blest," namely blessing the giver and the receiver. Coming to an end of playing and returning to your way of life is also "twice blest" because it is good for you and it is good for your player friend. In returning to your more natural temperament, which might be caretaking, loving, or analyzing will enhance those activities as you have been enlivened by playing, adventuring, and experimenting. You will be yourself but you will be better at being yourself for having experienced a different part of life.

Chapter 6

Challenges for Caretakers

CARETAKERS ARE MORE ACTIVE than people of other temperaments. They are busier. They work more. They do more. They certainly do more than players, and usually do more than lovers and analysts. All this doing, however, often leads caretakers to the problems that they have in life, problems that primarily have to do with property and secondarily to do with how property affects their relationships. Because their orientation is primarily towards property, they often become overwhelmed by the sheer amount of property in their lives. Equally important is the difficulty they have in relationships because they actually care more for property than they do for people. However outlandish it sounds to value property over people, this is not something wrong with caretakers. As with all temperaments, it is one's strength to a fault that gets people in trouble. In the case of caretakers, it is their caring for property to such an extent that they neglect the other equally important aspects of life. In this examination we will look at the physical, psychological, and relational challenges that occur with caretakers' *caretaking to a fault*. Then, we will discuss how people of other temperaments can deal effectively with the caretakers in their lives. It is not necessary for caretakers to change any more than it is necessary for players, analysts, and lovers to change, but it is necessary for caretakers to govern their strengths first and then add to their strengths. Since the caretaker temperament reflects Ron's primary orientation to life, he will often speak in first person as one representative of the caretaker temperament.

CHALLENGES FOR CARETAKERS

1. Materialistic

Caretakers attend to property first and foremost. Recall that we identified caretakers as people who see property as having *intrinsic spiritual value*, something that is very hard for people of the other temperaments to understand. Their care of property is normal and good by itself. It is not in the care of property that caretakers have difficulty; rather, it is their caring for property so much that they neglect the other elements in life, namely the love of people that is central to lovers, the looking for meaning that is central to analysts, and the experience and joy that is central to players. Caretakers can be so property-aware that physical things are in their faces and minds all the time. They see things, they like things, and they care for things. But they can care for things to a fault. We have used the expression *to a fault* for players, and we will use it for analysts and lovers as well.

Doing something "to a fault" occurs when people *lose themselves* in what they do naturally. We will see that analysts can lose themselves in thinking and lovers can lose themselves in people, just as players can lose themselves in play. Caretakers often lose themselves in the care of property. There is nothing wrong about caring for property, but there is something wrong about caring for property if it *interferes with the rest of life*. A caretaker who spends hours nightly caring for his car has been seduced by the care of the car and has lost himself. The care of his car may have encroached on care of himself, care for people, and even care for other property. The care of his car is no longer the care of something that has intrinsic and spiritual value; rather, the car *itself* has become valuable, rather than its potential use of the car. Caring for his car has then become an *obsession* instead of a love, just as all obsessions start out as things that we love. Obsession with property and the care of property is materialism.

Caretakers are not materialistic by nature. Materialism is the valuing of material things *above* all else and *in place of* all else. At their best *caretakers just want to take care of property; they don't have to own it.* They are not hoarders. Caretakers would be plenty satisfied if everyone took care of their property as they do. People of other temperaments don't see property as intrinsically spiritual and valuable the way caretakers do. Lovers see people as intrinsically spiritual; analysts see meaning as intrinsically spiritual; and players see experience as intrinsically spiritual. The larger truth is that all of these things are spiritual. So, caretakers do what all people do: they think everyone else should value what they value. Since people of other temperaments don't take care of property the way they do, caretakers get lost in caring for everyone's property. Because the care of property is always screaming at them, they can get lost in its care. This is grounds for materialism: the care of property to the exclusion of everything else. At their worst, caretakers can become critical of people who don't take care of property the way they do. I just had a conversation with a man with a caretaker temperament. He said that he gets easily angry at the way everyone mistreats property. After a few minutes of discussion, he came to realize that it is his love for property that first led to disappointment when he saw property neglected. He had not recognized his disappointment, much less his love of property. Rather, he raced right into being angry at the guy who disregarded the care of property. We will discuss the caretakers' inclination towards anger momentarily.

The man who cares so much for his furniture that he never uses it, the man who manicures his lawn and becomes an ogre with his neighbors because their dandelion seeds blow into his yard, and the man who immediately worries more about the condition of the car than his son when hearing of an accident are all caretakers who got lost in their caretaking: all of these people are caretakers…caretaking to a fault. Just as lost is the woman who insists on a clean house while she is also caring for her twin toddlers, the woman insists on washing all the dishes and all the clothes daily, and the woman who always works at her job until 7 PM to get it all done. Without an understanding of the ultimate use of property, namely the use people put to it, property becomes an *idol* rather than a *gift* of care for property.

I have met several millionaires in my lifetime, and they are an interesting lot. One of these men came by his millions almost by chance. He had known Warren Buffet of Berkshire Hathaway fame 50 years earlier and happened to invest in Buffet's early ventures. In a way, he came by his millions nearly by chance compared to his benefactor, Buffet, who came by his billions by wise and prudent investment. While Buffet has had a lifelong reputation of sharing his earnings with his employees, the fellow I met in my office was quite different in his life. I suspect that both of these wealthy people were caretakers, but they were quite different in how they also took care of things other than money. My client neglected his employees, his wife, and his children. When I met him, he was in a third unsuccessful marriage and was contending with some legal difficulties. Upon his request, I arranged to meet his children and was not so surprised that all of his children had been alienated from him in one way or another. Eventually, he "bought himself out" of his legal difficulties but was then caught by the results of his crime. No one wanted anything to do with him. He had obfuscated his love for people with a love for money. Another millionaire I have had as a patient has regularly worked up to 90 hours a week for most of the 30 years of his marriage and is bemused that his wife is happily spending money with abandon. Another millionaire I knew lost the love of his life because he insisted in a prenuptial agreement guaranteeing that his millions would stay with him if she were to divorce him. These several examples are of people who have become materialistic, not in the sense of hoarding, but of getting lost in the care of property.

Not all caretakers are millionaires nor are all millionaires caretakers but money does seem to be a difficulty with caretakers because money is so directly linked to property. Mature caretakers do not love money; they love the *care* of money, or perhaps the prudent use of money, which is something they do by nature. When they fall into *loving money instead of caring for it*, they are on a slippery slope from caretaking to materialism. They become stingy; they have fallen into feeling money itself is valuable rather than the wise spending and saving of money for ultimate use. When this happens, life becomes drained of energy because money itself has become an idol. Stinginess can become a way of life regardless of how much money a person has. At their best caretakers can be quite generous, giving away property or money, if also with prudence. If money and property become idols, caretakers' natural generosity fades.

It is a generous thing that caretakers do when they share their money with a worthy charity, when they turn someone else's lights off when they leave a room, or pick up scattered toilet paper in the bathroom, or shovel the neighbor's snow. As I look outside my office at this moment, it is snowing. I am prepared to get on the lawn tractor, now with a snow blade, and probably just plow the sidewalk of the whole block. But in doing so, if I do this generously, I will not expect anything in return. I will not expect someone to do the same for me sometime. There is nothing wrong with teaching your kids to turn the lights off, but there is something wrong with yelling at your four-year old when she forgot to turn them off. I have turned many-a-light off myself, so I am very aware of the felt need to save electrical dollars by switching lights off when they are not used, but I am also aware that a light can burn for hours at the cost of pennies, and that my friends and family may truly enjoy the light that these few pennies buy. My wife really likes light, preferably natural daylight, but she also enjoys lighting up the kitchen or the living room to bring out the brilliance of these places and spends many an hour enjoying the lights in her greenhouse. Many caretakers save pennies at the cost of the simple inexpensive pleasure that someone might have with three lights on in a room when one would be sufficient for them.

My undue focus on property and the undue care of property has caused a myriad of problems; personal, interpersonal, and ultimately financial. One of the most expensive mistakes I made had to do with the undue care of property during the years that Deb and I owned that large building; the former YMCA building in Council Bluffs. This turn of the century building looked like a good deal for $30,000 because it had 5 floors and 25,000 square feet of possible usage. I saw the big picture of possibly restoring this building to its former grandeur as a residence for our family as well as an office building for us and others. I did not count the cost of time, labor, and money going into such a restoration project. Most importantly, I did not see the value of converting a steam boiler heating system that was nearly a century old and very expensive to operate into a more efficient system of smaller furnaces, this despite the fact that many people tried to explain to me that I should update the heating plant. That mistake nearly led to a bankruptcy for us. I "took care" of the 1920's tube walled boiler but I didn't "take care" of the larger issue of making the building profitable. This was my largest financial mistake, but I made many others with my intent of being unduly conservative in expenditures and saving old things in place of buying something more efficient. Likewise, my relationship with Deb and with several other people suffered because I was not able to see the "forest for the trees," which was the larger picture. Not only did my caretaking "to a fault" cause financial and interpersonal problems, I have suffered physically and psychologically by focusing too much on saving property and pennies rather than on saving relationships and dollars. Without knowing it, I found myself controlling my family in the care of this property. Many caretakers do the same.

2. Controlling

Because caretakers "take control of life," they can be controlling, usually without knowing that they are adversely affecting other people. Their tendency to control is not actually a desire to *control people* but rather a desire to *control the use of property* and events surrounding property. The "controlling" that caretakers do might originate in a desire to be efficient but with a certain neglect of common courtesy. When caretakers tell people what to do with property, they are attempting to *help* their friends care for property. This "helping" is often perceived as "controlling," just as a player might want to "help" a friend enjoy life more by playing. Notice how your caretaker friends talk about property be it his car, his electrical box, or his bank account. Property is the medium through which caretakers relate to people. They do not know that people of other temperaments simply don't care about property the way they do, and they don't necessarily know that people might not be particularly interested in their talking about property. The underlying phenomenon that caretakers have when they think that property is being misused is that they are *hurt*. This emotional hurt is the same feeling players have when they can't play with their friends, and we will see that lovers and analysts experience hurt when they can't connect or understand.

When people get emotionally hurt, they look for ways to assuage that hurt: they try to fix the problem. Caretakers often think that people aren't taking care of property as they should be, so they do what all people do when they are hurt: they step right in and start taking control. When players are hurt, they start playing...instead of recognizing their love of playing. When analysts are hurt, they start analyzing...instead of recognizing their love of analysis. When lovers are hurt, they seek immediate connections…instead of recognizing their love of people. The mistake that caretakers make is the same that all people make: people tend to think that everyone else is like them. Worse yet, that other people *should* be like them. Caretakers mistakenly think that everyone *can and should* take care of property the way they do, and even treasure property the way they do. When caretakers are hurt, they tend to forget that they love property because property has spiritual value. By the way, caretakers don't generally know that they value property as "spiritual." As a result of this unrecognized feeling of hurt and the love that always underlies hurt, caretakers try to fix hurt by controlling what other people do with property.

Caretakers tend to step into the care of the property the way they think property should be cared for. They can push people out of the way, figuratively or literally, in order to take care of property without knowing that they have pushed someone. I recall many years ago, pushing Deb's hand away when she was loading the dishwasher, thinking that I could do better with my hand than hers. I simply thought that I could fit the glasses in better than she. I didn't even realize that I had pushed her hand away before she kindly reminded me that she has loaded the dishwasher before. I had been *hurt* by what seems an inefficient use of her hands (How silly does that sound?), but instead of recognizing my hurt and my desire to do the activity more efficiently, I just pushed her hand away from the project. In so doing, *I hurt her*. My focus had been on the activity, not the person. Hurt people hurt people. At that time, now many years past, I didn't know that I was hurt when I saw something that wasn't being done as I thought was right. I certainly didn't know that I hurt Deb when I pushed her hand away. I just knew what should be *done*, and so I did it. My doing, however, caused more problems than it solved. I thought I was doing the right thing. I thought I was doing the loving thing. In this circumstance though, I loved the activity and not the person doing the activity.

Because caretakers tend to be doing something all the time, they can mistakenly think that everyone else should be doing as much as they do. Caretakers are not just doing for doing sake. They are doing what they think is *necessary* to be done. Caretakers see something that needs to be done and they just do it. As we discussed in the last chapter, this characteristic can be wonderful, whether for employer, friend, or spouse. Do you have a spouse who after backing the car out of the garage, remembers that he had forgotten to get the water bottle that he likes to have in the car on a ride? Then, he is gone for 10 minutes, only to discover that in getting the water bottle, he also saw that the kitty's food was empty and so he filled it, saw that his son had left the toilet seat up, so he put it back down, remembered that you wanted to return those shoes to the store, and two other things. He was doing all these things because he saw them, he knew they needed to be done (sometime), and he could do them quickly. These little things took 10 minutes, 10 minutes you were waiting in the car wondering if he completely forgot you. You are understandably irritated by the delay, but you are in the difficult position of being irritated at his doing all these nice things…and neglecting you in the process.

When their friends aren't as interested in doing something all the time, caretakers can be offended and feel pressured into doing all this work that they think is *necessary* in their eyes. They think that if everyone would simply do what is necessary, as they do, all would be well with the world, namely the world of property. The pressure that caretakers often feel does not come from other people, but rather from caretakers themselves. Their sense of urgency to do what they think is the right thing spills over to the assumption that others should do the same things, not considering that other people have other priorities, other loves. In so doing caretakers don't realize that what is necessary is not the same in everyone's eyes. It's not necessary for everyone to save every sheet of paper that has an unused side so to be used again somewhere. It might be nice to do so and it may save a few pennies, but a caretaker office supervisor who insists on it is trying to force her values on her employees. It's not necessary for every dish to be placed in the dishwasher instead of the sink. Again, it might be nice and it might keep the kitchen in nice order, but it doesn't have to be done. It isn't necessary for everyone even if it feels necessary for the caretaker homemaker.

My father was largely caretaker by temperament. My brother, however, was of a much different personality, namely that of an analyst. I remember many times when my father tried in vain to get Bill to do something that he thought needed to be done. Dad would, for instance, begin to cut the lawn (whether or not it really needed to be cut), and then try to get my brother to help him finish the project. Battles frequently erupted between Bill and Dad over whether Bill was going to invest time and energy into one of my father's doings. Things were much different with Dad for me because I shared the same caretaker temperament with him. Life was regularly difficult for Bill dealing with an authority figure who demanded him to act like someone he was not. Dad frequently engaged in some project or other, many of which were of trivial value. In the days of his deterioration from Alzheimer's disease Dad would carry one empty jar or tin can at a time out to the garage where he had the trash can and deposit these items where he thought they belonged. It was not terribly difficult for me to go along with Dad's silly demands to walk out to the garage with one or two empty containers because it just took a minute for me to do it. But my brother would spend hours arguing about such work resisting Dad's tendency to control him with tasks that Bill considered to be trivial.

Caretakers do not mean to control people but they do controlling all the time. They just mean to take care of property, to do things in a routine, and to do them in what they consider to be an efficient manner. Unfortunately, care of property requires that *people care about property*. I could do the trivial short-lived tasks that pleased my father because, like my father, I cared about the cans being thrown away. My brother Bill didn't care about the cans. He cared about what he was reading in the moment or figuring out a math problem. So Dad's insistence regarding the cans felt like control to my brother. I can only guess my brother also felt demeaned frequently by a person who had a profoundly different value systems. Unfortunately, Bill was controlled by my father's nature whether or not he took the jar into the garage for deposit because he spent so much time resisting and arguing about jars and the like. A lot of energy is wasted in battles between caretakers and those around them, energy that might be better spent on the common ground of understanding one another. As I watched my brother battle with my father on things like cutting the lawn and doing the dishes, I only saw Bill's resistance to these caretaking activities. I didn't see that my father was trying to control Bill, namely to be like himself.

One final note on the business of controlling: not all controlling is done by caretakers. Many people exercise abusive controlling of people around them because of their insecurity, envy, or greed. As we shall continue to see as we study the challenges for all four temperaments, we see that everyone has the tendency to think and act like we are all the same and we should all have the same values. My caretaker father valued property as intrinsically spiritual and unfortunately attempted to force my analyst brother to view property in the same way. My brother didn't care about taking the garbage out because he valued meaning and figuring out a better way to manage the garbage and wanted dad to be like him. When we think and act that way, we end up trying to control other people. Caretakers just happen to do it with property and activity.

3. Unavailable

With all their doings, caretakers are so busy that they often don't have time for the people in their lives. It is hard to have a conversation with someone who is always on the run, always working, always between one task and another, and always thinking of the 16 things that have to be done. Such people are hard to pin down for a good conversation, good play, and simple relaxation. Ever tried to have a simple conversation, watch the sunset, or just "hang out" with your caretaker friend? You might get a minute, but not much more, and during that minute you get the feeling that he has more important things to do than sit with you. Caretakers do not understand how their busy-ness offends and hurts, and makes people think that they don't count in the caretaker's eyes. They may count, but doings and property usually count more. It's not so bad that property and doing is more important to the caretaker, but it's not good when there is never any time for simple conversation. When some piece of property is in need, or something needs to be done, this almost always takes precedence over talk, play, or relaxation.

A day for a caretaker is usually filled with more things to do than most other people might do in a week. In a typical day I may see about six or seven patients, respond to 20 emails, write up psychological evaluations, visit with our office manager, and conduct various phone conversations. Additionally, I play basketball three times a week, work out twice a week, routinely assist in cleaning up the kitchen or put in another load of laundry. Unfortunately, unless I watch myself very closely, these various activities keep me busy for at least 12 hours a day. It has taken me (and my analyst wife) years to really learn how to "just hang out", something both of our daughters have yearned to experience with us. It is much too easy for me to busy myself with business of one kind or another and be unavailable for fun and conversation. It seems that I don't have time to think about anything but some kind of work. It *seems* that way.

The caretakers I noted earlier have been largely unavailable: the millionaires, the perfect mother and wife, the perfectionist who manicured his guitar and BMW, and the corporate manager who works 70 hours a week. Each of these people regularly hears the complaint from their loved ones that they were too busy and unavailable. If someone is spending hours every night shining a car or a guitar or engaging their clients long past the family's dinner time, there is not much time left to attend to relationship matters. Just as easily, the mother who does the duties of mothering can be the same mother who fails to really attend to her children in simple playtime. The parent who works the 70 hours a week "to care for the family" may not, indeed, care for the family's emotional and relational needs.

Caretakers might take Buddha's alleged statement to heart: "Don't just do something; sit there." And we might add, "…and smell the roses, listen to the wind, think deeply, feel simply, just hang out…and let someone else pick up the milk on the way home." It is easy for me to say such things because I have learned the value of life beyond property, but this is extremely hard for most caretakers to do because their vision is always on things and how things need to be cared for. Another patient of mine has a cabin "up north" as we say in Wisconsin, and he truly loves to work on the landscape, repair the dock every spring, and cut wood for the fireplace. He can't understand why his lover wife would much prefer to hang out on the porch and watch the sunset. Sam has seen more sunrises than sunsets because he's usually up at 5 AM working. All this busy-ness and property management has another effect: anxiety.

4. **Anxious**

Caretakers are prone to some form of anxiety. They tend to worry about the future, which often leads to considering what might go wrong with something. The "future" is often just the day or two ahead with all that they think needs to be done. They have a list of things to do, a host of people to serve, an inhuman amount of work to be done at work, and a lot of property to take care of. The unavoidable tendency that these concerns brings to most caretakers is anxiety. They can easily get into thinking too much about the future and fearing the worst. They can even think of potential disasters that most likely will not happen but could happen. They want to control the future by thinking ahead of responsibilities as well as dangers. The things that they think need to be done in the future scream at them, like "It might snow tomorrow, so I better put my boots in the car tonight," "I'm not sure that Julie got the email I sent her yesterday, and she needs to know about the meeting we're having today," "I haven't checked the oil level in the car for a while. It might be low, which could be dangerous for the motor," "I have to remember to give the kids the Valentine cards for school tomorrow. They might forget to put them in their backpacks." Notice the operative word *might* in all of these concerns. One of the millionaires I referenced above regularly worries that he will lose something in the stock market even though he would still be a millionaire if he lost half his savings. "Might be" can easily drift into the feeling of danger or impending doom for caretakers. They can be overwhelmed about minor possible difficulties in the future.

Their desire to take care of things is admirable, but caretakers' worrying about the future does no one any good, especially them. We need to think and plan about the future, whether it is tomorrow, next year, or 30 years from now when retirement comes. Both of my parents were worriers more than thinkers and planners. Both of them had substantial caretaker elements in their personalities, my dad more than my mom. I often saw Dad fretting over something that was very unlikely to happen, like bankruptcy or foreclosure on the mortgage, or even paying a bill on time. My mom worried unnecessarily about how my brother and I might get hurt water skiing. I remember her hollering down at me when I had a bunch of adult friends who were water skiing asking whether I had "liability insurance in case someone got hurt." I retorted that I had an "umbrella insurance policy that covered everything." She knew better but deferred from further questioning. Mom's concern about our welfare was admirable, but it interrupted the process of my having fun with my friends. It took me years to overcome my inclination to worry too much about how something might need to be done rather than more efficiently taking the day as it comes meeting the trials and challenges of each day.

There is a developing professional literature called "psychoneuroimmunology." However complicated this term seems, it represents an important area of research around people staying well and people getting sick. Simply stated, the finding is that anxiety in any form causes physical distress and can cause physical and medical harm. Having just had a heart attack only a month ago, I am more than aware of how my heart is regulating in any given moment. This morning, as Deb and I lay in bed, I began to think about going back to work tomorrow after a week off. I started to think about how to manage our office in potential subzero weather next week. I thought about a neuropsychological report that I needed to finish; I thought about making sure that a therapist that I am training would be in the second session with a new patient; and I thought about several other things that needed to be done. As I thought about all these things, I noticed that my heart began to beat more swiftly. Immediately, I recognized that my brain had kicked my heart rate up so I could think more clearly and more quickly. I knew what was happening even though my brain churned my heart rate up without my consciously willing it to do so. As I lay there, I willed my mind to let go of the concerns of next week's weather and true enough, my heart rate settled down. Deb and I just took a brisk walk and when I told her of this morning's incident, she noted that she had actually felt my heart rate shift this morning while her hand was on my chest and wondered about it. It wasn't easy for me to admit that this shift in my physical being was due to anxiety! I actually didn't feel anxious, like worrying, but my heart was doing what it does when my brain determines that I need more blood in my brain.

There is a host of what are called "MUI's", medically undefined illnesses that are caused by anxiety in various forms. Caretakers are inclined to suffering anxiety and from MUI's. You might notice that the caretakers in your life tend to talk about their aches and pains. These difficulties come from very real physical discomfort or genuine medical disorders, but much of what is presented as medical or physical originates in worry and anxiety. Listening to someone's aches and pains can be irritating, but caretakers themselves tend to be irritable.

5. Irritable

Caretakers are inclined to irritability because they are thinking so much of what needs to be done, what has been done wrong, or what might go wrong in the future. They are easily irritated because there is a lot on their mind. It is a rare time that they just kick back and hang out. Rather, they are thinking of the several things that need to happen or might happen even if these potential tragedies most certainly won't happen. When they are interrupted in their activity or even in their thinking, they can be irritated by the interruption. Ben is one of those guys who provides well for his family by working overtime to provide the only family income, continues to work on remodeling his house, and gives his time at several volunteer activities. Unfortunately, Ben also suffers from a good deal of anxiety, which has now developed into an ulcer. He also finds himself irritable with all of his family members. He has tried hard to govern his anxiety but without much success. He told me he couldn't meditate for more than 15 seconds because his mind would race to other thoughts, usually about the six or seven things he needed to do. He feels bad about being irritable with his wife and children because he says that they are the most important things in his life. Yet he feels compelled to work hard, volunteer frequently, and always be thinking of the list of activities that need to be done. It is no small task for me to help Ben to reduce his anxiety while retaining his good caretaking tendency.

Ben is not the only man I have seen in my office who suffers from irritability. In fact, most of the men who come to my office get angry too easily. I just spent an hour with a man who comes to anger so quickly that he doesn't realize that his voice is raised and sometimes his arms are waving in the air, behavior that scares his family. Brian is certainly a caretaker and struggling to raise one son who is clearly a player and another who is an analyst. He can't understand why these kids don't value property the way he does. There is a whole program called "anger management" that helps people, mostly men, deal with their inclination to get angry. I do not subscribe to "managing anger" but rather to *preventing* anger in the first place. Some men fall into physical abuse because of their uncontrolled anger, but most caretaker people, male or female, just find themselves irritated much of the time. It is understandable that caretakers become irritable. At least it is understandable to them because they are doing more than everyone else. Sometimes they think, "I am doing everything and everyone else is doing *nothing*." You will not succeed in doing everything your caretaker father wants you to do. Nor will it help to tell him that he is just irritable and needs to put a lid on it. The caretaker, himself or herself, must find a way to get away from caretaking to a fault, and get back to simple caretaking within limits. In the meantime, caretakers will be inclined to complain about all the work they have to do and how everyone else needs to do more. Caretakers often take on too much, namely too much caretaking with the naïve belief that they should do something at the moment the something becomes obvious that it needs to be done.

It has been a hard lesson for me that there are times when I shouldn't do what I am capable of doing. I have slowly and painfully learned that just because I *can* do something doesn't mean that I *should* do it. I recall early last summer when this really came home to me. We had made our first "summer" trip to our simple cabin "up north" in Wisconsin, and I was just sitting on the porch when I caught myself thinking of all the things that I *could* do: get the pontoon boat ready for use by charging the battery and filling the gas tank; cutting wood for use in our fire place next winter; washing the dishes left after breakfast; re-varnish the oak end tables that are on either side of the couch I'm presently sitting on; sharpen the chain saw blade for future use. Note that Deb and I had only arrived at the cabin that day and I had already cut down two trees and cut the logs into smaller pieces, repaired the dock, put away the winter clothes, installed the clean shower curtain in the bathroom, put the paddle boat in the water, and cut the lawn. Why would I be thinking of doing all of these additional things instead of just hanging out on the porch and listening to the geese squawk as they fly by, watch the hummingbirds feed on the feeders, watch the deer cross the lake to the island not 50 meters from where I sit, not to mention play another game of Chinese checkers with my life's partner? Because I am a caretaker and I like to take care of things. I made mental note that there was nothing wrong with taking care of those cabin chores, but there is something wrong with caretaking *to a fault* where I don't really enjoy what I am doing and could fall into being irritated at something or someone. Sitting on that wonderful little porch proved a good life's lesson for me. I have learned to take my own advice by using what I call "the 4 questions related to doing something:"

- Does it need to be done?
- Can I do it?
- Do I want to do it?
- Should I do it?

Caretakers like me tend to forget to ask the third question and hence jump right from seeing that something needs to be done, together with the fact that he or she is capable of doing it, right into doing it without asking the crucial third question. Right now, I will set aside all my other thoughts of doing things and attend to what I really want to do, which is to finish this chapter. And in fact, I may not finish the chapter today, or perhaps not this entire week if I discover that I really don't want to do it. One thing for sure: I don't need to be irritable, not with myself, not with my beloved, and not with God. I need to attend to the joy of doing things without letting these things get in the way of my being a good person first, an honest person first, a loving person first, and then a caretaker second. In other words, I need to grow up and give up the naïve belief that I should do everything that I think needs to be done.

6. Naïve

People of all temperaments are naïve in the same way: they think that because it is easy for them to do something, like caretaking, loving, playing, and analyzing, it should be easy for everyone. Players think that it is easy for everyone to play all the time; analysts think it is easy for people to analyze all the time, lovers think it is easy for everyone to seek connection all the time, and caretakers think it is easy to take care of property. It is understandable that caretakers think this way but it is naïve and it is dangerous. It is dangerous because caretakers do not consider the energy that they expend in working and they don't understand that it is not always good to take care of their own property and it is not always good to take care of other people's property.

Mary is one of those people who gives her time and money easily and freely. She just loves to be generous, and few who know her would not be aware of her generosity. She gets lots of accolades for generosity and many people have profited from her gifts of time, property, and money. About 90% of the time, Mary's giving is well received and appreciated, but there are also times when Mary gives "to a fault." She gives when she doesn't want to give or at times when she is so exhausted that she shouldn't give what someone asks of her. She doesn't know when to stop. She doesn't know when to say "no." There is nothing wrong with Mary giving the 90% of the time because it serves her to give, and it serves her friends to be recipients of her generosity. However, it is wrong for Mary to give the other 10% of time and effort because she will feel drained and depleted. When that happens, she will get irritable. Her children certainly don't know the extent to which she works so that she can provide for them. They just see that Mom gives them all they ask for. Mary *naively* thinks that she could satisfy all of the wants of her family and friends because she thinks that it is "easy" to give to them what they want. She doesn't trust the feeling that she has no more to give, or equally important, it is not good for family to receive all that they want.

This week alone I had two men, Tom and Ben, come to my office saying that they have great trouble saying "no" to doing things, often things asked of them by other people. The Mary's, Tom's, and Ben's of the world, male or female, old or young, naively think that they have an endless amount of energy, interest, and ability to give everything to everybody. Many recipients of such boundless gifts are children who have not matured enough to realize that it is not good for them to have all they want. More dangerously, there are adults who have not matured beyond the 4-year-old belief that they should have all that they want. Caretakers do not naturally see the danger of such people. They just hear their wants and interpret them as needs and proceed with providing all they can in the name of caretaking, often exhausting themselves in the process.

A very important part of my own naiveté has had to do with my profession. My tendency in my early years of practice was to approach anyone who comes to my office as someone that I could help and should help. It took me many years of fruitless trying to help certain people to realize that I could not help everyone. Sometimes, I was not the right therapist for a particular person; sometimes the individual was looking for someone to cure the world of its sins; sometimes, I was just not mature enough to see the larger picture and worked on the assumption that a particular client could do what I thought they should be able to do. During these early years I slowly and painfully realized that I needed to give all that I had to give but not give more. This is a distinction that is very difficult for caretakers to make. We tend to skip over the "third question," namely, "Do I want to do it?" and certainly fail to ask the equally important question, "Am I capable of doing it?" Instead, the immature caretaker will naively assume that because they can, they should. This is perhaps one of the most difficult pieces of being a caretaker.

CHALLENGES FOR CARETAKERS EXPRESSING FEELINGS

Recall that there are four ways of expressing feelings: physically, emotionally, cognitively, and actively. Caretakers express their feelings in activity. Their activity usually takes the form of production or repair, but it almost always has to do with some physical object, whether the furniture in the living room, the car in the garage, dishes in the kitchen, or papers on the desk. Both caretakers and players are action oriented, but caretakers' action orientation is toward *doing* something more than *experiencing* something the way players express their feelings. Do you remember Dickens' famous beginning of his *Tale of Two Cities*? "It was the best of times. It was the worst of times." Caretakers experience the best of times when they are doing and they experience the worst of times when they overdo it.

We noted that caretakers are all about business and busy-ness. Nothing wrong with being busy, but there is something terribly wrong with being so busy that you fail to communicate who you are and what you feel. Caretakers are especially prone to being blinded by their own doing in place of the alternate expressions of feeling. They are joyful when they produce but often unhappy when there is nothing for them to attend to. When there is a lack of activity or production that seems meaningful to them, they often become irritable or anxious, characteristics we have already addressed above. To avoid these dangers caretakers need to recognize that production brings them joy, but joy can come in other ways, namely physically, emotionally, or cognitively. Equally importantly, joy can come from good conversations, simple contemplation, or the "sweetness of doing nothing" as the Italians say, *dolce far niente*. Furthermore, caretakers need to simply be disappointed, sad, or hurt when they can't finish something in a timely fashion just as they need to learn to sad and disappointed when others don't attend to property. If they succeed in this transition of feelings, they can more easily learn to find joy in the other characteristics such as analysis, connection and play. This is a maturing process that brings about contentment that we will address in chapter nine.

Let me tell you about Jack. Jack works all the time, often 90 hours a week during tax time because he is a tax accountant. You might think this would be mostly in the months of March and April before the tax filing deadline. But Jack takes it a step further: he works an average of 65 hours *every week of the year*. Understandably, this leaves little time for the things that players do (play), lovers do (connect), and analysts do (discuss). If confronted, he always says something like, "Well, I'm working to care for my family. I'm preparing for our retirement. I'm not working for me." This statement is not entirely true, especially the last statement because he is, indeed, working for him because he loves working. Jack displays his feelings in working all the time just like many other caretakers, and then mistakenly thinks that he has successfully communicated his feelings, his passion, and his love to his family. He has not succeeded in that endeavor because he thinks it should be obvious that he is communicating these things through his work. He is not. When Grace, his wife, challenges him about working all the time, he will temporarily give into her demands for a while but then go back to furiously working 65 hours a week. While he is seemingly giving into Grace's demands for attention, he is secretly on his laptop working into the late hours, sometimes getting up in the middle of the night to do so. You might think that Jack expresses his feeling singularly in production, but this is not entirely the case. He "plays" at work, often with crunching numbers; he "connects with people," often customers with whom he has learned to engage; he engages in "thinking" like analysts, but almost all the time looking at how much money he can make, save, and protect. No one knows that he plays, loves, and thinks because all they see is his working.

As a caretaker Jack's predominant emotional expression is joy, just as it is for players, but his joy is almost exclusively related to production. He loves his kids and he loves his wife and wants good things for them, yes, but when he is honest about himself, he reports that he is happiest when at work saving tax money for his customers and sheepishly admits he is even happy when he pulls out his laptop late at night after Grace is asleep and works on one of his accounts. Like other caretakers he can enjoy doing household chores, when he isn't overtired from all the office work he has done.

With all his success at work, Jack is usually joyful, but he can fall into bouts of anxiety when things don't go well for him. As we have already noted above, caretakers tend toward anxiety because, like Jack, they can become overly dependent on production and the mistaken notion that doing is the solution for all things. When he can't quite get the numbers to work for a client, he tries all the more, works all the harder and longer and finds the anxiety creeping in because he might not "get it done". True to the caretaker's nature, anxiety takes the form of irritability. He gets mad instead of feeling sad that he can't work the numbers to his satisfaction. He becomes irritable and demanding when his family interrupts him and asks for his time. Unfortunately, his wife and kids see his anger and can only assume that he is just an angry person and have learned to stay clear when he comes home late. They don't see the disappointment that Jack feels when he can't succeed the way he desires, and they don't see that when he does stop working, he is too tired to play. Jack doesn't know how to say "Gosh, I really would like to finish my work before the weekend comes around. I am sad that I couldn't finish that account today. Kids, give me a little time with your mom to just sit then we can go out and play." If he could, he would feel better and his family would understand him better.

Sadness unrecognized for what it is, a loss of something loved, can lead to depression for caretakers, but more frequently anger is the problem. This is not to say that anger is wrong *per se*. It is the undue expression of anger, the intensity of anger, and the frequency of anger that displays the darker side of caretakers, which should more accurately be described as the emotionally immature side of their character. For a caretaker person to mature, he must first learn that taking care of things does not always successfully communicate feelings. He needs to add to caretaking the elements of feeling expression of the other temperaments and to govern his tendency to get angry when things don't go his way. This amounts to learning that in addition to the joy they feel in life, often in producing, they need to realize that joy always ends, and when it does, there needs to be a time of sorrow, disappointment, or hurt, all of which also end. In order to prevent the anger that they so easily come to, caretakers must accept the centrality of sadness in one's emotional life. Anyone dealing with caretakers needs to be aware of their strengths, their limitations, their feeling expression, and their emotional expression. This is no small task.

SUCCESSFUL ENGAGEMENT WITH CARETAKERS

1. Value Their Contributions

Caretakers do more than people of other temperaments. Sometimes, this is hard to see. You might think that you do "just as much as they do," but that is unlikely. You just work hard and do what you think is best to do. If you're an analyst, you're working in your head all the time trying to do the best thing at the best time. If you're a lover, you might work hard at relationships, or if you're a player, you might see yourself working hard to play and entertain, but no one takes care of things as much as caretakers…nor should they. You don't have to do as much as your caretaker husband does, but you need to see how much he does…even if he is less interested in a hug.

It is hard to value someone who does things that you don't think are important like washing every dish as it is dirtied. It is equally hard to value someone who seemingly cares for the couch more than sitting on the couch with you. It is hard to value the work someone does who gets in your way and tells you how to do something you choose to do in your way. It is harder still to value a caretaker's work when their caretaking work is obviously more important to them than your work in life, be it loving people, play, or ideas. Even so, if you can stand back and simply see what your caretaker does in a day's time, you will see that s/he is making an important contribution to the world. Yes, much of what they do may seem trivial and unimportant to you, but most of what they do is absolutely necessary. Ever notice that the sheets are always in the laundry, cleaned, and put back on the bed? Notice how the kids' schoolwork is always on the kitchen table ready to be done right after dinner? Your spouse "just did it" without asking you to help. Notice the extra work that your secretary did and then didn't even charge you for the extra hour? She didn't need to. She just saw that the office needed the work done. It is these little actions, often unrecognized, that are the very best of a caretaker.

Seeing what caretakers do leads to appreciating them. Appreciation should stand on its own. This means recognizing what you do like, appreciate, and value about the caretaker. Especially with a caretaker there can be no "I really appreciate what you do, *but*…." Such comparisons will not make sense to the caretaker. Remember caretakers are very concrete in their production. They do not look for meaning like an analysts might, or to have fun like a player would. They are actually more close to lovers in this because they perceive their production as a means of connection. If you note the good in one breath and immediate compare it to what you don't like, you will find that your caretaker will dismiss the comparison and stick to "why can't you just appreciate what I do?" When this happens, you will lose your audience. It is important in dealing with your caretaker to keep the criticisms and disappointments separate from the appreciations. You will get much further down the road if you keep this in mind.

Appreciating a caretaker can be a challenge because of what they *haven't done*, like love you the way you want to be loved (if you're a lover,) sit and play games on a weekend (if you're a player,) or be interested in your latest idea (if you're an analyst). In appreciating a caretaker you often have to feel your own sadness for a while because the appreciating might seem like simply giving in and agreeing that they should work all the time.

If that is what you are doing, then you just tolerating, not loving your caretaker. You need to take a step beyond seeing what your caretaker spouse, work associate, or friend has not done, and see what they have done. You need to appreciate them for who they are not what you think they should be. Being aware of your disappointment, and yet holding back on expressing feelings is what we call *containing* your feelings. This is setting your disappointment aside for the minute and see that he loves a part of the world that is different from the way you love the world (connection, experience, or meaning). Caretakers don't need you to like all that they do, but they do need your appreciation of what they do. Knowing that you don't like everything your caretaker friend does is about you and your value system, not what is wrong with the caretaker. What your caretaker friends do and how much they do is about them. Sometimes, appreciating a caretaker means that you need to contain the dislike for the time being, and perhaps come back to it later. We discussed containment of feelings, or governing your feelings, without repressing your feelings in *I Want to Tell You How I Feel*.

Caretakers need to be appreciated despite the fact that they don't actually look for appreciations because working and care of property is so natural to them. You might think that they are seeking appreciation in this work, seeking approval, but such is not the case, even so, as much as they do not *seek* appreciation, they *need* it. They need it just as much as you need it for what you love, be it people, ideas, or play. It will do your caretaker friend good to be appreciated. He might even dismiss your appreciation with a glance, or say, "that's nothing" or "I'm not looking for approval." But he needs to be appreciated. If you appreciate caretakers' work, you will discover that they will actually mature into doing *less* and be available more because appreciation of someone is an act of love. Love always has a positive effect. When a caretaker is appreciated, they feel loved and accepted in their value system. When a caretaker feels loved and valued for their work it becomes easier for them to begin to see the larger world, and to mature beyond the "just doing".

2. Dealing with the Phenomenon of Being Bored with Caretakers

Caretakers can be boring to many people, especially people who have a different temperament. By no means are they boring to everyone all the time but their tendency towards repetition can easily shift others into a state of boredom. Furthermore, they are boring even to other caretakers. There is no shame in being bored with what caretakers say or do. You simply are not interested in what they say, which they tend to say over and over again. It is not interesting to watch a caretaker work all the time, and it is even more boring to listen to her telling you what she has done, what she plans to do, or what somebody else has done. To deal with the boredom factor in relationships with most caretakers you have to admit that you are not always as interested in what they are interested in. This is hard work because you have to know that you are not interested without expressing your boredom. Just like you have to know what you don't like and keep that to yourself when you are appreciating a caretaker, you have to know that you are bored without accusing them of being boring. You don't have to be interested in what your caretaker friend says or does, but if you are to be a good friend and truly develop a relationship with her, you have to set aside your feelings of boredom and learn about your friend. Despite how we started out this paragraph, the truth is, your caretaker friend is not *boring*; you are *bored* with her. When you are bored with someone, realize that that person, himself, isn't boring. You are bored with him. Know that you are bored but don't say it. Find a better way of dealing with words and ways that are boring *to you*.

Caretakers have a tendency of saying the same thing twice…or thrice…or over and over again. This is just their way. They tend to talk about things as if the talking is a representation of what life is about. Talking for a caretaker is a form of "doing". Telling you what they did is a way of doing it again. You can find a comfortable way of dealing with the caretaker in your life by admitting to yourself that you simply don't care what she is saying to you while you are caring about them. You don't have to be mean spirited but you do have to admit it to yourself. Then, you will be able to manage it. Admitting to yourself what you are feeling is always the first step. This will keep you from interrupting a story that you're being told with such responses like "you have already told me that." If you can accept that you don't care about all of what she is saying, you will find a way to be patient for a bit, listening to something that is not interesting to you, just out of an act of kindness. Listening kindly to a caretaker that you love means letting the repetitions come, all the while appreciating them and reminding yourself that this story is energizing for them. Remember when caretakers tell you what they did it is a way of doing it again. Living with and loving Ron as an extroverted caretaker has taught me patience. Wading through the patience of repeated stories, for example, now gives me a pleasant joy. I am now more able to hear a story…again…and simply experience his inner joy alongside of him. Give your caretaker her due: listening only. It will be good for her and it will be good for you. After a while though, you may need to find a way out of a conversation that has no meaning, much less excitement to you and you need to find a comfortable way out of the conversation or the room. If you are careful in your departure having given your caretaker her due for a few minutes or a couple of stories, she will feel better but also realize that you are not as interested in how she put the dishes in the dishwasher, the book in the bookcase, or folded the kids' clothes.

Deb has honed this art of being appreciative of my tendency to talk about what I have done, am doing, or will do in the future. I used to come home and tell her every hour I spent with all of my clients that day, or every piece of wood I put up in the barn, or everything that I wanted to do tomorrow. There have been times when Deb has needed to tell me that she is finished listening for now or that it would be better for her to hear about something later in the evening after she has finished a project. This is much better for me as a caretaker than to catch a rolling of her eyes or a sigh when I am telling her about something I have done or want to do, or forbid, for her to simply blurt out how bored she is. I have learned from her gracious challenge to my talking too much about doing things that I can enjoy doing and talking about doing without dominating the conversation. With Deb's patient listening to me, I have come to recognize on my own when I have said enough or done enough. All of us, given enough time, can naturally mature beyond the limits of our temperament. I could never have matured beyond boring people with my doings except by the means of Deb's gracious listening to me being me. Then, I have learned to listen and engage her desire in conversation, namely analysis, problem-solving, and understanding the complexities of the universe.

3. Avoid Tolerating

It is too easy to slip into tolerating a caretaker. If you are living or working with a caretaker there is no getting away from their working. It is always in your face. If you are partnered with a caretaker in some way, whether in a marriage or a committed relationship, you are in danger "just tolerating." He might be taking care of the property in the home, the work at the office, or the plans for the neighborhood outing, but in all areas his doing will be so in your face that eventually you will want to have him stop and, when he doesn't, you will tend to give in which is what leads to tolerating. More than once have caretakers heard from their loved ones or friends "Please, just stop working, will you?" They don't usually stop. They might just look at you quizzically because their focus is on what needs to be done or retort that they just have one more thing they want to do and, while they do "that one more thing", you just sigh and begin to become disinterested in the caretaker.

As we noted above, learning to appreciate a caretaker requires you to be both patient and to sometimes contain your own feelings for a while. These are acts of kindness and love. Tolerating is neither kind nor loving. Tolerating comes when you haven't learned to contain your feelings and you put up with something that isn't good for you instead of dismissing yourself kindly when you have had your fill. More often, people begin to tolerate a caretaker's work and all that goes with it, like his irritability and his being tired all the time, or his repetitive nature. If you are in love with someone with this temperament, it is all the more difficult because you see all the work she has done. Recently, in a session with a couple, the woman said to her husband who is a caretaker, "Allen, you push yourself all the time." This statement by Allen's wife is evidence of her resenting his working all the time. It took me some time to help her make a clearer statement of how she really felt, "Allen, I love you. Because you work so much, I don't see enough of you. I would like us to find more time together." As you might guess, Allen's wife happens to be a lover by temperament but any temperament could easily say the same thing.

If you are working for someone with a caretaking temperament, you can easily give in and tolerate that your boss doesn't seem to care that you have a family and don't want to work until 8 PM every other night. If your college friend is a caretaker, you might get quite bored with them wanting to spend every Friday night in the library. It doesn't matter how you came to tolerating, however understandable it is, toleration is your fault because you went beyond the goodness of containment and slipped into toleration. When we discussed appreciation above, we talked about the goodness of containing your feelings while the caretaker is doing and talking. Containment is holding your feelings for a time while you give time to someone else. Tolerating is not the same as containment. Tolerating is giving in time and time again when something is less than good for you. How many times have you just rolled your eyes and slumped down when your caretaker wife wants to do just one more chore and you sit in boredom or frustration waiting on her to be done? Caretakers do not need to be tolerated. Toleration always leads to some kind of divorce, whether quitting a job, firing an employee, ending a friendship, or filing for a formal divorce from a partner.

If you are tolerating someone, you have given in to that person. Giving is great. Giving money is charitable. Giving time is gracious. Giving your life is the ultimate gift of love. But *giving in* is not the same as *giving*. It is a slippery slope from *giving* to someone to *giving into* them. It is especially easy for caretakers to fall into giving in because at first, you so much like what they do, until what they do is all they do. You have to take responsibility for having given in however you did it. At some time in your life with your caretaker friend or loved one, you gave in, and when you did that, you set yourself up for tolerating. You did the dishes when you wanted to take a walk after dinner.

You went to the same vacation campground when you wanted to try out a cruise. You took the kids to all their games because it was important that your spouse finish her work. Tolerating always comes from giving in.

Tolerating is bad for you and bad for the caretaker. When a caretaker is tolerated, they are no longer appreciated. When you tolerate a caretaker, or anyone else for that matter, you become dulled and disconnected and become judgmental. You have to know the difference between kindness and containment and something that is bad for you. When it becomes bad for you, it is your responsibility to know how you are being affected and for you to take action and excuse yourself from the caretaker.

In a nutshell, find a balance of appreciating what your caretaker friend does without giving in to doing too much yourself or tolerating him. Find a delicate way of expressing both your appreciation for his work and your need for some other kind of love…like connecting, playing, or discussing. Like with all the other temperaments, knowing how you feel, learning to contain your feelings for a time when it is kind, and then trusting your limits are all important. In dealing with caretakers, like dealing with any other temperament, there is much joy and there is much sadness.

Keep this in mind: we all love, but we love different things and in different ways. Regardless of how hard it might be for you to understand it, caretakers care for property above all else. If you get a grasp of this most difficult concept, you will love them more and help them mature just as you mature in the way you love. *Again*, let me quote Shakespeare from the *Merchant of Venice*, "you are twice blest." You are blessed because of the act of love and she is blessed because of having been loved. The balance of fostering appreciation, preventing giving in and tolerating, and clearly stating your own feelings will make your caretaker and you "twice blest."

Chapter 7

Challenges for Analysts

PEOPLE OF ALL TEMPERAMENTS have trouble communicating. For analysts, it can be especially hard. The key for successful living and successful relationships is the ability to communicate, mostly about how you feel, what you think, and what you do. It is not too hard to talk about what you do. It is quite hard, however, to communicate what you think, but it is immensely difficult to communicate what you feel. If you try to communicate your feelings through what you think, like analysts do, the process is nearly always a failure. Good communication primarily involves first *knowing* what you feel and then successfully communicating your feelings. When we fail at communicating what we feel, we will not be understood because miscommunication *always* leads to misunderstanding. Even though analysts desire understanding above all else, they frequently fail at communicating and being understood.

Although everyone has some trouble with communication, and ultimately with being misunderstood, analysts are the most misunderstood of the four temperaments, a fact that is ironically tragic. Because of their passion for understanding, analysts often fail to communicate and consequently are not understood. What is important in this is that analysts don't always grasp that understanding itself does not necessarily naturally lead to communicating what you understand. In Chapter 3 we described analysts as people who seek to understand as much as possible, and in that seeking to understand analysts are interested in the discovery of truth. It is in their very attempts to speak what they understand and what truth they have found that leads to their not being understood. Worse yet, they are often judged as being unsympathetic, critical, or argumentative and often, downright "unfeeling". In their essence they are none of these things. Analysts are not particularly good at communicating their essence, and it is in this failure that analysts have their greatest challenges in life.

Analysts, like all the temperaments, mistakenly believe that other people are just like them. We say this in every chapter because of the significance of this great and common flaw. Players think everyone should be gung-ho on experience. Caretakers think everyone should value property the way they do, and lovers think everyone should be seeking connection. For their part, analysts assume that others are just as interested in information and truth as they are. They usually operate under the assumption that everyone wants to hear the truth regardless of what the truth is and that everyone should be able to hear the truth spoken unvarnished and unadulterated. Keep in mind that analysts play with information, they produce analyses, and they seek connection by disseminating the truth they have found. Unfortunately, when analysts speak in their effort to connect, they often present information that doesn't communicate adequately. They often fail to recognize that the information they present doesn't forge a connection with other people despite the fact that same information is gold to them. So much of why analysts suffer in relationships is entangled in this communication difficulty. As we detail the challenges of the analyst in this chapter, note how these specific challenges relate to their world view, which is a deep desire for information and truth.

CHALLENGES FOR ANALYSTS

1. Perceived Criticalness

Analysts are often perceived as being "critical," meaning that they are fault-finding or "always look on the dark side." In fact, analysts are none of these things: not critical, not fault-finding, and most certainly not looking at the dark side. They are most certainly never *intending* to be critical. Yet they are *perceived* as being critical. This *perceived criticalness* is a very important aspect of how analysts engage the world, including the world of people. It shows up in just about every characteristic pertaining to the analyst, as you will learn throughout this chapter. The problem with analysts lies with their primary passion for finding and expressing truth as they perceive it. The Holy Grail for analysts is a truth that they have discovered by having gathered all the possible information available to them. When analysts speak, what they say is usually based on all they have learned, studied, and analyzed in a consolidated form. When they have coalesced all that information and thought, they often just "blurt" out some statement based on the truth that they have found. Analysts don't mince words; they don't take into consideration how their words might sound, if their audience grasps the context or not, or that their statement might offend the listener. At a moment of discovery, they are excited and just want to speak the truth, but their presentation of that truth is unimportant to them. Recall Chapter 3 where we discussed that analysts are primarily trying to *make the world a better place*. This "blurting" has to do with making the world a better place. They see how things are and how they could be improved. You might hear them say, "This is the way it should be" or "This is what you should do." What a listener doesn't know is that her analyst friend has been observing, musing, thinking, feeling, and analyzing long before she makes a summary statement. To an unaware listener, the analyst simply sounds like a know-it-all.

Because the analysts' seeking of truth often takes the form of problem-solving, they can appear to be interruptive, boastful, harsh, and critical. They are none of these things, and most certainly not know-it-all people. We might assert that analysts are the least arrogant of the four temperaments because they know that they don't know everything. They just want to know everything. How could it be that people with a basic desire to make the world a better place have such difficulties in communicating this passion and end up being perceived as critical? Analysts have such a heart for truth, problem-solving, and problem-preventing that they get excited about learning something new, something important, some new part of the overall truth of life, and want to share it. It is this desire to share what they have learned that gets them into social difficulty.

Indeed, analysts take a *critical look at things*, meaning that they look deeply at things, in order to understand how something isn't working well. Importantly, there is another piece to this *perceived criticalness* that they display. Not only do analysts seek to find answers when things aren't right, they actively look for things that could go wrong so as to prevent problems. They jump at the chance to point out what is going to go wrong as well as what isn't already right. It is very easy to interpret an analyst as "always looking at what is wrong" compared to their intention of making things better. Many years ago, when we lived in Newfoundland, we would drive across the province on the TCH, the Trans-Canada Highway. It was often a bit of a challenge because of the scarcity of "convenience" services, like an espresso-serving coffee shop. Once, after we had moved back to the States and returned to St John's for a visit, we were driving the TCH again and I bemoaned that we wouldn't find any espresso. Ron suggested that we might, but I emphatically declared "There isn't any espresso on the TCH!" Low and behold, in our years of absence, various espresso shops had popped up. When we did find one, after all my bemoaning, Ron laughed and said "there isn't any on the TCH!" Now, whenever I engage in my "what is wrong first analysis," he will simply quip, "Oh, there isn't any on the TCH!" which has become a friendly hint that I am assuming a problem when maybe there isn't a problem to be fixed. Not having a problem though, is actually difficult for an analyst. The old adage "If it isn't broken, don't fix it." is about a far cry from the analyst as you can get. It is this need to find the flaw in order to improve that often makes the analyst appear so critical.

The dilemma for analysts is that they just love problems, or more accurately, love to see how a problem might be prevented or resolved. They see how property can be better utilized or more safe or how some unexpected environmental factor might be dangerous or damaging. They see how an explanation of insurance benefits is less than clear. They see how an idea or theory can be expanded or clarified. They see how people could be happier if they would take a more honest look at themselves. They see how relationships could be better if the partners would work harder at understanding each other. Their observations about how something could be better might seem trivial and even critical to other people but it is enticing and energizing to an analyst. Unfortunately, in their seeing how something could be better, they are inclined to speak about what is wrong, and in doing so they are *perceived as critical*.

The tendency for analysts to comment on what is wrong often leads to people being offended, or put off to say the least. It is one thing to critique a movie, which is composed of actors playing the parts they represent, but it is quite another to critique an individual who is a real person playing himself in life. Even if we see the whole picture, both what is right and what is wrong, we tend to focus on what is wrong and make comments accordingly. We analysts can be heard saying something strongly, like, "This is certainly a stupid design!" or "That isn't how that should be done!" or "Why can't they see that what they are doing is dead wrong." Even in direct relational encounters analysts will often make exclamations like "Don't do it that way!" or use rhetorical questions like, "What are you doing that for? Why are you doing it that way?" I know that when I make such declarative criticisms, they are emotionally driven, but at the moment of speaking, I feel compelled to identify the flaw, whether in product, people, word, or action and disregard my passion behind it.

Analysts critique people in the same way they critique property, ideas, and movies. In their critiquing, analysts do not intend to be unkind to people; they intend to be helpful—by criticizing them, however paradoxical that sounds. They desire that their analyses and examinations bring light to people so that they can have a better life. However, their suggestions often fall on deaf ears and hurt hearts. No one can hear criticism, however right it is, without feeling hurt, a fact that eludes most analysts. The essential desire that analysts have, which is to help people and make life better for them, is often lost in what they say, when they say it, and how they say it. Again, it is sad that they do not realize that their desire to help a person have a better life is *perceived as critical*.

We frequently encounter marital or relationship problems in our office of which probably 90% have to do with miscommunication. When it comes to the difficulty that analysts have in the realm of communication, it is often related to the way they say things, not what they say. Ron has been working with a middle-aged couple who have been experiencing long-term marital difficulties, mostly in the form of frequent disagreements and arguments. Furthermore, there were some extended family difficulties that tended to make the marital relationship even more difficult because the couple took "different sides" in some of these family conflicts. The wife was distinctly an analyst by nature, while her husband was mostly a lover by temperament. The husband presented the fact that his wife tended "to be critical of everything and everyone." The wife didn't see herself that way, and in fact thought she was really being quite loving of her husband and their adult children. She admitted that she had some occasional relational difficulties with the spouses of her children but tended to see these as minor and due to these younger people as being "'defensive" and "immature." Over time, I began to work with the wife separately. I began to hear firsthand many stories that had led to marital and family conflict, almost all of them having to do with this woman's perception of what was "right" to do and "wrong" to do. She talked several times about an incident where her daughter-in-law came into the house with dirty shoes and "made a complete mess of the foyer." Now, lots of people don't like mud brought into their homes, but for this analyst and her daughter-in-law, the conflict wasn't really about the mud, it was about the woman's seemingly unrelenting explanation of how people can avoid such things. The conflict became about the explanations from the analyst rather than the mud brought in by the daughter. The husband told Ron that his wife "explained" to the entire family multiple times over the course of a weekend how to prevent bringing mud into the house. As the story unfolded, I learned that the daughter-in-law apologized for the mud incident, but the discussion didn't end there. This woman felt compelled to talk about the "irresponsibility" of mud coming into the house and how it could be avoided, which is what ultimately fed more conflict.

If this woman had been a caretaker, the apology probably wouldn't even have been necessary. She would have just mopped the floor. If she had been a lover, she might have dismissed it and suggested that the muddy dog could come in, too. If she had been a player, she could have suggested they go out for a mud fight. In truth, the analyst woman just wanted to share her understanding of how certain shoe treads collect mud more readily than others, and that certain paths in the park are lower in grade and so collect more run off, and, if people could take that into account, then less mud would be carried in on their shoes. No doubt, she sought to engage emotionally with information.

Her husband and her daughter-in-law did not grasp this concept, that this woman's corrective information was her wanting to connect the family. Note how sad it was for this good woman, who simply wanted to be reasonable and responsible, to offend the very people she wanted to help.

Ron's brother, Bill was a good friend of mine for a long time. He was an extremely bright and well-read person. I think Bill knew more about more things than anyone I have ever known. We were friends, I think, mostly because we shared this analyst stuff, although at the time, we did not have our current vocabulary for it. We just knew we were similar while being so different from most of the other people in our families. I can recall many times that Bill would tell Ron or other members of his family something based on what he had read or had figured out. At the time, I didn't perceive his instructions as critical. I could see that he was knowledgeable about some fact and that his opinion was well-researched and well-reasoned. It was not infrequent, for example, that Bill, while sipping on coffee sitting around the table, would casually instruct his mother and say something like, "Mother, there is a better way to load the dishwasher." Then, he might say to Ron or me, "I don't understand why Mother won't listen to my instruction." Margaret would voice herself with something like "I have done dishes my whole life…and I like…" to which Bill would easily interrupt, "What one likes isn't the same as what is right or best." Bill could counter any defense with more correction complete with documented information that confirmed his position. In this instance, I actively recall that he had researched how to load this particular brand of dishwasher. Even though Bill may have been right in his analysis, he was clearly wrong in his way of speaking his analysis. As with many analysts, Bill thought that it was more important to see "improvements" than cater to preferences. As I look back at Bill, I see an intelligent, spiritually driven, generous man who was often misunderstood, especially by the people whom he loved the most. How sad to see greatness misunderstood as arrogance.

The more analysts mature in life, the less they comment on what is wrong, and the more they express how something could be improved. Most people, however, are not particularly mature in emotional and social development, and analysts are not the exception. A mature analyst can be content to "just know for themselves" and not demand that the environment understand what they know. They generally don't know how to say "You know, if ever you are interested, I have an idea of how that project could be improved" or "If ever interested, I have some ideas on that." The challenge for analysts is for them to accept that most people are simply not as interested in how the world works and how it could work better. They do not grasp that everything they know is not obvious to others.

2. "It's Obvious (to me)"

I find myself thinking this frequently and saying it occasionally. I used to say it more often but I have learned to keep such thoughts to myself because saying, "It's obvious" so easily can be heard as a kind of arrogance. I don't mean it that way. I don't mean to say that everyone else is stupid because they don't see what I see or know what I know. I just see a lot, which then puts me in the unenviable position of seeing more than most people see. When I use the phrase, "see a lot," understand that I use the verb "see" to represent the information that I have accumulated, perhaps through any of my five senses. When I *see* something that seems obvious to me, I have to remember that not all people see the same thing, nor are they interested in what interests me. As a bit of a naturalist and a gardener, I enjoy seeing the array that Nature always has for us and frequently find myself commenting on the beauty that She offers us. Ron doesn't regard nature the way that I do, nor does he care much about nature. He doesn't see the new red rose blooming in June, partly because he is red/green color blind, but also because he simply doesn't care as much as I do about such things. I know he is being kind to listen to my nearly constant comments about nature and he never dismisses my observations. However, I have to admit that I am simply disappointed that he doesn't see and doesn't care about nature the way I do. When we walk past that rose, I see the beauty of it, yes, but just as equally I see everything that surrounds the rose: the foliage, the fence line, the rocks and the pots as well. It is all so obvious to me. When I work with analysts in my office, I try to help them understand that this "seeing" that we do is a gift to us, not a gift that everyone has, and not a gift that everyone should have.

I watched Ron with amusement recently when we rented a car. We did the paperwork, the rental agent handed us the fob and off we went to get the car. As we approached the car, Ron pressed what he thought was the unlock button only to find the panic siren going off. It was "obvious" to the 20-something rental agent how the fob worked, but not to Ron. The rental guy could have told Ron something like, "This is the key fob. It is a remote start. Press the lock button then the start button. You don't need to put this fob into any slot, but you can." He already knew all of this and assumed that any other intelligent person would know it. He didn't know that Ron still drives his 20-year-old Mustang that is simple to unlock and start with a "real key". The agent came up and took the fob from Ron somewhat begrudgingly and ceased the siren then told Ron how to use it. He wasn't crude, but it was clear that he thought Ron should already know what he knew. *It was obvious to him.* Analysts often react similarly when what is obvious to them isn't obvious to someone else.

There is a lot that is "obvious" to analysts because they watch more, think more, and analyze more than the people with other temperaments. Very frequently, analysts know something so well that they, like the car agent, simply skip the steps that would make a matter understandable to someone else. As an analyst, it takes an incredible amount of energy for me to step by step communicate how I got to the burst of information I might spout out. It is like having to gear down to my lowest level of thinking and start back up. I know at this stage in my life that most people need or at least appreciate some of the back story, or foundation of understanding. Recall that we analysts love to collect information. We want the back stories too, like how we learned something, but we just don't like to relate the back stories when we are offering suggestions or corrections. Once we have understood something, to retread that information is simply not fun. So, when the conclusion is presented without any back story or prep by an analyst, it is often received as if the conclusion is out of context because our listeners are still in the early grasping of the information.

This morning, Ron and I were sipping espresso talking about our clients on the docket for the day and he noted that a couple of his analyst men were failing miserably at communicating their feelings. Ron noted that James, a longtime client of his, frequently responds to his suggestions with comments like: "Yes, I already know that. That's obvious." Ron suggested that it was a defense mechanism. After a few moments, I suggested that in addition to James seeming a bit "defensive," he was wanting to get to the point and not review how he got there. James' response, "Yes, I know that," seemed abrupt to Ron, but I saw the situation of an analyst wanting to get on with fixing the problem with some kind of strategy, not belabor old information. I frequently use the phrase "I already know that," much like Ron's client does. I reminded Ron that I do the same kind of abrupt responding when something is already obvious to me, like when he might explain the basic rudiments instead of a specific strategy in working a Sudoku problem. Indeed, "I already know that" sounds defensive because it is, but it is also a truth for an analyst.

The "I already know that" piece of the analysts' nature has to do with boredom. All people get bored in some way. Players get bored when they can't experience something and are forced to just sit and read. Caretakers get bored when they can't do something productive. Lovers get bored with things that aren't immediately relational. We analysts get bored with any information that is repetitive. Sometimes, when I am told redundant information, I just want to shout out, "Tell me something I don't already know. Don't give me the same stuff I have already figured out!" When something makes sense to analysts, they are ready to get on with something else, something new, and something more challenging and therefore more interesting. We analysts seem defensive whereas, in fact, we are just bored with information that seems irrelevant or repetitive. I am currently working with a client who, having just begun a new job, is in an introductory probation period as she becomes familiar with her new responsibilities. She is more than skilled for the job, strong analyst that she is, but she finds great frustration in having to fulfill the requirements of the probation, which include exercises in demonstrating her knowledge set. She clearly knows the rudiments of her job, but it is painstaking for her to go through a "meaningless" process of demonstrating how she knows what she knows. She reports that she isn't sure she can maintain this job because of how boring it is just to get past initial probation. For an analyst to have to delay their minds with the already known is tedious and unfulfilling. My client is frustrated with this probationary period because it is boring for her but I suspect she looks defensive.

3. Intentionality is Everything

Defensiveness is often a result of *intention*. How many times have you heard someone say, "You're taking this the wrong way," "I didn't mean it that way," or worse yet, "Why are you so defensive?" People say these things because they haven't communicated successfully and assume that the problem in communication lies with the listener, not themselves. Miscommunication and the judgments that result occur every day with every person, and they are the heart of difficulties in every relationship. A professor can't blame her students for not understanding her lecture, and you can't blame your friend for not understanding what you said. This fact is hard for everyone but it is hardest for analysts because, as we have already noted many times, their *intention* is to communicate knowledge, and in so doing find truth, central elements in every analyst.

The paradox that occurs with every person of every temperament is this: *you hurt someone but didn't intend to hurt that person*. Likely, you have been trying to help your friend, or simply communicate something that you felt or thought. A few hours ago, we lowered our flag to half-staff for Memorial Day. As I was watching Ron do this respectable chore, I commented that the flag was too low. His immediate response, a common one when I "correct" him was, "I am not there yet," which meant that he was still adjusting the flag and for me to please hold my suggestions. I was unaware that he was tying on a rope extension and wasn't yet in the place of positioning the flag. I didn't see all of what he was doing. I just saw the improper height of the flag, not his efforts to extend the rope. Ron was *caretaking* by extending the rope and I was *analyzing* the appropriate level of the flag. I wanted the flag to be in the best possible position. Ron didn't care about the exact position because he was doing the task of extending the rope. In my instruction or correction, I might have hurt Ron, who from his standpoint, was doing what he knew to do. When I heard Ron say, "I'm not there yet," I knew to say no more and wait until he finished his caretaking before I did my analysis. Once he finished repairing the rope, he asked me to let him know when the flag was at the right height. I did. Then, I promptly acknowledged my appreciation for him taking care of the flag. Can you see how this situation could have deteriorated into "defensiveness" with one of us attacking the other? In this situation, it would have been very easy for me to defend myself with, "I was just wanting to be sure you knew where the flag was supposed to be!" And, had Ron reacted angrily at me saying something like, "Do you think I'm stupid? I am fixing the rope." I could have easily retorted, "Well, I didn't know the rope wasn't long enough!" Any of those retorts would have been offensive, especially between a caretaker and an analyst.

A simple apology for offending is often in order but it hard for most people to say because they *didn't intend to offend.* It is a rare time that someone of any temperament or type could graciously say, "I am sorry for offending or hurting you." We analysts can be the worst at being able to do this because our intention was to inform, correct, and improve, not to hurt. It often eludes us that our intention is half of the story; the other half is the effect. Wanting to have the flag set properly at half-staff to honor the fallen is admirable. Interrupting a caretaker who is doing his chosen duty the way he sees fit is offensive, just as it would be offensive for a caretaker to interrupt an analyst doing the very same thing with a desire for a perfect half-staff.

I remember a time some 30 years ago when Ron and I were in a group setting associated with a church we had been attending. On this particular night in question, we related the fact that our older daughter, Krissie, wanted to marry someone although she was only just graduating from high school, planning to go to college, and wasn't quite yet 18. This was one of many difficult times we had with dear Krissie, primarily a player as we have previously noted, but also with a good bit of the lover temperament. This was a time we had hoped to simply share our conflicted feelings about wanting Krissie to make her own decisions in life and yet render the best that we could in this situation. Most certainly, we didn't think she should marry and had talked to her quite a bit about it, but alas, our discussions did not lead where we hoped it would, so we did our best to love her and encourage her without further direction, much less criticism of her desire to marry at such an early age. We expected that this friendly church group setting would allow us to share our feelings and concern, but we were not prepared to hear a comment from one of the group members, Sam, who was most certainly an analyst by temperament. Sam spoke almost immediately after we had relayed the story of Krissie and suggested in clear and precise terms that we should most certainly not allow Krissie to marry and do our best to instruct her on the error of her ways. When Sam had finished his suggestion, Ron simply stated that he was "hurt" by what Sam had said, and then explained that we were simply sharing our grave concern along with other mixed feelings about Krissie's intention to marry. I still remember what Sam said: *"You can't possibly be hurt because I had not intended to hurt you."*

It is very difficult for analysts, like Sam, to understand that analysis spoken to someone can have a negative emotional effect despite their good intention to help. This is often the case with analysts who can jump right in with a solution, when a solution isn't what is being asked for. Analysts assume a solution is always in order instead of "just hearing" someone's feelings. As we said before, it is especially important for analysts to see that intention is half the story whereas the other half is effect. The truth-seeking and truth-telling that so typifies most analysts is quite similar to the philosophy of the ancient Cynics of Greece who espoused *parrhesia*, which can be loosely translated as truth-telling which sometimes rejects social protocol with its candor or frankness. Ancient Cynics were not "cynical" in the contemporary understanding of the term, but rather those who trusted that truth itself would cure any ill, whether a country or an individual person.

Recall from chapter 3 that truth-seeking and truth-speaking are central to an analysts' way of going about life and central to what they say. Furthermore, truth, like beauty, is sometimes in the eye of the beholder. Analysts think that truth is good, therefore speaking truth must be good and the effects of truth speaking should be secondary. As a result, when we speak just a few of our thoughts, and find that these few words hurt people, we are nonplussed. On one hand, we are like everybody else and it is painful for us to hurt others. On the other hand, we have to step back and shake our heads at how truth-speaking can hurt someone. It is a large step for us analysts to consider that positive intentions can solicit negative results. An even larger step is learning to gauge when to withhold our truth-speaking when we suspect that it might wound someone. What is interesting in this whole discussion of how analysts seek truth and speak truth is the fact that they actually keep most of their thoughts and analyses to themselves. In doing so, they can be quite self-critical.

4. **Self-critical**

Truth seeking and truth speaking is so important to analysts that most of their waking moments and thoughts are about truth. They seek diligently to understand the world, including the world of people, and they are often very incisive and insightful in their analyses. Yet, as with all people, analysts are sometimes wrong in their analyses. As if it weren't enough for an analyst to work diligently to understand the whole truth and then be wrong, even a little wrong, it is even harder for them to admit the error of their analysis. This challenge of admitting to error, first to themselves, and then to other people, is incredibly painful for analysts. Rather than simply acknowledging that they might have missed something, they will be inclined to give you several reasons why they made a mistake. This is very similar to when analysts have been told that what they said was hurtful, they go into an explanation of *why* they said what they did instead of facing the emotional truth of the situation. A simple apology is difficult for them. It is a great leap of maturity for analysts to see that however well-intentioned their words or actions were, and however well thought-out their analyses were, they are sometimes simply wrong. This disinclination to admit to error and simply apologize can make the analyst seem "defensive" at best and arrogant at worse. Instead of owning up to their error, analysts want to *explain how* or *why* the error came about. To really understand analysts, you need to know that their seemingly defensive explanations are a desire to do the right thing, but when they see that they have actually done the wrong thing, they are terribly upset with themselves.

It is bad enough when analysts hurt people with their suggestions and corrections, but when they have made some erroneous judgment, said something that was not accurate, or made a mistake in some kind of action, they are really at a loss and then do what analysts do best, analyze themselves, but always with great harshness. Analysts hold very high standards for everyone around them, something that can be difficult for their family and friends, but they hold even higher standards for themselves. They think that they should always do the right thing, never make a mistake, and certainly think ahead for any possible contingency. You might think that the analyst could simply admit that he has made a mistake, render some kind of apology, learn from his mistake, and go on. Caretakers do this. Analysts don't. They are not good at the simple "my bad" statements that come more easily to caretakers, nor are they emotionally as sensitive as the lover to offer a compassionate apology, and certainly, they are not even close to the nonchalant, carefree "oops" of a player. If you think that your analyst friend is hard on you or your children, you have no idea of how hard he is on himself even though he rarely admits to it.

I recall a couple of things that I did wrong this week, but when I even think of these errors, minor as they might have been, I feel a tinge of distress. As an analyst, it takes me longer to process my errors. "My bad" slips out of Ron's mouth easily, but not true for me. A few weeks ago, we were up north at our cabin and enjoying our leisure. I began tending to patch of lilies that line the back of our cabin. I noticed a good deal of what I call "devil's knot," which is a particularly wicked invasive ground cover. Ron said he had already sprayed the area with weed and grass killer, a kind of "kill all" chemical, but he had been careful to avoid spraying the lilies. Later, as Ron was mowing grass in the area, I leisurely inspected the lily patch, saw no evidence that the spray he had used had been effective and so I "just sprayed again", the whole thing, invasive ground cover and the lilies. Two days later, sitting on the cabin porch thoroughly enjoying the hummingbirds do their dog fighting antics, I mentioned "oh, by the way, I resprayed the lilies, let's go see if we got the devil's knot." We walked back to the lily patch and to my utter dismay, everything had wilted, not just the devils' knot but the lilies, too. I was beside myself. Immediately, and privately, I began racing in my mind, reflecting back on the action I took and in true analyst form began a self-barrage of criticism: "I was carless in my work, I should have waited longer to see if Ron's application took effect, I should have researched the product, I should have applied the chemical directly onto the devils' knot instead of spraying at large." These citations all lead to the emotional criticism of "How could I do such a thing? Why didn't I think it through? I should have known better! How ignorant of me! I would never use kill-all spray in my gardens, why in the world would I do it here, at the cabin?" This mistake was grievous. It was AWFUL! As a gardener, it was grief. As an analyst, it was despair. I went for a long lonely walk. It took me more than an hour to bring myself out of my own bereavement so that I could face my error and apologize to Ron, the lilies, and the universe at large. The whole process was, in the end, as it should be, both humbling and necessary. The next day, still saddened, I attempted to amend my error by pulling up all the lilies, removing any remnants of the invasion, washing off the lilies, flushing the soil and then one by one, replanting them with a repentant prayer. Luckily, when we returned this last weekend, to my great delight, most of the lilies had somehow weathered the storm of my error. I offer this admission of error and confession of sorts because you're not going to hear such things from your analyst friends too often. Know this: they feel much worse than you can possibly know when they have made a mistake. The greater the implications of the mistake, the greater their distress. The difficulty that analysts have with seeing their mistakes, admitting to them to other people, and looking defensive can make them look a bit odd.

5. The Oddness, the Uniqueness of the Analyst

Every temperament is unique, and every person in each temperament is unique. Analysts, however, are generally more unique than the other three temperaments. Lovers are better at loving people than the rest of us, but we all love people. Players are better at playing, but we all play. We all do some kind of caretaking, even if caretakers do more of it. However, we do not all do the kind of regular and intensive analysis that analysts do. Their nearly constant gathering and sifting through information is not any kind of simple analysis. It has an intensity that goes way beyond understanding of something. They want to understand the whole picture, the ins and outs of something, the causes and origins of things, and most importantly how to improve on things and prevent problems. It is very likely that the brain of an analyst is much more active than the brains of people who do not share their temperamental orientation. This nearly constant intensive analysis tends to make analysts hard to understand but also makes them unique in the way they go about life.

Sometimes analysts simply want to be unique. They want to be different from other people. When I explain to analyst clients they are, indeed, "analysts," together with all that means, they always feel a tremendous sense of relief. Being an analyst "makes sense to them" and they feel relief that someone acknowledges, in positive terms, *what* they are, *how* they think, *how* they feel, and *how* they operate in the world. They feel recognized for *who* they are, including their oddness. Clearly, they have often felt "odd" but the oddness, their uniqueness now is a piece of their preferred identity.

We analysts know that being "unique" can seem odd to other people. For the most part, analysts accept this perception that others have of them, but they don't tend to fret about what other people think of them. They know that their accumulation and, more specifically, their presentation of knowledge makes them a bit of a misfit in society. *Odd* as it seems, knowing that others think you are odd, is just part of the drill for analysts. Because analysts' orientation is mostly about information, they are not too concerned about the other elements of life, many of them particularly social, like what they look like and how they operate and how people perceive them. This lack of social concern contributes to their strong independence which in due course, adds to their oddness. They often like to live in unique places, dress in unique ways, speak in unique terms. They generally have unique ideas and unique lives. All of this uniqueness makes them hard to understand—and sometimes hard to like—because they don't fit into typical norms.

Analysts' unique nature is not primarily by their design or by some desire to "just be different." Rather, it erupts from their intense desire for truth and the dissemination of truth. If social norms and expectations get in the way of what they do, how they dress, or how they speak, analysts tend more to disregard such norms rather than to adjust to norms. Their unique or odd physical and social presentation is mostly due to the fact that they are disinclined to care much about how things look. In fact, they disregard the appearance of others as much as they disregard their own appearance. They are just not interested in appearance because they are so interested in essence. They look under the surface for this essence: under the surface of what one wears, under the surface of what one says, and under the surface of what one does. A frequent byword for analysts is *authentic*. They want to be authentic and seek for authenticity in all circumstances. For analysts, what is visible is never the real essence; it is only the surface.

Analysts spend so much time looking under the surface of what is said or done that they sometimes neglect to see the surface itself. Furthermore, they often speak in unique or complex ways because they are searching for words and phrases that speak to the essence of their thoughts more than how they might communicate in ways that people can understand them. This unique nature of speech and appearance can seem weird to other people. Ron's analyst brother, Bill, was quite taken with his favorite philosopher, Soren Kierkegaard, who once said that he wrote in obtuse ways so that people would have to *work hard* to understand him. Bill often spoke in such a way that even I, another analyst had to work hard to understand him. I just read a bit of Martin Buber's *I and Thou* in which he used terms like "I-ness, Thou-ness, I-Thou-ness, and I-it-ness to such an extent that I had to put the book down and muse how Buber, great as he was, probably didn't communicate to most people who read his work.

I can think of many analysts that I have known over the years, and with most of them, I recall how they simply looked a bit odd, talked a bit odd or behaved a bit odd. A fellow who officed in the same building where Ron and I officed often stood in a way that made him look contorted, almost as if he were trying to twist his body out of proportion. I doubt that he was trying to contort, much less trying to be odd. Rather, he just disregarded how his posture might appear to others because his interest was on things more important to him. A woman analyst we both knew quite well always wore clothes that made her look like a hippie even though she was quite conservative in her way of life. One time, many years ago, a client of mine asked me if I owned any other dresses because I apparently wore the same dress every time I saw her. These days, I actually rotate my clothes in my closet so I know what I have already worn in a given period of time. This is a reasonable procedure I have adopted to accommodate to the social atmosphere, but in fact, I don't care a hoot what people might think of what I'm wearing on any given day. I might care, but I don't care if anyone else cares.

Ron tells me about a time that he hosted a pot luck game night for a group of his men friends. After they had eaten their dinner and played some games and it came time for the dessert, Ron went to the kitchen with two of his guests, Marty and George, to retrieve the dessert for the evening. When the three of them got to the kitchen to fetch the special cake that Marty had baked, they saw that George's dog had been feasting on it. Marty and Ron stared at the cake and then at each other with great disbelief. As a caretaker, Ron was immediately taken by the loss of property and said something like, "Well, that's too bad." Marty, lover by nature, expressed a similar disappointment because he was looking forward to sharing his carefully prepared cake for the party. George, the analyst, looked at the cake, looked at his dog, and said, "Wow, that's odd. I don't know why he did that. He never does such things." Ron was appalled be George's seeming disregard of the disappointment that was staring them in the face. It is possible that George felt sad that the dessert was lost for the party, but he didn't say so. Rather, he said over and over again how he "didn't understand" why his dog ate the cake. Having seen this situation as an opportunity for expressed disappointment and apology, Ron waited to hear something apologetic from George and eventually said, "George, isn't this a time you simply apologize and express regret for what your dog has done?" "Sure, of course, it's too bad. Gee, I'm sorry," but then quickly added, "I just don't know why my dog did that."

In our friendly relationship, my caretaker husband and I tease each other about the "weaknesses" of our personality types and temperaments. I tease him about being "simple" in his approach to the world and of people, and he teases me about looking "weird" or sounding "weird" when I have a unique analysis of something or someone. Ron often reminds me of a time many years ago when we were in church waiting for a Bible study to begin. Evidently, I was out in the hallway doing yoga stretches while some inquisitive church members watched me go through these exercises. It made sense to me to do something meaningful while I was waiting for something else to be meaningful. I don't actually remember the incident, but I can surmise that I might simply have been stretching to relax my body and mind and prepare for a good discussion. Stretching wasn't "odd" to me. It made sense to me. It didn't matter that it didn't make sense to anyone else.

6. Talking

Everybody likes to talk. Even introverts like to talk when they have a kept audience. So, for the most part, if you're willing to listen, most people will want to talk to you. You don't even have to ask questions because people are eager to talk without provocation. That fact is one of the reasons psychotherapy is so popular, as we therapists know, is because people want and need to talk. When Ron began our business nearly fifty years ago, the motto was, "When people talk, we listen." One of the primary reasons we wrote *I Want to Tell You How I Feel* is to convey the importance of talking and listening, particularly talking about your feelings and listening to other people's feelings. Talking and being heard is a rudimentary piece of our North American culture, if not an inherent nature of all human kind.

Analysts are no different. Even though many analysts are private people, they still want to talk given the chance to do so. Players are eager to talk about what excitement they have experienced and more often, what they can't wait to do. Lovers want to tell you about the joys and sorrows of their relationships, and caretakers want to tell you what they have done or what needs to be done. Analysts want to tell you what they know and what they think. As we have noted, analysts have often gathered so much information that, when they get a chance to have someone listen to them, they can talk for a long time. Listening to analysts can be exhaustive for a couple of reasons. One they have so much to say, but also, they go at such a clip and with so much information that you can get lost trying to follow what seems like "rabbit trails".

Analysts often suffer in conversations because their listeners are unable to stay with them long enough to hear all that they want to say. Their presented content is often overwhelming to most listeners. As a result of having the experience of losing their listeners, analysts sometime speak with great speed so as to disseminate as much information as quickly as they can knowing that they could lose their audience at any moment without getting to the core of what they want to say. I have one analyst client with whom I literally have to put my hand out to slow her talk down. Often, analysts are so confident in their persuasion that they insist others hear them out. Ron told me about a friend of his with whom he plays basketball who talks so furiously regarding his theological persuasion that he continues to talk even as Ron is up and leaving the gym. Analysts try so hard to communicate that when someone doesn't grasp what they are saying, they try all the harder to explain their point making their content even more elaborate. People can become befuddled with what they are hearing from an analyst and feel a bit awkward while pretending to understand what they're being told. Listeners in these situations feel like they are being *talked at*, not talked to. It is just hard to have conversation with analysts.

Analysts generally know more than the rest of us, and they certainly have analyzed things more than we have, but this can be a real problem when it comes to having a simple conversation with someone. Analysts can switch from one idea or theory to another without much of a transition making it difficult for most listeners to follow their train of thought. Very frequently, their minds are literally faster than their mouths and so they begin one sentence and before they finish it, they begin their next thought. They tend to be unaware that listeners may become disinterested or even confused when listening to this breadth of information and ideas. Analysts often haven't learned to allow for back-and-forth conversation, which would require them to listen to what other people think is important. Unfortunately, this opportunity of listening and learning often eludes them because they are less interested in experience, relationships, and production that is the heart of what players, lovers, and caretakers talk about.

Many years ago, Ron and I were at a concert with his brother and some friends. Bill had just spent a month alone memorizing *The Four Quartets* by T.S. Eliot. After the concert, we all went for drinks and conversation. In the midst of the conversation regarding the music, Bill quoted some of Eliot's poem because he had, during the concert, made an analytical connection between the music and what Eliot penned. Unfortunately, he was the only one who had this musical-poetic connection. His comment, though eloquent, simply didn't fit in the conversation. In those moments, Bill was alone in his understanding as well as alone in the company of friends. Knowing all T.S. Eliot's *Quartets* is remarkable, but it can also be a conversation stopper more than a conversation enhancer. Bill was attempting to engage people with information but he was unsuccessful. The moment spoke to me about how often analysts are left out or avoided because of their lack of give-and-take conversation. For the analyst, a lot of what they say is, in their minds, as simple as A, B, C. For the listener, it feels like an Einsteinian equation and they are caught in not understanding. Sometimes, more often than not, the analysts' insertions are just interruptive and confrontive. Analysts can say something like, "No, you're wrong about that. The real truth is that..." Such a way of responding by criticizing can really put people off even though the analyst is trying to relate to the other person. In this situation, analysts think they are relating by dispensing information and ideas rather than discussing or dialoging. Analysts tend to think of a conversation as lecture and audience. They can speak and they can listen, but they are not good at doing both in a free-floating verbal interaction. Information-giving can be interesting, but it doesn't make relationships develop and contributes to the loneliness of analysts.

While many analysts might have the tendency to talk too much, too fast, or out of turn, there are an equal number of times when they keep their thoughts entirely to themselves. It can be very pleasurable for an analyst to privately muse in their own thoughts and feelings while seemingly disregard or be disinterested in others. Unfortunately, these days when everyone seems to be a diagnostician of mental health problems, in addition to being seen as arrogant when they are verbally energetic, analysts can be "diagnosed" as being avoidant, depressed, or even autistic when they are in retreat. At best in these quiet times, they are contemplative. At worst, however, they are simply lonely, lonely for someone to talk to, discuss, analyze, and understand the world all the while familiar with not being understood.

7. Lonely

The loneliness that analysts experience is because their primary interest is in truth, not in relationships, not in property, and not particularly in play. It isn't that they don't hope for or desire relationships. Analysts anticipate relationships much the same way everyone else does. They assume they will find people who are like them and then they will go about enjoying life together. Analysts' default way of relating to people is in the belief that others will be able to meet their level of understanding about things. They assume others will value truth and understanding over other factors like simple companionship that is so central to lovers, working together that caretakers prefer to do, or engage in some physical experience that is typical of players. Often, when analysts can't find commonality with their friends and family, they will forfeit relational interaction to a large extent and attempt to be content with their own thoughts and musings.

Many, perhaps most analysts are introverted by nature so they do not require the amount of connections that people of other temperaments seek. In this privacy they tend to enjoy leaving the world of people for the world of ideas and possibilities. In doing so analysts spend a good deal of time thinking by themselves, reading by themselves, and analyzing by themselves. They treasure what they have learned and understand and are energized by their understanding. Theirs is a largely self-directed way of life, both self-enhancing and self-effacing. Analysts want the freedom to examine the world on their own first and foremost, and only secondarily engage people in order to listen, learn, and analyze. Furthermore, since much of the life of an analyst is being alone gathering information and analyzing information, there isn't much time left over to earnestly practice the rudiments of interpersonal engagement. As a result, they don't spend enough time with other people to adequately develop friendship and intimacy.

Analysts often have not mastered the give-and-take that is so central in conversation. Once they have satisfied their need for solitude and in-depth examination they return to the world of people and dispense the information they have gathered in their odd and often intrusive analyst way. It is this re-engagement with people that is difficult for analysts. Failing to find a person who is willing to relate in the analyst way, analysts can simply become frustrated in relationships and determine that it is simply easier to be alone. Many analysts who have examined their analytic nature begin to conclude that they will never be compatible with others. When analysts feel the social rejection that often comes to them, they can conclude that the world is not ready for them, and so they will just have to bear with a rejecting and misunderstanding world. Analysts want someone to share with as much as anyone else does, but it often comes at too steep a price. Sharing life with someone who is never quite as interested in what you are, much less has the patience to engage what you have learned and comprehend begins to weaken the passion of being an analyst in the context of a relationship. This is often when analysts feel their loneliest.

It is not intrinsically lonely to be alone with one's thoughts. If being alone is a time to think, feel, experience, analyze, and gather information, analysts are fine with it and find it refreshing and satisfying. It is usually in the reengagement with others that the loneliness is takes hold. Then, like all of the temperaments they use their best gift to a fault. Analysts begin to use their ability to be solitary as a consistent escape from people. Analysts need to guard against the "just easier to be alone" in order to ward off isolation. If it is done right, analysts profit from their time alone and return to the social world invigorated, refreshed, and certainly with more information and a better understanding of the world. But it is important for an analyst to mature in giving time and energy to learning the give-and-take of engaging in daily chores like caretakers, engaging in frivolous playing like players and engaging in compassionate and comforting relationships as lovers do.

I sat with a wonderful analyst woman, Elizabeth, last week who, after relating a very difficult conflict with her best friend, asked why her friend couldn't "get" her opinion of what she should do in life. I reminded her about being an analyst and that her ability to perceive the bigger picture goes beyond some people. As we discussed this situation, Elizabeth sat back in her chair with a sigh, began to cry and simply said, "I feel like an odd duck in so many of my circles. It is lonely knowing what I know." Being the "odd duck" certainly contributes to the loneliness of analysts, but even more significant is the absence of reciprocity of perception and understanding. In Elizabeth's words, "Seeking to share my understanding isolates me from the people with whom I most want to connect." Absolutely true. While it might seem on the outside that analysts have simply not mastered the give-and-take that is so central in conversation, the deeper truth is that the analysts' passion for understanding and truth trumps social ease and even intimate relationships. As another analyst client of mine said not too long ago in a bit more straightforward way, "It is just fricking lonely to know what I know!" This is not arrogance. It is the painful awareness that analysts often know more than other people know, just as players experience more than others, caretakers work more than others, and lovers love more than others.

CHALLENGES FOR ANALYSTS EXPRESSING FEELINGS

Analysts have the greatest challenge when it comes to expressing feelings and are the hardest of all temperaments to read emotionally. As we have noted, analysts are often seen as "unfeeling," or worse yet, "cold" in their way of life. Nothing could be farther from the truth. Analysts express feelings all the time and they are just as emotional as everyone else, but they don't wear their emotions on their sleeves, so they often fail to communicate their feelings. Recall that analysts' feelings are best expressed in their cognition, namely their thinking, evaluating, musing, and in analysis. Unfortunately, as we have just discussed, analysts *seem* to be critical and unhappy about things, which is far from the truth.

When analysts express their feelings cognitively, they are indeed expressing feelings, but it doesn't always seem that way. The very paradigm that we have presented in expressing feelings proposes that there are four ways of such expression: physical, emotional, cognitive, and active. When analysts communicate their feelings cognitively, which is their natural way, they don't seem to be communicating feelings because "feelings" are too often associated with emotion.

So, on one hand, it seems that analysts aren't "emotional" because they are the least visibly emotional of all the temperaments. On the other hand, however, given their depth of thought and internal processing you can often see scowls on their faces and it might look like they are angry or distraught when they aren't, they are just thinking. Many times, in our early years together when I attempted to express my feelings, I heard from Ron that I don't tell him my feelings. In those early years, that was very frustrating to me because I was aware of having feelings and aware of my attempts to *explain them*. These years, I have learned to broach my expression of feelings with phrases such as "I have something emotional to say" or "I have deep feelings on this". Then, I proceed to speak myself. I do this so that Ron knows I have important feelings about something and that I will work towards speaking feelings even though I am doing so via thoughts.

The manner in which we analysts communicate our feelings is too often with a *seemingly* rough, gruff, or harsh tone. If analysts want to communicate their feelings and emotions, they need to realize that their words do not adequately reflect what they really feel. Consider the analyst woman I mentioned who spouted out, "It is just fricking lonely to know what I know!" That statement sounds more egotistical and angry than self-revealing. I know this woman well and she is not an angry person. She is a lonely person. She just happens to be an analyst who looks and sounds angry.

It takes great effort on my part in working with other analysts to assist them in recognizing that they are frequently hurt by other people. It is just too easy for analysts to go into their customary arena of explaining the situation or gear up for finding a solution instead of feeling hurt. My client Elizabeth is suffering greatly from her loneliness and sense of isolation. At least three times in one session with Elizabeth I had to lean forward, gesture with my hand in a slowdown motion and say, "No, don't think yet, just feel this loneliness for a few more moments." It is just too easy for an analyst, when they are experiencing emotion, to try to explain what they feel or to figure out what someone else is feeling. This, of course, only adds to their dilemma. They are simply gathering and disseminating more information in place of allowing emotion to be recognized and run its course. It took me a number of years to come to the place where I can say to Ron what I am feeling in terms that he could understand, primarily using terms like disappointing, sad, and hurt. Ron would ask me how I felt about something he had done or said and I would inevitably respond with something like, "Well, I think that…" Ron, bless his heart, was patient and asked me again what I felt. I simply didn't comprehend that explaining my hurt wasn't the same as experiencing my hurt, much less communicating my feelings to the most important person in my life. To know an analyst and to eventually love an analyst, you have to understand how hard it is for analysts to express the emotional aspects of feelings.

SUCCESSFUL ENGAGEMENT WITH ANALYSTS

1. Value What Analysts Give to the World

Analysts want to make the world a better place and help people to become better people. That includes making *you* a better person. They have no ill will at heart in wanting things to be better. We grant that it is often hard to deal with analysts' critical appearance, but analysts are *not critical* by nature, rather they take a *critical look* at things, which is to say that they look deeply at things as well as people with the intent of making all things better. If you can keep in mind that analysts mean no harm…quite the opposite…they mean to help, you will be able to adapt to their nature. More importantly, you will be able to see the gift they have for the world. Our fondest hope in the writing of this book is that we help people understand and appreciate one another in their temperamental gifts.

Understanding and valuing analysts' nature is primarily seeing that they bring something very special to the world: insight and the desire for improvement. Keeping this in mind, you will be more able to see their hearts are pure and their minds are clear even if their words are not always socially fluent. You can see your wife's desire to have the kitchen functional and useful as she deliberates for months over new appliances. You can see your husband's desire to keep the car running at its best when he insists on changing the oil sooner than the manufacturer's suggestion. You will be able to see your friend's comments about what you did wrong when you repaired the porch as his desire to help you make a better porch. You will be able to see your son's desire to have a perfect science project even it is two weeks late due to his fastidiousness. Additionally, you will be able to see your employee as trying to make the job better when he suggests trying something that seems impractical or peculiar to your accustomed ways. All of these analysts are trying to make things better, even you.

2. **Avoid Arguments with Analysts**
You will rarely win. She might be right; she might be wrong, but she will defeat you either way because she has so much information at her disposal, and she will more likely be able to think of ways of winning the argument with effective analysis and effective debate techniques. Some might think that analysts actually *enjoy* arguments. More accurately, they enjoy *debates* where they can display their use of all the information that they know, and they enjoy gathering more information if you have any to offer. Equally important, they enjoy such intensive discussions for the simple joy of bantering ideas and theories back and forth not aware that it feels like a fight to you. If you're a lover, you are always looking for harmony and want to avoid debates and subsequent arguments that separate people. If you're a player, you probably don't care about the information, but you could get caught in arguing because you initially find it exciting only to soon discover that arguments are not fun. If you're a caretaker, you might look at the information but without the critical eye, and could easily end up angry at your analyst friend because they just won't get how simple something is.

Avoiding arguments tends to mean avoiding debates with analysts. If you find yourself initially challenging something that your analyst family member or friend says, you may find that the discussion about information has turned into a debate of right or wrong, my way or your way. It is not easy to find a way to avoid such things. The better thing to do when you hear something from the analyst which has offended or hurt you is to note that you are hurt but also know that expressing your hurt will not be the primary thing that the analyst is interested in. In these circumstances, it is better to contain your hurt for another time. This "containing of your feelings" is central in any conversation and in any relationship, which we discussed in our *Feelings* book. Remember, your analyst friend is looking for a discussion and a debate where she can express all that she knows about the subject. Don't get caught in thinking this discussion is about the expression of feelings. In these circumstances, try listening, asking questions, and giving yourself an opportunity to hear something that you never knew or don't understand. This giving the analyst due time for debate may be an act of sacrificial love on your part. It is not patronizing the analyst but giving her an opportunity to be analytical and in so being, be at her best. Do this and you will find that she might actually be interested in what you have to say and more capable of hearing your feelings.

3. Careful Use of the Term "Hurt"

We heartily believe that the feeling of hurt is one of the most important things that occur in human relationships. In fact, hurt occurs in many circumstances that are not relational, like when you make a mistake…and feel hurt, or when you see someone else in pain…and feel hurt, or when your favorite team loses a game…and feel hurt. Hurt always comes from love, or more specifically from the loss of something you love. Hurt is unavoidable in human relationships, and in fact is an unavoidable experience in everyday life. This is true with any temperament. When you are dealing with analysts, you need to know that you are hurt but be careful in the use or expression of hurt. Hurt is not a word that is in an analyst's vocabulary. Remember that they will tend to side step it with further explanations.

Having said that, it is not always wise to avoid saying that you're hurt with analysts. Sometimes, it is absolutely necessary, particularly if you're in an intimate relationship, whether romantic or friendship. I could have expressed hurt more with the colleague I spoke of who, many years ago, said I couldn't have been hurt be because he didn't intend to hurt, but I determined that the social situation did not render me that opportunity. On other occasions, however, I have found it necessary to say that I was hurt in order to save the relationship. If an intimate friend has truly wounded me by what he has said (or more rarely, by what he has done), it behooves me to carefully explain that I know that he didn't mean to hurt me, but nevertheless, I was, indeed, hurt. This rarely goes well and is never easy, but it is not good for analysts in an intimate relationship to have free reign to express things that are hurtful. They need to be corrected and they need to be informed of the importance of hurt. You can say something like, "Luke, I know that your intention is always to help the world and help me. I need to say, however, that what you just said hurt me emotionally. I know your hurt wasn't intentional, but the words you just used seemed critical of me and what I stand for." Know this: Even if you say something this carefully constructed, you will get the analyst's defenses up and he will explain why he said what he said. He might even go further with some kind of an additional hurtful statement, like, "Well if you don't want to hear the truth, then I'll just keep my mouth shut." If you are speaking with a life's partner who is analytical by nature, or a very good friend, you have to weather the storm here. You have to come back and reiterate that what you are feeling is about feelings, not about facts or information. You can improve the relationship eventually but in the short range, the analyst will not know what to say or do. Be prepared for a couple of rounds until they begin to grasp that you are speaking emotional material rather than what they consider to be factual material.

As we have noted, analysts are hurt as much as anyone else but they do not register hurt like everyone else and are very much less able to express their own hurt which contributes to their lack of ability to hear about hurt from someone else. They are less inclined to be aware that they are hurt and even less inclined to speak it. They are hurt, but they just don't use the word and are rarely aware that they have been hurt. They much prefer to analyze a situation with hurt in it than experience hurt. As we noted in Chapter 3, analysts believe truth is the core of reality, which means that they first look for what is a logistical truth in the situation before they consider emotional truth.

We have spoken of the challenges that analysts both present and experience in life. If you can learn to understand and accept your analyst friends, you will be better and they will be better.

Chapter 8

Challenges for Lovers

LOVE IS NEVER WRONG. But when love is demonstrated, it can cause hurt, however odd that might seem. More accurately, loving someone can bring tremendous difficulties, both to the one who is loving and the one who is being loved. The challenges that people with the lover temperament have relate to their immense ability to love and their profound awareness of emotional hurt. They are always ready to love and always aware of hurt, whether their own hurt or other people's hurt. While wonderful, beautiful, and godly, this intense awareness of their own feelings and other people's feelings can be very problematic, both for the lover and for the person loved. While love itself is never wrong, loving can be done at the *wrong* time, with the *wrong* words, in the *wrong* place, or in the *wrong* way. It is very hard for lovers to comprehend that love can cause problems in life, but it is essential that lovers realize that love expressed can be challenging, sometimes hurtful, and even harmful. In this chapter, you will note that *connection*, which is the basic characteristic of lovers, can be "a gift to a fault." As we discuss the challenges that lovers have in the following pages, we want to emphasize that not all lovers are alike, and not all lovers have these same challenges. In fact, probably no lover has all of them, but in our experience most lovers have some of these challenges.

CHALLENGES FOR LOVERS

1. Separations Are Difficult

Gary is a lover whom I have known for many years and watched him as he struggled with relationships. I jokingly told him that he didn't have an *attachment disorder,* which is a formal diagnosis for a person who didn't get properly attached to a mother figure. I told my friend that he had a *detachment* disorder, meaning that he has a hard time *detaching* from people despite the fact that he has no trouble *attaching* to people. In fact, he had struggled with two very dysfunctional marriages, each for years, before he finally pulled the plug and began to grapple with his lover nature and truly find himself. He also had a history of struggling to separate from certain friends who had regularly taken advantage of him. He even struggled to separate from his former in-laws who were clearly harmful for him. He just couldn't stand the pain of detaching from someone, even if that someone was harmful to him. Why didn't he separate from people who were harmful? He loved them. All of them.

Lovers have particular difficulty with relational losses, whether these losses are permanent, like a death or divorce, or temporary, like a friend simply leaving after a friendly visit. Lovers can experience any loss, even a temporary departure, as a harsh rift. They feel a separation as a loss that takes something away from them. Remember that lovers' life orientation is *connection,* so when that connection is broken, even temporarily, they feel the loss as a mild disappointment, all the way to extremely painful. As natural that it feels for lovers to connect with people, it feels very unnatural for them to separate from people. Lovers are smart enough to know that they will have all kinds of separations in the world, but in their heart of hearts they would prefer to never leave anyone, nor for anyone to leave them.

It doesn't matter whether the "leaving" is for an hour, a day, a week, or a lifetime: separation is always difficult for a lover. Lovers will attempt to extend the separation process or avoid it altogether. When the time for departure comes, you can see that the lover is distressed, a bit sad, or even a bit agitated. At the moment of departure, the lover feels the loss of the beautiful connection of one common soul into two separate souls. We cannot say enough about the beauty and godliness of the union that lovers have with other people. In these pages, however, we want to identify the tremendous challenges that lovers face every time they lose someone, or might lose someone, even if that loss is temporary. Lovers live to love, they live to connect, and they are most alive when they are loving and connecting. When they suffer a loss or a potential loss, they feel a kind of death, namely the death of the union of two souls. So, naturally lovers do their best to postpone any kind of separation and extend the time of parting so as to forestall the loss of this union. This postponement or avoidance of separation can create immense difficulties for them and for those people that they love.

Both of my (Ron) parents were blessed with the lover temperament…and cursed with it. My parents both sought to connect with me, albeit in different ways. When my mother had not seen me for some time, she would put her hands on my shoulders and look straight into my eyes as if she were simply absorbing me. My dad would connect with me in other ways, often with joking, but the purpose was the same: connection. As I look back at the years of childhood and adolescence I had with them, I see how they were always looking for ways to connect with me. They would listen to me, especially if I were having some kind of problem, whether it was social, academic, or athletic. They seemed to live through my failures and other problems, and equally enjoyed my successes. Any kind of my separating from them, whether large or small, was a challenge. In fact, small separations often ballooned into extended times of separation because of their desire to always be connected with me. When I lived hundreds of miles away in my early adulthood, reconnecting was always immensely joyful, but departures were particularly difficult. When it was time for my own family and me to depart, I felt this tremendous tug to stay at their house. My dad would often pull out a $100 bill as a way of assuaging his grief of my departure. My mother would hug me until I couldn't breathe. Both of them would find ways to extend our departure with gifts, hugs, and always one more "I love you" as we were driving away. My departure must have seemed to them like they would never see me again. Now, years later, I understand that they felt the grief that all lovers feel at a departure of a loved one. Fifty years ago, I didn't understand the purpose of their delaying my departure and I didn't like it. I just wanted to get on with life, to get back to my own home and family.

Given that neither of us has a primary lover temperament, Deb and I have always found these extended departures from lover family and friends uncomfortable at the least and irritating at the most. When the simple departure is extended, even by minutes, we feel a kind of clinging from the lover person that is very uncomfortable for us. It is generally beyond a lover's understanding that an extended departure replete with shuffling of the feet, the last-minute gift, the one more hug for the road can be emotionally depleting for non-lovers. We have learned that departures are longer than necessary for us, but not long enough for the lover. More importantly, these extensions of contact might offend one's sense of purpose. Recall that I am a caretaker by nature: I just want to do something like say good bye and get in the car and drive home. I am not particularly interested in finding connection with someone, much less extending this connection beyond a quick goodbye. Deb, an analyst by nature, is more interested in the content, meaning and purpose than in human connection. The fact that we are not interested in extending a departure can be immensely painful to people who want to continue in emotional connection. Due to their natural awareness of emotional hurt, lovers do their best to avoid hurt at all costs, even the cost of extending a departure from people who simply want to get away. It seems that the lover feels something like, "How can they want to leave me while I am loving them?"

The essence of this "detachment" difficulty that lovers have is their love of connection, both physical connection and emotional connection. As we have discussed, lovers have an "us first, you second, and me third" philosophy. This view of life makes relationships paramount, so much so that lovers often lose sight of themselves or the other person in favor of this feeling of connection. The loving and connecting that lovers tend to do results from their desire to love, share, give, and otherwise connect, but in so doing, lovers forget about their own wants and needs. As a result, their wants and needs are pushed to the side in favor of other people's feelings. So, when faced with a separation, a lover can feel a deep sense of loss, which is a loss of *self.* Very often lovers have given so much to the other person in the attempt to connect, that when they lose the other person, they feel a loss of self.

If a lover has had a good time with his friend, he not only wants the good time to continue, he wants it to never end because the good time is about *us*. The lover feels something like, "*We* are having a good time, so let's never stop." Lovers don't feel so much that *they themselves* are having a good time. It is all about *us*. When they are having a good time, lovers don't distinguish between their own feelings and others' feelings. This weekend we enjoyed sharing breakfast with some friends of ours. When Deb and I were ready to leave the lover man employed us to have another cup of coffee along with the query, "Sure you need to leave so soon?" His simple question was really a statement of feeling sad. His sadness was not profound or overwhelming; it was simply the way he communicated that he enjoyed the company and departing was hard.

Departures and separations are difficult for lovers when there has been a good time, but they are even more difficult when there has been a bad time. If a lover has had a difficult time with his friend, he wants to settle the problem, that is, feel reunited, before they separate. He doesn't want to be left with the bad taste in his mouth that they are disconnected or offended with one another. As a result, the extensions of departures can be extended well beyond any value that might come by staying longer. Many couples have told me of arguments that have lasted for hours, sometimes well into the middle of the night. When I think of an extended argument, I think that it is better to get away from the other person, get my head in order, and then find a way to get back together. Note, this is my caretaker way of engaging people. Lovers don't think the way I do. I think something like, "I've enjoyed this time together but now it is no longer profitable, so it is time to leave." Furthermore, if I have what appears to be an increasing unpleasantness to a conversation, I start planning my departure while looking forward to startling afresh at another time. This is not how lovers think. Their thinking is something like, "It's been good so let's continue with this good." Likewise, if the conversation has been less than good, they think, "We haven't found a connection, so we have to continue to talk and argue and find some resolution because we can't depart with ill feelings." If a discussion has somehow deteriorated into an argument, lovers want to settle them right now…at any cost. The cost is often an argument that lasts all night, a departure at the front door that lasts for an hour, or a hundred texts sent to the departed friend. I was stunned the other day when a client told me he received dozens of texts from a woman after he said he didn't want to go on a *second* date. These kinds of extensions of separation create tremendous problems for lovers. In this kind of desperate desire to forestall and prevent the separation, the lover actually causes more harm than good by creating further discord and increased desire by the other to separate. At a time of departure, it can be very hard for lovers to feel that there is a real difference between the other person and themselves. A lover might even say something like, "Don't leave feeling upset with me!" without knowing that the plea itself can further separate their friend from them. To some degree, lovers neglect other people's desire and need for separateness.

As we have noted in most chapters, we all think that everyone should be like us, whatever temperament we have. It's hard for me to understand why people fail to value property the way I do as a caretaker. It's hard for Deb to grasp that most people are not as interested in gathering information and understanding so as to find meaning in life. Players can't grasp that most people don't want to play all the time. It is nearly impossible for lovers to accept that everyone doesn't want constant connection. Many lovers find themselves in therapists' offices bemoaning the lack of connections in their relationships or some painful separations that they have had. They say that they are lonely and complain that the people in their lives are not as available to them as they would like them to be. When they are separated from people and alone, they can feel quite overwhelmed with loneliness, and this feeling often leads to anger.

2. Outbursts of Anger

Lovers are the most gracious and sacrificial of the four temperaments, but they can also be the meanest. It is remarkable how angry lovers can get. They can be vicious in words and dangerous physically. The reasons for these outbursts are almost always related to some kind of disconnection. It is important to keep in mind that anger is a defensive mechanism often used to protect against feeling sadness. When lovers feel a disconnect and don't know how to simply feel the sad of that disconnect, they tend to go to anger. People of all temperaments tend to bypass hurt and accompanying sadness and go to the defensive feeling of anger, but this is especially true with lovers. The outbursts that lovers sometimes display is related to their tendency to "give to a fault" or, in actuality, "connect to a fault." They work so hard to achieve connection and harmony that someone would "reject" their connection is taken as a gross affront. When their efforts at connection fail to work, they race by hurt and sadness right into anger. Their desire for harmony and connection thwarted, they can become everything but harmonious. Remember that lovers tend to feel hurt by any kind of separation and may feel that a small difference of opinion or separation is permanent. Lovers can become really angry with the person who has initiated the separation. It is not a pretty sight, and few people understand that this anger-at-the-loss feeling really has to do with sadness of having lost a connection. This can be the simplest departure at the door, the end of a phone conversation or even a forgotten birthday card. It is not easy to understand how a person with such a gift of generosity and connection can turn on a dime into someone who is so unkind.

What happens to turn the most generous person into someone very unlikable? It is the lover's desire for emotional connection *at all costs*. Lovers rarely count the cost of connection. Their desire for connection often comes with an emotional blindness to differences that exist in all people. Their love for someone quite simply overshadows differences that may seem obvious to everyone else. They can truly dislike a part of someone that they love but put this dislike aside because they love the person. Later, they may feel resentful that they didn't get much in return for their love. But they do not think of the consequences of loving freely and carelessly. The difference or dislike that a lover might feel can be mild or major, but if they deny these feelings, they can pay an enormous price and eventually exact revenge on the person that they have loved. Have you ever had the experience of hearing someone go on and on about what is wrong with someone else? Most of us hear these kinds of complaints all the time. But then have you found yourself suggesting to your friend that she should end the relationship? What you hear in response from your distressed friend is, "…but I love her." Your friend who might do nothing but complain about the person she loves cannot conceive of leaving the relationship, or even making some minor adjustment to it. In your friend's mind, there is an underlying belief that all arguments can be resolved; all differences can be bridged; and all relationships can be healed. This phenomenon of complaining about someone but being unable to separate from that person means that your friend has tolerated the person in his life without regard for the cost of tolerating. Toleration always leads to resentment. Resentment always leads to some kind of anger, and for lovers, the anger can be demonstrated as rage. We believe that this anger is exacerbated because the "us" part of a relationship has usurped the "I" part of a relationship.

Lovers put "all of their eggs in one basket," and the basket is love. They are the song, "Love is All You Need." In our therapeutic work with lovers they often have no idea their partners were different from them. Often, they are fully unprepared to see and to admit that someone they love might be profoundly different than they are. Consider the program that lovers follow: (1) love first, (2) enjoy the person next, (3) give all that they have, (4) avoid seeing the differences between other people and themselves, (5) repress the feelings of disappointment of these differences, (6) give more, give all, (7) give in, (8) feel the anger building, (9) try to avoid feeling anger, and finally (10) explode. This can take days or years. Repression of feelings, particularly feelings of disappointment, always leads to anger sometime later. Repression of anger always lead to outbursts because the initial disappointment and anger builds within the person to a boiling point. Note that the lover's program starts with love and often ends with an outburst of anger. Without consciously thinking, the lover assumes that her friend has the same orientation to connection and a desire to avoid any kind of difference in value or feelings. In a way, lovers tend to feel, "I feel it, and so you should feel it." We try to help lovers interrupt this program at the point of seeing the differences, which is tantamount to helping lovers feel sad for a while so they can find ways to connect and understand that they can't always connect. However, this is no easy task because in the lover's mind, "love is all and love can cure all that ails us."

The outbursts of anger that so often typify a lover, if only occasionally, are due to the fact that they have not fully come to grips with the disparity between their own feelings and desires and those of other people. Without knowing it, lovers move from having feelings and beliefs to believing that their friends and family have the same feelings and beliefs. What can happen in a developing loving relationship between a lover and another person is that the lover moves into love more quickly than the other person and then gets upset because the other doesn't share the same intensity of love, sameness and connection. Likewise, in a developing relationship the lover can give to a fault, give without regard of the consequences, which may be giving to someone who does not or cannot share the same amount of love.

Over the course of a developing relationship, lovers often have given too much of themselves. They often feel exhausted but are often unaware that they have created this exhaustion by their excessive giving. Their exhaustion leads to frustration, then to resentment, and then to anger. At these times, lovers feel something like, "Hey, I have been giving to you and loving you and listening to you, but you aren't giving anything to me in return." This is a very interesting feeling because true love does not expect anything in return. *Love that is real is good for the person who is loving regardless the outcome.* It might also be good for the recipient, but it is really good for the person who loves. People with the lover temperament are very good at enjoying the act of loving, but *when they slip from giving to giving in, they are, in fact, not loving anymore.* They are expecting something in return. It at these times that the lover can seemingly change from a Dr. Jekyll to Mr. Hyde. It is not a pretty sight.

I (Ron) have been slapped by three women in my life, all of them people with a lover temperament. All three of these slaps occurred in my adulthood. All of them were the result of my separating from these people in some way. I once challenged my mother's firm desire that I should do something that I did not want to do. This occurred maybe 40 years ago and I have no memory about the actual difference of opinion we had. However, I do remember her becoming so irate with me that she slapped me. About the same time in history, a good friend slapped me because I just wanted to leave her presence because it was obvious (to me) that we couldn't settle our difference of opinion at the time. I remember that she stood in front of me wanting to hug me and keep me in the conversation. I resisted her desire for this physical connection. That's when she slapped me. The third incident happened long ago and was with a patient that I was seeing at the time. She came into my private office space unannounced, and physically grabbed me and demanded that I see her. I restrained her and asked her to leave. She slapped me. Not only was I surprised at being slapped, I was even more surprised by the reaction of these three women when I restrained them (emotionally and or physically). In all three cases, I found myself in the presence of a woman who was completely out of sorts and sobbing uncontrollably. I didn't know it at the time, but what had happened in all three of these situations is that I had evidently broken the unified soul experience that they had felt, and now they were *adrift* alone. I didn't understand this phenomenon 40 years ago. I understand it today. I understand that they loved me and couldn't tolerate the differences we had in how, when, and where we loved people. In all of these circumstances, I saw some kind of unavoidable conflict and chose to separate myself from it. They saw the necessity of connection and agreement and were fighting to keep the connection.

3. Avoiding Conflict

The difficulty that lovers have with separation, as well as their occasional outbursts, is related to the difficulty they have with conflict. Because they are so good at harmony and connecting, they are less good at disharmony and disconnecting, as we noted above. Neither are they particularly good at simple debate, which ideally involves a discussion of opposing views, opinions, and thoughts more than emotion. It doesn't naturally occur to lovers that there will be differences of thought, beliefs, and opinions among people, which eventually lead to differences in feelings. Many lovers, particularly lovers who are not emotionally mature, believe that everyone should see the same thing, like the same thing, and agree on all things. If a lover thinks a particular flower is beautiful, she thinks that the friend by her side should also see the beauty of this flower. If the lover has a particular political persuasion, she not only thinks that her friend should have the same opinion, but assumes they do.

The "I feel it, so you should feel it," or "I like it so you should like it" phenomenon with lovers can easily lead to a conflict when the other person has a different feeling or opinion. While we might consider that this perspective is naïve, we need to make primary note that this "we are all in this world together" feeling is not something *wrong* with lovers: it is something *right* about them. Lovers see the potential for agreement and connectedness and want everyone to feel it. They just want to be together with their friends, and they want their friends to be connected to them. They don't want people to have different opinions and feelings, whether they are of beauty, politics, religion, or anything else.

Many years ago, I (Deb) was shopping with a good friend for household décor, namely wallpaper for our new house. Looking through wall paper samples, my friend saw something that she really, really liked. Excitedly, she showed me. I also really, really liked the paper. We talked of the loveliness of the color and pattern and shared an intimate affection with each other because of the love of this particular paper. While we both thought the wallpaper was beautiful, I knew that it wouldn't fit in my dining room where I needed to use it. I was convinced that the lack of natural light would darken the appearance of the paper and it wouldn't be as beautiful. When I said that I had decided against the paper, my friend… in a true lover way…said, "but *we* like this paper." Notice the first-person plural pronoun *we* that my friend used when I said no to the paper. At the time, I didn't fully appreciate that our mutual love for the paper and our mutual love for each other were combined. With the perspective of hindsight, I can now recognize that with both of us loving the wallpaper and then my deciding against it felt like a "separation" between us that she felt hurt. My friend felt "us" and I felt "I" and "you." She did not separate the love she had for me and the love that we had for the wallpaper, and as a result, when I said no to the wall paper, it felt that I was saying no to the "we".

When confronted with some kind of difference of opinion or feeling, lovers immediately try to *correct* this difference assuming that something is *wrong* with difference. Lovers try to "correct" this difference in one of three ways: (1) by adjusting their own beliefs; (2) by trying to convince their friends to take on their belief or opinion; or (3) by being quiet. They might give some credence to their friend's opinion or belief, but this acquiescence is often short lived. In the first effort, the lover might actually say something like, "Well, if that is what you think is right, I can believe that," suggesting that her believing with you will form a union from which your opinion might eventually change. In the second effort, lovers will often continue to bring up the difference and often ask rhetorical a question like "Don't you think we really feel the same about this topic," or they might make dismissive statements like "We really do feel the same, we are just using different words." In the third effort, they will go into a silence, all the while feeling hurt, but not communicating it. This is where they are more likely to end up in anger after a while. If the lover can't find enough commonality, she will try fervently to either excuse it or fabricate a temporary union. This trying to find commonality, or even trying to force commonality often leads to conflict, and the lover is not prepared for it because any of the attempts they make to salve over differences, is simply another attempt to make a connection.

A few months ago, we had to have our car towed. When we got the bill for the tow, it was $100 more than what the man quoted us when he met us on the road. Furthermore, we thought that the charge to drive 60 miles was a bit steep. I decided to write a kind letter to the garage and challenge both the extra $100 and the total cost as compared to other local towing companies. A few days after I sent the letter, a woman showed up at my office door and identified herself as from the towing garage. This seemingly very kind lady explained to me that the people she worked for were good people and suggested that I should appreciate their goodness even though I had never met them. She also mentioned how their kids had evidently been bullied at school, which she felt was terrible. She made no mention of the charge, the overcharge, or my letter. She only spoke of how good the people were that owned the towing shop. Her intent was for me to love her employer and his family the way she did. I saw that this was her intent and kindly ended the conversation after a couple of minutes. She left quite unhappy even though I had not challenged anything she said nor agreed to retract my letter of complaint. I thought about asking something like, "I thought the customer is always right." or otherwise engage in a discussion of the towing charge, but it seemed the better part of wisdom to keep the discussion as short as possible. It was all about connection in her mind. It wasn't about right or wrong. It wasn't about money. It wasn't about the ethic of holding to a quoted price. It was about the pain this lady experienced in apparent conflict.

Within the last year, I had the opportunity of expressing my political opinions to two good friends, men who are of vastly different political persuasion than me. One friend is a caretaker and one is a lover. Both are good men, individuals of great faith and solid characters and both have been quite successful in life. When I expressed my political persuasion to my caretaker friend, he said something like, "Well, it is probably good that we not discuss this issue, right, Ron?" When my lover friend heard my political opinion, he was visibly distressed and launched into how we both believe certain things about our country and our faith. He did his very best to persuade me that I was wrong, not by saying so, but by trying to persuade me of what "we" believed. I knew it was not possible to honestly debate the facts with either of these friends because both were emotionally postured, but it was much more difficult to excuse myself from discussion with my lover friend because of his obvious hurt with our differences. My lover friend's implicit belief was not unlike the nice lady from the tow truck firm: I should agree with him because he so *deeply felt* his political position.

Lovers' skills at resolving conflict are usually undeveloped because they have only learned to use one of their primary ways of dealing with conflict: ingratiating, emotionalizing, or avoiding. As a result, lovers rarely face up to the real differences that exist between people, regardless of what the differences might be. Why do lovers avoid difference of opinion, belief, or feelings? Are they simply stubborn? No. Are they arrogant? No. Are they stupid? Certainly not. They are connected...and they want to stay connected. When they don't feel connection, they feel pain. Lovers feel that such differences of opinion or value are essentially trivial, and that all people should somehow get along—if they would only love each other better. Hence, lovers bring to their relationships an unspoken feeling that conflict should never exist. When conflict does happen, lovers are really overwhelmed and confused. They want the conflict to end as soon as possible—at any cost. Sometimes, the cost is the outbursts of anger, as we have discussed. More often, they passively yield, which just stores their anger for some later eruption. Lovers are not angry people; they do not have some kind of anger issue; they don't need anger management. They need to find ways to process the immense amount of pain that they experience every day of their lives.

4. Hyperaware of Pain

Why are lovers so pain-adverse? Are they afraid or unaware of their pain? No. Are they unaware of someone else's pain? Certainly not. They are aware of everyone's pain: yours, theirs and everyone else's all the time. Lovers don't distinguish between their own emotional pain and that of others. Lovers are so empathic that they can feel the pain someone else has immediately. As a result of this hyperawareness of pain, they look for ways to assuage this pain in any way possible. That is why Ron's mother always looked into his eyes when she first saw him after a time of absence. She wanted to see if he was in any sort of pain so she could share it with him and perhaps assist in healing it. Before she was able to heal it, she had to *feel this pain with Ron*. If Ron were happy, his mother wanted to be happy with him. If Ron were sad, she wanted to be sad with him. We know that there is a lot of pain in the world, some small, some large. Unfortunately, lovers are so pain-aware that they cannot avoid feeling others' pain almost immediately.

This phenomenon of feeling others' pain immediately puts lovers in the face of pain almost all the time. At the same time of feeling people's pain, they wish to heal this pain as quickly as possible because they experience pain as so intolerable. They want to be together in pain just as they want to be together in joy. Many years ago, Deb and our daughter Krissie were having lunch in downtown Madison. Deb proceeded to tell Krissie that she was going to have hip replacement surgery. Krissie, possessing a good deal of the lover temperament immediately said she would schedule herself off work for several days. Deb, the analyst, stopped her in her tracks by saying that she didn't want her there. Before Deb could soften the blow by reminding Krissie that she is a very private person and would prefer to take the immediate recovery alone, Krissie was crestfallen. She could not conceive of anyone wanting to be alone in such a situation. Krissie just assumed that Deb would want someone with her in her recovery. The basic philosophical notion among lovers is that there should be no pain …ever, and when there is, certainly someone should not go through it alone. While lovers would readily admit philosophically that pain is unavoidable, they actually believe that pain shouldn't exist in the world. Furthermore, they believe that pain comes from difference of opinion and feeling, and these differences lead to disconnection, which is something to be avoided at all costs. Much of lovers' avoidance of conflict resides in their desire to assuage pain. Lovers seek so diligently to find harmony and connection and avoid pain that they have great difficulty in seeing genuine personality differences, cultural differences, philosophical differences, and value differences that are quite normal.

It is painful for all people to face differences of any kind because differences have important emotional components. When I value something, whether it would be my political or my philosophical belief, my cultural norm, or my passion, this valuing always has an emotional component. While this emotional component of belief exists in all people, the emotional component of connection is much stronger with lovers. When there is a difference between what a lover values and what his friend values, it is much more painful for the lover than for his friend. Lovers will do everything in their power to avoid the potential conflict implicit in a difference in valuing something. Lovers tend to look the other way when they encounter a difference of opinion with someone whom they love. The difference of opinion, however, is not the problem; the problem is with the emotion attached to the opinion. While emotion is central to humankind and certainly necessary for successful living, emotion can get lovers tangled up, dependent, and lost. They too easily give in.

5. Giving In

Lovers are quite generous by nature and enjoy giving to people. They give their time, they give their money, and they give themselves. They would give the metaphorical shirt off their back or their left arm if someone needed it. They would gladly sacrifice their lives if they were truly called upon to do so in the name of love. The generosity that lovers have knows no bounds. They do not think about giving; they just give. The problem that lovers have is not in the giving. The problem is the *giving in* that they often do. The "giving in" that lovers do is quite subtle, so subtle in fact, that they do not know that they are giving in. There is a slippery slope between giving and giving in, and lovers often quickly slide into giving in. They do not seem to distinguish between giving and giving in. When I give something out of a *spirit of love*, I am giving graciously. This kind of giving does not expect anything in return because it is sufficient to have the joy of loving someone by giving something to that person. Giving in is not done in the spirit of love; it is done in the *spirit of fear*. Specifically, fear of losing connection. Lovers cross this boundary from love to fear without acknowledging that their giving in is fear-based, not love-based. When lovers have crossed this boundary from love to fear, they are giving something that they do not want to give, do not have to give, and shouldn't give. When lovers slide into giving in, they also slide into expectation and they will unavoidably feel resentful because they are not feeling connection in return. *Giving that is love-based does not expect anything in return; giving that is fear-based leads to an expectation of some kind of return on the investment.* Love is not an investment; it is intrinsically spiritual and satisfying in itself. The outbursts of anger that you see with lovers come because they have given when they shouldn't have given, which means that they have given in.

Recently, I (Ron) was asked to evaluate a local pastor who had been having some trouble in his congregation. It seems that some of his parishioners had taken offense with his ministry and somewhat with the way he conducted his personal life. When I saw Bruce, it was immediately clear to me that he had a lover temperament. In the few times that I have seen Pastor Bruce he has said many times how he cannot understand why he is not appreciated. Much of what Bruce does in his ministry amounts to talking to people who are hurting, and then counseling them. When I saw him yesterday, he talked about how he had spent most of the last 48 hours ministering to a family that was only marginally involved in the church. This family had suffered from the slow death of the father in the family. Bruce talked about how he had helped this family, preached a good sermon at the funeral service, and otherwise served these people. Bruce truly loved these people and gave them an immense amount of time in the form of comfort. Because he spent so much time with this family, he neglected some of his other pastoral duties. He thought he was doing the right thing, the "Christ-like" thing as he conceived it: giving all that he had to people who were in obvious need. He expected that people in his congregation would understand and appreciate his generosity of time. He was so enthralled with what he did in the moment of loving one family that he was blind to the rest of his environment, namely the rest of his church. There is nothing wrong with Bruce loving this family and giving what he had to give to them in the form of love, but in his giving all his time to this needy family, he unconsciously thought that everyone else in the congregation should feel the way he did. Furthermore, this family never came back to Bruce's church, something he just couldn't understand. While he didn't state that he felt "they owed it" to him, he mentioned that with all he had done, he thought maybe they would really want to join his flock and become part of the church family. Likely, Bruce was way over his head in trying to help these people, and ended up being very disappointed with them for not coming back to church as well as being disappointed in his congregation for failing to appreciate all his giving…which was not giving at all; it was giving in.

The *giving in* that lovers do can lead to a deep disappointment like Pastor Bruce felt or it can lead to more grave situations. Giving in can be as simple as giving a panhandler a dollar because you are "supposed to take care of the poor" yet be critical because you think that panhandler should "just get a job." These small times of giving in are not so important because they can be faced and forgotten after a bit of complaining. However, if giving in to such small things out of fear of disapproval, or of what others might think of you continue, they tend to build up over time bringing the lover to a more deeply rooted place of resentment.

When a lover has given in over and over in a relationship, the situation becomes more serious and the consequence is not just an irritated disappointment but a resentment that can lead to a potential loss of self. This happens very frequently with lovers and it can lead to years of unhappiness, outbursts of anger, and addictive coping. Even worse, sometimes it leads to remaining in a neglectful or even abusive relationship. Lovers often become involved in difficult relationships much more often than people with the other three temperaments. Lovers can find themselves stuck in these difficult and even dangerous relationships because they did not comprehend that their loving efforts would not change the other person. How did they give in? They gave in with the perception that if they continue to love enough, their love will change the other person. This, above all, is where the lover loves to a fault. They are blind sighted to dangers and impossibilities of change because they "just want to love". They gave out of love and then slipped into giving in to the false belief that they can "just love enough" by tolerating what they don't like, what they think is wrong, or by not having enough sense of their independent self that would make them realize that the relationship is unviable. They forfeit the "me" for "we" in these circumstances. They move from the generous act of giving to the fear-based act of giving in. They are stuck in such relationships because they are expecting the person to "change" and "return the favor" of being loved. Remember that love does not need a return of the favor. When lovers are in these difficult relationships, they can't seem to get out of them because they can't see their part in it: they can't see that they have been wrong in their perception and continued to give in until it seemingly was too late to get out of the relationship. They tend to blame the abuser rather than seeing how they fell from love to fear. We have seen lover people stay in unsatisfactory relationships for years and decades waiting for their partners to "change" and "appreciate" what the lover is doing.

By no means do we suggest that lovers create the abuse that they suffer. Far from it. We know that there are abusive and mean-spirited people in the world and they can be an easy trap for many people. There is never any excuse for abuse of any kind. Our intent here is to highlight the tendency lovers have to get into neglectful and abusive relationships and feel unable to get out of them because of their having slipped from giving to giving in.

It is not only in so-called abusive relationships where lovers get caught. Lovers also tend to get caught in "needy" relationships. They see the initial need of someone and without comprehending the extensiveness of that need they make their best efforts of taking care of them only to find that no matter what they give, it is never enough. It is likely that Pastor Bruce was involved with a family who needed more care and direction than he could realistically provide. People in all the helping professions need to come to grips with the fact that "needy" people never get enough love and attention. Lovers get into these relationships because they wish to assuage the pain of the person not knowing that truly dependent people often are so lost in their pain that they feel truly helpless. Time spent with such a truly needy and helpless person can be a genuine act of generosity, but lovers tend to fall into the "over giving" and then become stuck in the relationship. Lovers feel stuck in such relationships because of their great difficulty of disconnecting. It is almost impossible for a lover to actually leave a truly needy person because it feels like abandonment to them. Even when the relationship becomes obviously damaging to the lover, it is excruciatingly painful for a lover to separate.

Giving leads to good feelings, both for the giver and the receiver. *Giving in* always leads to resentment and further difficulty in separating. This tendency to give in and resent can then lead to other problems, like outbursts of anger or even to depression. The real danger that exists for lovers in their tendency to avoid conflict by giving in is that they will continue to hold the same opinion but resent the other person who has seemingly won the conflict. Worse yet, lovers can turn to what is sometimes called passive-aggressive behavior to get even with their friends. Passive-aggressiveness is a way of silently expressing one's feelings behind the scenes, but experiencing these feelings in a critical, hurtful way. The truth that usually escapes lovers is that one can never give in to one's feelings and opinions without resentment following. We often say to people: "Give your money; give your time; give your left arm; give your life if need be. But don't give in." What often occurs when people give in (instead of giving) is that they complain about others not giving in.

6. **Focus on Hurt and Tendency to Complain**
Lovers look for hurt that needs healing, particularly emotional hurt. They connect with people primarily through feeling their hurt and then sympathizing with them. Naturally, lovers look for hurts in their friends and family members in order to help them find a way to heal. The side effect of this seeing and feeling others' hurt is that they have a hurt-based perception of humankind. In a way, they look for what is wrong in life, namely how someone has been hurt in life. People of all temperaments look for what is wrong in order to correct it: analysts look for what is wrong with people or procedures to make things more efficient; caretakers look for what is wrong with the way property is managed; players look for what is wrong in people's experience. In their looking to help people who are hurting, lovers tend to see emotional hurt more than anything else. Because everyone has some kind of hurt somewhere in their psychological system, lovers can easily find hurt in anyone at any time.

Because of their focus on hurt, lovers can be more aware of the hurt in another person than the other person may be. Sometimes, lovers believe they feel someone else's hurt even though the other person is not actually in pain. This phenomenon puts the lover's friend in a difficult situation. It is certainly possible that the friend needs to face, feel, and finish their hurt, but it also possible that the hurting friend is not willing to feel their hurt at the time, not able to feel this hurt, or may not actually be hurt. Lovers are so good at feeling and expressing hurt that the very word "hurt" rolls off their lips with ease. They don't think of hurt as terrible or forever lasting but rather a signal or invitation to intercede. Non-lovers may have a much different perspective of hurt, especially if it is their own. The awareness of others' hurt also creates a dilemma for lovers when they feel their friend's hurt in their own soul. Recently, I had a session with a couple, the husband being caretaker and the wife being a lover. The husband is a medical professional and works very hard in his practice. Sometimes when he comes home, he speaks of the great pain that some of his patients suffer and how that makes him sad and that he wished he could do more for them. In our recent session, the wife said, "James, you work too much and too hard. You push yourself too much." The caretaker received her words as criticism of his care for his patients. When he voiced his felt criticism, she became immediately defensive and said "She was only trying to ease his distress." I helped the wife reframe her words that reflected the essence of what she felt, "James, I love you very much, and when I see you working so hard, I feel hurt myself. I just want to be with you in your pain. We went on to deal with the hard work the husband was doing and his compassion for his patients. Eventually, we got to the place where they could both deal with their hurt, but not as quickly as the wife wanted it done. In this case, James needed to feel his compassion for his patients as a catharsis so he could be refreshed for the next day's work. His wife needed to simply love him in his hurt rather than trying to fix his hurt. Lovers don't always tolerate hurt much before they bring it to the surface. They have difficulty allowing hurt to be present without interceding. People of other temperaments usually don't want to focus on hurt, whether their own or the hurt that the lover feels.

Some of the hurt that lovers find in others may not be significant to the other people and so may not need to be identified and attended to. Lovers' focus on others' hurts might actually cause more harm than good because some emotional hurt simply needs to run its course without interruption or expression. Many times our hurt is just a natural part of our experience and it just needs to be there, unexpressed. Other times, hurt can be an eventual catalyst for change. People can resent having their hidden hurts unveiled and probed. Lovers think that it is always good to identify hurt and believe that hurt should always be recognized so it can be shared and healed. They may not know that hurt might simply run a course of sadness until the sadness has ended. As a result of lovers' desire to share all hurts, lovers can easily become intrusive, which leads their friends to resisting them. Just this morning, I worked with a client who is a very strong lover. She reported that her week was quite difficult because her partner was not very kind when she was loving him. She noted that her partner seems to be most critical when she is working the hardest to be loving. Apparently, in a recent encounter with her partner, she said that she asked her partner what was bothering him, and when he told her, she responded with "I feel exactly the same way," and went on to tell her partner about her own experience. She then told me, that it was very disappointing that her efforts to, "share his hurt," were taken as a criticism and that "He just pushed me away." She said, "How can wanting to love him be wrong?" This young lover woman doesn't yet know that her insistence of connecting with someone actually caused more conflict and more separation. She cannot yet see that she simply got in the way of his feelings and he needed to separate from her.

This felt rejection that lovers experience can lead them to complain about people. "What is wrong with her? I'm just trying to be a good friend." This puts lovers in a difficult position because their intent is to love, but when this love is rejected, they are unable to see how their gesture of love, however well intentioned, was not necessarily good for the other person. The complaining about people not necessarily wanting to face and feel some particular hurt is a very unfortunate result of a lack of awareness of how their wanting to help, sometimes hurts.

It is not only with other people where lovers tend to "complain." In their tendency to see what needs help, what hurts, and what is wrong, they are also inclined to speak of what is wrong in their own lives. Lovers, much more than persons with the other temperaments, are inclined to express their physical, emotional, and relational distress. They do not see that their talking about their ailments amounts to complaining because they are seeking that common bond that is so central to lovers. They just want to connect with someone, and the primary way of connecting for them is through shared pain. When they express their hurts, whether physical, emotional, or relational, they are hoping that someone else will feel toward them the way they feel toward other people. They are looking to have someone *feel what they feel* and do what they would do, attend to their hurt. When they complain about something, they don't want answers and suggestions. They want to experience a sympathetic connection with the other person. The woman who frequently comes home to talk about the people at her work usually complains about what her associates said, didn't say, did, or didn't do. Her talking about her work associates might seem like complaining to her husband, but she is trying to unload the pain she intuitively or outright shared among her colleagues during the day. She doesn't need to hear some suggestion by her caretaking husband that she should quit her job, nor does she need to hear from her analyst friend what psychological problem she might have. She certainly doesn't need her player friend to make some jovial remark about her workmates. She wants someone to say, "I'm sorry; that must be so difficult!" Unfortunately, lovers' tendency to talk about their disappointments, ailments or conflicts via complaining is a put-off to most people.

I have a man in my practice who happens to also be a church counselor. I have seen Jerry off and on for nearly 20 years, sometimes as therapist, sometimes as colleague, and sometimes as coach. He trusts me and truly loves me like lovers tend to do. I looked over my therapy notes the other day that I keep for Jerry and noted that the very first session I had with him was, "Experiences a lot of hurt; can't seem to get out of it; always seems to be someone else's fault." I just saw him yesterday, and I found that my progress note included nearly the same thing: "Continues to focus on his hurt and lack of attention from others." All the times I have seen Jerry have been littered with hurt, and the complaints that go with it: including his grandchildren who are not doing well, both of his daughters who are not doing what he thinks they should do, and of course, his two ex-wives who most certainly didn't do what he thinks that they should have done. Yesterday, I heard of a new girlfriend who called it quits and devastated him. He shook his head as he said "I don't understand why she couldn't just listen to me." He has no idea of his part in his deteriorated relationships, but I suspect it is his tendency to look for connection by always talking about hurt.

Any comment on what is wrong by any person regardless of their temperament will tend to have a negative impact. Lovers' expressions of what is wrong are misunderstood and felt as complaints rather than attempts at connection just like analysts' suggestions are received as criticisms, not helpful suggestions. A lover who comes home talking about discord at work could easily be misunderstood as complaining. A lover who talks about her physical ailments (overweight, back pain, or whatever), will eventually be avoided by her listeners who perceive her as always talking about her physical problems. We both have misunderstood and misinterpreted lovers' expressions of hurt in themselves as complaints rather than attempts at connection. Lovers who seem to be complaining are really saying, "Please feel this hurt with me for a bit, and I will feel better." The very thing that lovers need-connection with other people-is the very thing that they lose because of their tendency to complain about what hurts. As with all temperaments, lovers fail to understand that their way of life is not the same as others.

7. Limited Understanding of Human Differences

Lovers know that hurts and conflicts exist in the world, but they believe that these things should not exist. They believe that conflicts exist because people do not love each other enough and don't share their hurts with each other. There is a certain philosophical truth in this belief: hurts and conflicts exist because of misunderstanding and misstatements between people. If everyone thought the way lovers think, there would be fewer conflicts, divorces, and wars. We are not all lovers, nor should we be. Furthermore, there is much more to the story of living and relating than loving people the way lovers do all the time, something that lovers have a very hard time accepting. In their minds love conquers all. It doesn't.

While analysts might be the best at seeing human differences, lovers are the least aware of this important ingredient of human psychological functioning. Lovers may listen patiently to a lecture I might give on the nature of human differences, and then after my lecture, say something like, "But Dr. Johnson, don't you believe that if we just loved each other, these differences really wouldn't be important?" I have often been offended by lovers' *tolerating* my own type and temperament as they continued to believe that I just *refuse* see that the only really important aspect of life is loving and connecting to people. A friend of mine once told me that I was really a lover at heart, that I hid my loving from other people by hiding my feelings from other people. She said that she "saw through" my hiding and caretaker facade to my real loving nature that she certainly knew was there. To this person's immense surprise, I was offended. Without meaning to do so, this person did not see the godly part of my caretaking. She only saw the godly part of loving. I have written letters to lovers attempting to explain my way of life, namely that my way is not always lover-like in approach. These letters, however carefully written, have almost always fallen on deaf ears; and worse yet, I have often offended lovers receiving my words. It doesn't seem to matter how much I praise and appreciate the person with a lover temperament, if I am not able to love like they love, they seem to feel that something is wrong with me, and I need to be fixed in some way. It is very hard for persons who do not have a lover temperament to encounter lovers' constant tendency to diminish differences rather than to uphold them as different ways of operating in the world.

Everyone loves, but everyone loves different things and everyone loves in different ways, something that eludes lovers whose love is largely for people and connections with people. Analysts love understanding, problem-solving, and truth. Players love experience, discovery and frivolous fun. Caretakers love property and the care of property. Lovers' loving nature can bring great joy to people, but players' cavalier way of life can seem "wrong" to lovers who want to connect. Caretakers can easily be offensive to lovers because they care about anything and everything but, "You don't care about me!" Analysts, who help the world understand things, can be often dismissed by lovers who believe love of truth is less valuable than love of people. Analysts often suffer the most at the hands of lovers who dismiss them as cold or simply unkind. Lovers don't see that analysts, caretakers, and players are loving in their own ways. Lovers' distinct love for connection, however godly that is, tends to blind them to other forms of love, ways that are good for people.

The lack of a true appreciation of psychological differences among people goes beyond temperament. Other differences include those of personality type, gender, intelligences, and culture. Extroverted lovers wrongly believe that introverts should share all their feelings the way they do. Lover men think that women should love in the way they do, perhaps by being particularly sexual, while lover women might want a whole lot more cuddling. Lovers who are Caucasian might misunderstand the ways that Latinos, Asians, or African-Americans operate. They might, for instance, appreciate the deep family connection that tends to be so central in the Latino community, but not understand the reticence of emotional expression that tends to be the operation of many Asian communities. Again, we see that the flaw lovers make is in their thinking, "I feel it, so you should feel it the same way I feel it."

It is paradoxical that lovers are really generous and giving to other people while at the same time being less than accepting of people who do not share their desire for connection. When someone is not particularly interested in connection, they personalize it as rejection. When lovers begin to really understand and accept the differences between people, it is hard for them, often painful for them because separations seem so awful. For lovers, perhaps more than any other temperament, when they first come to grasp that differences abound, it is shattering for them. Their belief system is so entwined with connection that when they face the differences of others, especially value systems other than loving, it baffles them, it is nonsensical to them. We work diligently with lovers first to appreciate their gift of love and secondly to understand the other gifts of personality and then to find a way to integrate rather than dismiss the differences through their loving nature.

8. Dependent

We work hard to avoid the common nomenclature of psychiatric diagnoses as a way to understand people. Rather, we use temperament and other tools as ways of understanding how people operate and find that we can tackle the challenges that people have in life with an understanding of their psychological nature rather than identifying them with some kind of disorder. Even so, it is hard to clarify the lover temperament without pointing out their tendency to overuse their desire for connection and get caught in various forms of dependency, very often being *dependent on connection*. Lovers tend to get into relationships prematurely and stay in harmful relationships too long. Sadly, we see many relationships with people who have essentially been unhappy for years or decades yet with the abiding hope that some kind of magic will occur so that the relationship can thrive. Too often, lovers tolerate and find ways to survive in a relationship that has long ago become neglectful, hurtful, or even abusive. In fact, the longer a relationship is, the harder it is for a lover to end it because they feel unavoidably tied to someone and feel that they can't get out and be alone.

Because of the primary desire for connection, lovers tend to have trouble being alone peacefully. Their inability to be alone often leads lovers to end a relationship only when they have found someone else with whom to connect. Most divorces occur because one partner has found someone else, which is most common with lovers. Moreover, the lover can seemingly change from being deeply in love with one person and then somehow love someone else with just as deep a love in a relatively short time. A young man I saw recently was nearly suicidal because his wife asked for a divorce. I spent multiple hours with him over a week or two trying to shore him up while he was grieving terribly about the loss of "the love of his life." In the midst of his grieving, however, he got on a dating site, met another woman, and soon was texting and talking to her several hours a day. They went from brief emailing to extensive texting, to hours of talking, to a couple of meetings, to sleeping together, and then moving in together all within a matter of several weeks. I have learned that once a lover "loves" someone, there is little that can be said to assuage the lover from going headlong into a deep relationship. This whole phenomenon made me think of the song written by Stephen Stills with the line, "If you can't be with the one you love, love the one you're with."

CHALLENGES FOR LOVERS EXPRESSING FEELINGS

In Chapter 4, we discussed how lovers experience feelings and how they express emotions. We noted that the primary experience of feeling for lovers is emotional, which is distinct from the other experiences of feelings like physical, cognitive, and active that the other three temperaments favor. More importantly, because their primary feeling expression is emotional, they express themselves emotionally more than people of other temperaments. The difficulties that all people have with the experience of feelings and the expression of emotion is that they often fail to communicate how they feel. Lovers are no different.

We noted that lovers share with analysts the predominant emotion of sadness in their daily lives. This is not to say that they are sad all the time or depressed, but rather they love so intently and frequently, that their emotional experience of loss is more obvious than people of the other temperaments. The beauty of this feeling experience of sadness is that it is related to the fact that they have loved something (usually someone). The danger with their frequent feeling of sadness is that they can be perceived as unhappy all the time. They are not unhappy all the time, but they do tend to express their unhappiness easily, which can be interpreted, not only as complaining, but as depression or general unhappiness. Lovers have an equally deep feeling of joy inside of them which is also related to their loving and connecting with people. Because lovers believe connection and harmony should be the norm, when they feel it, it often is portrayed as a simple satisfaction rather than an overt experience of joy. We have pointed out that all the temperaments have their own share of joy and sadness, but lovers are less inclined to share this deep feeling of joy as they are to express the sadness and hurt that so often experience. People who aren't lovers by nature don't really understand how much joy a lover has in connection because they hear more about the sadness related to separation and loss, than the joy of loving. The tendency that lovers have to "complain" and speak of what is "wrong" is not that they are negative or unhappy, but rather that they see hurt and unhappiness in themselves and in other people, and then want to assuage it. Unfortunately, when they speak so easily about hurt and disappointment, they frequently do not adequately communicate their love for people and desire for healing. They can do better by noting the many things that they love, particularly the people they love, and the connections that they love. Then, their expressions of hurt and disappointment might be better heard.

We have spoken about the tendency that lovers have to explosions of anger, which are quite distinct from their deep-seated loving nature. They come to anger because they experience a loss of some connection despite their efforts to maintain connections at nearly any cost. Perhaps truer to a lovers' nature is fear of losing connection. If they could face that they might lose a connection, they could more easily be sad of it and allow disconnections to naturally occur. Feeling the sad rather than the fear is usually too great so they resort to the post-disconnection anger. In our offices we work hard to assist lovers to become more trusting of their sadness and to recognize that all loss is based on love. Recognizing that joy and sadness are equally natural in love is the task. Then they can love with joy and lose with sadness instead of defending in fear or reacting in anger.

It behooves lovers to know that they are particularly acute with emotional awareness and emotional expression, a combination that is quite strong and something that many other people do not share. It also behooves them to learn to govern their expressions of emotion so as not to be misunderstood and avoided. Understanding their depth of love and connection and the valuable ability they have to express emotion is the heart of what it means for a lover to be content in life. Lovers who have successfully matured in emotional expression have learned that they are not particularly good with the expression of anger, which is to say that they have difficulty in governing the tendency to quickly move from disappointment to anger. A maturing lover person realizes that she is frequently disappointed and hurt…as all people are, but that it is not always necessary to speak of it. Lovers who have successfully matured in emotional expression have also learned that the sadness in a lost connection is inevitable and that to love someone is about disconnecting as well as connecting. Governing feelings and emotions is no easy task. It is not repression of such feelings and emotions; it is the knowing how you feel and expressing those feelings at the right time and with the right essence…love.

SUCCESSFUL ENGAGEMENT WITH LOVERS

1. Appreciate Lovers' Ability to Love People

We have said this of all four temperaments: If you are to deal effectively with other people, you have to understand how they operate, and in this discussion, you have to understand what lovers value, how they love, and how they express feelings and emotions. Keep in mind that lovers are all about connections, that they are better at connecting, and that they are better at giving than you are. This does not mean that they are better than you are, and it most certainly doesn't mean that they love more than you love. It means that love for lovers is all about the "we" part of a relationship, not the "I" and "you" parts. Keeping this in mind will help you appreciate the lovers in your life. You will be able to hear what they say and see what they do with an appreciation of their immense gift of loving people and loving connections with people.

You can take a step further beyond appreciation lovers' way of loving by understanding the tendency that lovers have to complain. Realize that they do not see themselves as complaining, but rather are expressing their disappointment, sadness, and hurt that they so easily and frequently see in the world through which they hope to establish connection. Lovers are acutely aware of such things, probably more than you are even though you have just as much hurt as they do. You just keep it to yourself; they don't. You might not bother to say that your arm hurts like they do; you might not express the hurt you feel when you read about starvation in Somalia; you might not worry about a disagreement between your lover friend and you. You love just as much as your lover friend loves, but you don't necessarily express the hurt that is associated with loving and losing. While it might seem to you that lovers are always talking about some kind of hurt, keep in mind that they speak about hurt because they are keenly aware of the love they have for people and the losses that all people have every day. You don't have to be so aware of such things; they do.

2. Engage as Much as Possible in Connections

This is the heart of lovers' way of life. They wake up every day looking for some kind of connection, and they go to bed every night remembering the connections that they had. They are good at connecting, they are good at giving, and they are good at forgiving. You can have one of the best things in life, namely having a together experience with your lover friend and come away a better person because you have been loved by someone who is very good at loving. Keeping in mind the connecting nature of lovers will help you understand that you need to connect and you need to be loved. Furthermore, you need the healing that comes best at the hands of lovers. You can avail yourself of this connecting, healing, physical loving, and emotional loving that comes best from lovers. You don't necessarily have to return the favor because lovers simply enjoy loving and healing more than you do. It is important to appreciate it, though, and when you can share a hug with a lover, it is about the best gift you can give them.

3. Protect Yourself from Enmeshment

Sharing with a lover is good. Enmeshing with a lover is not good. Enmeshment is lovers using of their gift to a fault. All of the temperaments can too easily use their gifts to a fault. Caretakers disregard people and their needs by working too hard and too long. Analysts can just as easily over-kill their gift of analysis and disregard others. Players are no different, they can become irresponsible and dangerous in their play and hurt others. When lovers want to connect, they want to feel the beauty of two souls together in some way and for a moment to have no distinction between the lover and the loved one. This is godly and valuable. The danger of enmeshment is that the person gets lost in the connection or sees the connection as the only way to love and in so doing, truly disregards the individual with whom they are enmeshing. Lovers tend to become dependent in their relationships because they cannot tolerate separation and being alone. While there is nothing but good intention in lovers' giving, touching, and healing, it is your responsibility to limit those gifts when you do not need or want them. There are times when you simply do not want to talk, nor to be touched, nor to share hurt. You can't be honest in a relationship with a lover if you fail to set your own limits. The oddity of this phenomenon, as Ecclesiastes says, there is a time for everything, a time to love and a time to refrain from loving. It is up to you to trust when it is time for refraining. These are times when you need to be yourself, value your own way of life, and be separate from your lover friend or partner.

If you are to successfully live with, love with, and like lovers, you will have to know when connection is no longer good for you. You will note this in your body first, like the feeling that you have to get out of bed after great sex, that you have to end a good conversation because you are fulfilled and don't need any more talk, or you have to stop playing or working with someone because you need to be alone. You might even have to see that your lover partner in life is no longer good for you because s/he seems to be asking for more connection than you can provide. If you end something with a lover, whether it is a conversation or a marriage, be prepared for great disappointment coming your way.

4. Expect Lovers' Disappointment at Any Separation

Lovers are good at connecting, but they are less good at disconnecting. They are good at becoming one with another person, but they are less good at separating and being separate people again. You will need to be the one to end the night's conversation, the sexual engagement, the work or play together. Your lover friend or life's partner will not like it; they will be disappointed in the separation and your departure. Let them be disappointed and leave it at that. They will be disappointed. They will get over it, eventually.

Remember that lovers are good at connecting which is good for them and usually good for the people with whom they connect. They are also good at recognizing the disappointment that comes when they separate from people, whether briefly or permanently. Be very careful to avoid giving in to lovers when they want to continue conversation or other engagement because they are staving off the disappointment and hurt that always accompanies separation. You might be good at separation, whether briefly or permanently. They are not. It is your responsibility to be honest with yourself when you need a break, and then be honest with your lover friend and kindly and carefully end the encounter. This is not easy to do.

Love is the greatest of gifts, so the Apostle Paul said. As well, countless prophets and poets throughout history speak eloquently of the centrality of love. We need love. We need the lovers in our lives. To successfully relate to lovers is to appreciate their gift as you appreciate your own gifts, which is the topic we now wish to address.

Chapter 9

Maturing Your Temperament

AS WE NOTED IN the introduction, indeed, it is both exciting and challenging to live life when you have a good understanding of yourself. And, as we have noted, there are many good ways of developing self-understanding. We have attempted to add to the spectrum of self-understanding by introducing the concept of temperament. Granting that other ways of understanding oneself are quite valuable to many people, we have suggested that understanding one's temperament can help people understand themselves better and understand other people better. We suggest that regardless of one's station of life, people can profit from learning and utilizing the concept of temperament in their lives. Furthermore, people can utilize the concept of temperament regardless of their vocation, family, friends, geographical location, or their philosophical orientation to life.

Life can be exciting, meaningful, productive, and loving if you operate successfully out of your own temperament. Excitement is not just for players, meaning is not just for analysts, production is not just for caretakers, and loving is not just for lovers. We all look for excitement, production, meaning, and love of people in some way. In fact, a life of maturity and contentment must include the primary elements of each of the four temperaments. Succeeding in life is based first on understanding and valuing oneself including one's temperament, but continued success requires maturing beyond one's temperament. In his great wisdom C.J. Jung suggested that each of us is born with a preference in personality functions, but he went on to suggest that to be truly successful in life a person needed to move beyond self-understanding and self-acceptance of one's natural personality operations. Jung suggested that people need to spend much of the first half of life in self-understanding and self-expression, but they then needed to mature beyond what they are naturally by seeing a broader picture. We heartily think that the broader picture includes these three pieces of development: (1) know yourself, love yourself and communicate yourself, (2) know others and learn to love them, and (3) add to yourself new features of thinking, feeling, acting and communicating in the world that are more natural to others. We suggest that this process is *personal maturity*.

Maturity doesn't mean changing. We tell our patients daily that maturity is about adding to yourself, not changing yourself. Continuing to understand and add to your nature is the essence of personal maturity and always leads to social maturity, which is essentially understanding and valuing other people. Social maturity is about enlarging self to include others. Ideally, children do this when they are free to be themselves and engage others who may or may not be like them. Learning to share a toy with a friend is recognizing that you are not alone in the world and the world is not about just what you want and what you like. It is no different for us adults as we recognize our own temperament, embrace it, engage it, and live our lives through it. The natural and necessary step beyond this self-recognition is an increased recognition of others and learning from them other aspects of how we can engage life. Throughout this book we have attempted to communicate the value of each temperament and the giftedness of each temperament. We have also looked at the difficulties and challenges that each temperament has. Equally important is the challenge of engaging people with different temperament-based value systems and behavior, challenges that too often lead to unnecessary conflict and hurt. Hurt and disappointment are intrinsically unavoidable in life, but damaging conflict can be thwarted by gaining an ever-increasing grasp of temperament together with all its joys and sorrows.

In this chapter we will briefly review the gifts of each temperament and confirm how the goodness of each temperament graces the world. We will discuss how important effective communication is with each temperament. Also, throughout this chapter we will spend time discussing the centrality of personal maturity and how it naturally leads to social maturity. We also will discuss how both personal maturity and social maturity are challenging. We close this chapter by highlighting the essential virtue of maturity and the contentment it brings to people. Socrates said, "Know thyself." Shakespeare is renown in his quote "to thine own self be true." The gospel of Mark instructs us to love our neighbor as well as we love ourselves. Philosophy, literature, and religion recognize that self-love, self-respect, and self-acceptance are the foundation of maturity. Building on that foundation and coming to contentment in life require us to "know others" but then go beyond knowing others. We need to add what we learn about other people to our own character.

UNDERSTAND, ACCEPT, AND ENJOY YOURSELF

There Is Nothing Wrong with You
This statement is the cornerstone of our understanding of people, but it is a statement that is easily misunderstood. We are compelled to start with this statement, *there is nothing wrong with you,* in order to adequately discuss how people can find contentment in life. Psychology unfortunately has absorbed the psychiatric understanding of people, namely what is *wrong* with them, usually with the plethora of diagnoses like depression, anxiety, bipolar disorder, ADHD, PTSD, and the myriad of other *disorder*-based diagnoses. We do not dispute that there are people who suffer greatly from these disorders, nor do we dispute the obvious fact that everyone has times of anxiety and depression, but we believe that a psychiatric diagnosis does not give an individual a foundation for self-understanding. Rather, such diagnoses imply that a basic self-understanding is primarily related to something that is wrong with you. Furthermore, this pathology-based understanding suggests that whatever is wrong with you can be *fixed*, whether by medication or some change that you institute in your life. Instead of suggesting that you have a disorder that needs to be *fixed*, we believe that you need to *mature* in life, both personally and socially. We believe that if you understand your temperament first, perhaps in conjunction with other characteristics of personality, history, brain

functioning, cultural development, and personal development, you will be able to successfully deal with the *ups and downs* in life and, as Kipling says, "treat those two imposters the same."

To say that there is nothing wrong with you does not suggest that you never say anything that is wrong, nor does it suggest that you never do anything that is wrong. In the previous four chapters, we have discussed the challenges people of all four temperaments have. There is no doubt that lovers fuse too easily with people and get immeasurably hurt in the process. Likewise, caretakers, analysts, and players have equally difficult challenges largely because we all tend to operate on the default assumption that everyone has the same value system as we do. We all make grave errors in our engaging the world of work and the world of people, often because we operate so singularly out of our temperaments. Our suggestion that there is nothing wrong with you is a statement that reflects our belief that at one's basic core self, there is a goodness, a godliness, and a purpose in life that needs to unfold in life, particularly in work and relationships. The first ingredient of self-awareness should not be some diagnosis but rather seeing the good things about you, particularly the good things about your temperament.

There Is Something Very Good about You
Finding what is "good about you" is central to the process of maturity, and when added to accepting what is good about others then sets the stage for contentment in life. This understanding that there is something very good about you is central to any good psychology, any good psychotherapy, any good philosophy, or any good theology. We do not present the idea of temperament as the sole element of basic human goodness, but rather as one important reflection of this goodness. Basic goodness can also be reflected in the giftedness in intelligence, as well as many other features of life, such as social skills, intuitive perception, spiritual discipline, social customs and many other factors in developing self-understanding and maturity. Seeing the good things about ourselves does not lead to arrogance but rather to a foundation of self-confidence from which I can mature. If I have a confidence in being myself, I will then be able to have confidence in letting others be themselves. We have all heard statements like, "I have the right to be myself," which is

generally a statement born out of personal defensiveness, not out of personal awareness. This defensive statement is usually spoken by people who do not really value themselves because they are not fully aware of themselves or who have not had the opportunity to be appreciated for being the way they are. "I have a right to be myself" usually suggests that the person can do whatever they want to do, which most certainly is not true in life. Truly seeing one's basic goodness does not have primarily to do with what one says or does. At its foundation understanding your basic goodness is the best of self-love. It is not always *liking* what you do, and it has nothing whatsoever to do with what someone else thinks of you. Knowing your basic goodness is about respecting your value system. We think that the goodness of temperament might be the most important and valuable way of understanding yourself, as well as a most valuable way of understanding other people. Let's take a few pages and review the goodness of each temperament.

The goodness about being a player is joy: seeking joy, finding joy, and making joy. This is the heart of a player's nature. Players primarily seek experience in life, almost always physical and very often emotional, intellectual, and verbal. The player mantra is something like, "let's play", but it is more than just playing at something. The basic goodness of seeking experience is just that: *experiential*, not theoretical, not necessarily practical, and not even necessarily people-loving. Players can be theoretical and practical, and they can love people dearly, but they first love *experience*. Certainly, it is not always good to jump right into something as players often do, but it is generally good for players to experience something because experience helps them understand the world better. Furthermore, players help other people understand the intrinsic value of experience. When you really understand yourself as a player, you will be able to enjoy yourself. You will enjoy the discovering, exploring, engaging that together form the basis of who you are. Additionally, you will enjoy the laughing, teasing, joking, engaging, running, and poking that gives you momentary excitement. You will see that these activities are joy-inspiring to you and they are fun. You will see that you are meant to enjoy the world in any way possible and then help other people find joy. You will understand the potential for fun, joy, and pleasure in all things, in all situations, and in all people. You will become confident in your player way, but your confidence will be in your nature and in your intention, not in other people's appreciation of your play, much less their involvement in it. When you see the basic goodness of your player nature, you will find joy at your fingertips much of the time, and you will bring joy to the world. For several years, both of us have taken it upon ourselves the task and privilege of responding to a stranger, like a store cashier, with a statement that reflects our player nature and hopefully encourages others to play. Deb, when she is at the grocery store and the cashier says "Have a good day" will respond with something like, "Yes, I am really going to try to have some fun today. I hope you have some time to play today, too." This response often takes the unsuspecting cashier by surprise and is often received as an encouragement. Ron has taken to responding to people's question, "How are you?" with, "Couldn't be better, couldn't be better!" These are small ways of "playing" in which we seek to bring a small bit of joy to the people we meet. With both of us having a substantial amount of player personality we want to share fun and joy with others. We feel obliged to encourage play. We see this as our *noblesse oblige* (noble obligation) as players to share the art of play. I (Ron) find genuine joy at being the butt of the joke on the basketball court because I know that I am least skilled among the players and certainly the oldest. Today, for instance, I quoted something from Shakespeare's Hamlet while we were finishing our last game. Someone asked me how I knew Shakespeare, and I said that I "knew him well" as if to refer to my having lived in the 1600's. Giving others the privilege to laugh at me is a way of playing. Play can be so much fun when it is understood and appreciated, and it can bring so much joy to people.

The goodness of caretakers' productivity is just as profound as the goodness of players' joy inclination. Their manta could easily be Nike's "just do it!" As we have discussed, players and caretakers have a certain propensity towards things physical, but caretakers' interest in things differs substantially from players' interest in things. Caretakers take care of things, primarily physical property. This care of property brings safety to the world, which is perhaps the central gift that they have for the world. Caretakers are the folks who do the simple things like re-stocking the toilet paper and the valuable things like keeping the oil changed in the car, and the profound things like Thomas Crapper (yes, his real name) did in the 1800's when he developed what we now know as the toilet. Caretakers in their best role currently could easily be those who are advocating for environmental stewardship. If you are a caretaker, seeing your basic goodness is understanding that you value property above all else. Valuing property is not some kind of materialism. You don't value property *above* people; you value property *for* people. You enjoy basic caretaking activities, like doing dishes or cutting the lawn; and you enjoy taking care of people by doing such things. Know that you have a privilege of taking care of the world of property and people, and that this privilege is also a deeply felt obligation that honors the nobility of your temperament. You bring security and safety to the world. If it weren't for you, many things would be wasted, and many people would be undernourished. You should be proud.

When you truly understand your wonderful caretaking nature, you will not be governed by it. You will see that you have been given a gift: a gift of taking care of things. When you accept that your caretaking is a gift, you will appreciate the fact that you have this gift, and you can use it to take care of the world and its property. You will continue to enjoy working and being busy. You will also continue to take care of property more than other people do, and you will probably work more than other people. This does not make you a *better* person; it makes you a person who is a *good person*. You are rarely dismayed that something doesn't work because you just jump right into fixing it. When you use your gift of caretaking as a passion, it will not only give you great self-confidence, it will lead you to an important humility, the humility that other people have different gifts.

The goodness of analysts is that they seek to make the world a better place. Whereas caretakers want to protect and preserve things from harm, analysts want to understand and improve things. Caretakers' primary gift is in the care of property, whereas analysts have a wider vision that includes property but also includes ideas and people. Recall that analysts are problem-centered, namely looking to prevent problems but also to solve problems by understanding and figuring them out. If you are an analyst, it is of central importance that you grasp this view you have of the world: seeing the world, then seeing what is wrong, then seeing what could go wrong, and then looking for ways to solve things that are wrong, and then preventing other things from going wrong. Remember also that analysts are perhaps the least self-serving in an important way because they take an impassionate view at what is wrong, whether with property, people, ideas, or themselves. Then, they go about trying to figure out the cause and cure of the problems that exist in these genres. Analysts give to the world something that people of the other three temperaments can't bring: a courageously honest look at what is true, how to value what is good and improve what needs improvement.

Analysts can make this profound contribution to the world when they realize that they know more than most people. This is the *noblesse oblige* that analysts must engage in order to give to the world what they have to give. Analysts simply enjoy gathering information, whether by observing nature, reading books, scanning the internet, listening to podcasts, or just thinking and musing. Their love of information feeds their deeper desire for meaning, which then results in their making their positive impact on the world. If you are an analyst, the most honorable thing you can do is to realize that you watch more, think more, and know more than everyone else, but that this does not make you a better person or a smarter person. It makes you a good person who is highly aware but also very different person than players and caretakers, and substantially different from lovers.

The goodness of lovers is in their generosity and sacrifice, which is certainly the essence of how we truly love people. There is so much that lovers bring to the world. We simply could not survive as a human race if we did not have lovers and the love they bring to the world. We spoke of the basic nature of lovers in Chapter 4 with an emphasis on the generous-sacrificial nature that they have. Like all gifts, lovers' gift of sacrificial love comes naturally to them. There is no second thought. If you ask them why they might love you or do something for you, their reply is a shake of head, with "of course I love you." There is no explanation. They need no reason. They just love you. It is centrally important for lovers to see that they have the gift of love, particularly the love of people, and that this is their noble obligation. They are called upon not only to give and to be sacrificial but also to display these gifts for the world to see how we could all love each other better. It is not easy for lovers to believe that they actually love people better than the rest of us.

The second element of basic goodness of lovers is their ability to see the "we" more the "I" or the "you". This means that lovers intrinsically understand that there is something new, something special, and something godly about the connection that two people can have. They understand that when two people really connect, they create a new entity, the "we" as we call it, which is more than the "I" and the "you." Lovers "just feel it" when they are connected to other people, and they bring this feeling of connection to all whom they love. As lovers come to see that they have an opportunity to love people and connect with people more than the rest of us, they can truly be at their best.

Keeping this idea that "there is something very good about you" central provides the basis for self-confidence, personal maturity, personal development, and ultimately social maturity. While personal maturity is largely related to knowing how you feel, social maturity is knowing how other people feel. If I know both of these things, I will be able to communicate more effectively.

IMPROVING COMMUNICATION SKILLS

Keeping Your Foundation Foundational

In the best of times each temperament should be enjoying the fullness of who they are through their *expression* of life. Players would be dancing, running and skipping, teasing, cajoling, telling jokes and finding adventures of thrill and dare. Caretakers would be washing the cars, changing the diapers, doing the business, tending the sick in the hospital and making lists of all the things they've yet to do from dusk to dawn. Lovers would be reaching out to hug you, stroking your hair, holding your hand and emitting oohs, and aahs with everything you share about yourself. Analysts would be thinking and pondering, and gathering all the information they could possibly gather spinning them into great ideas. Like children, we all need some time to indulge our whims of temperament without constraint. We should play, and care-take, and love, and analyze with abandon. We should all exercise personal expression of our temperament on a routine basis. This type of abandonment is about relying on your foundation. For the rest of times, however, we have to go beyond the privileged joy of *expression* and do the more arduous work of *communicating* with others. Unfortunately, in most circumstances, communicating with others involves words.

Communicating Yourself Is More than Expressing Yourself

Occasionally, our friend and neighbor, Lonnie, roofer *par excellence*, walks over just to chat. Not too many years ago Lonnie, with our feeble assistance, re-roofed our 100 + year old house in metal. When he comes over to visit, he often recalls how he managed the difficult intricacies of our very steep and sloped roof. While it might sound like Lonnie is talking about roofing techniques, he is really talking about his personal foundation of being a caretaker and the joy he experiences in having taken care of us and our old house. He rarely, if ever, actually says that he is proud of his work or that it was a challenging project. Instead, he talks about materials and techniques involved because that is his caretaker language. Lonnie could just as easily come and stand outside our house and point to the roof with an approving nod as confirmation of how he took care of us. Because we know Lonnie's caretaker temperament such a wordless nod would communicate to us as an *expression of his temperament*. However, Lonnie would need to "say" more than a nod to his regular customers if he wants to succeed in communicating himself and his work. The *expression* of our temperaments, like with Lonnie's standing back and admiring his work, might come easily but finding words for the expression of one's temperament is often hard. For most of us, the *expression* of our temperaments comes easily. Adding words to the expression is much harder.

Words are wonderful things much of the time. We would not want to do without words in life. Words are required for us to understand each other, do our professional work, and write this book. Words serve us well and do great at communicating most aspects of life. Words are designed for the common good of people. They are the common denominator in day-to-day activities at home, at school, at work and in social circles. We cannot go through life without them, be they spoken, gestured, signed or written. When we want to communicate, we usually have to work to find the words that communicate best. This is particularly true when we are speaking out of our temperament which, by the way, is almost all the time. The only way for us to communicate well is for us to know our own temperament and the temperament-based words that come along with each temperament.

When you do use words to *communicate* yourself as compared to *expressing* yourself, there are a couple of things to remember. First, keep in mind that words are not facts; they are not ideas; they are not reality *per se*. Words are *representations* of facts, ideas, and reality. When you try to explain yourself and reveal yourself, perhaps about your temperament, you will find it necessary to use words that are approximate representations of yourself and your temperament. Use words as much as you can and as much as you dare always keeping in mind that *these words are not you, but only a representation of you.* Then, when you are making your attempt and it isn't quite right you can easily say something like, "I really want to express myself, but words aren't working very well. This is my bad. Let me try again." Ron is especially good at this, far better than I am. When we are engaged in emotional talk and I don't grasp something and begin to get defensive, he will readily say, "Hey, this is my bad. I am not communicating. Let me try this again, dear." This is a gift he gives to me in the truce of wanting to *communicate* himself rather than just express himself. To be able to render this kind of *mea culpa* you have to have confidence in yourself, including your temperament, not necessarily confidence in the words you use. Remember, expressing yourself does not necessarily equate with communicating yourself.

As we have emphasized in our previous books, feelings are central in any human communications. We have discussed how each temperament tends to express feelings. We wish only to emphasize the point that when we really want to tell someone something about ourselves, we need to be aware that *we are always talking about feelings* regardless of the words we use. Remember, the words themselves are not your feelings, but only a representation of your feelings. Furthermore, while we treasure the idea of temperament in personality and in communication, temperament is but one reflection of our inner feelings. Just like words are not our feelings, our temperament is not the same as our feelings either. Temperament is the foundation of our selves and reflects how we both experience and express our feelings. If you recognize that your feelings are very central to your soul, very personal, and very spiritual, you will also know that feelings are not definable. So, when you wish to communicate yourself, keep in mind that you are speaking out of your temperament, which in turn is a reflection of your soul. This will keep your foundation secure even if your words or actions are less than perfect in communication.

Miscommunication Is Simply Sad

In *The Positive Power of Sadness*, we made a case for stating that sadness is a "love problem." Our point in this statement is this: The only reason we are ever sad is because we have lost something that we love. When I try to communicate myself, be it through words or actions, and fail in that endeavor, the result is that I am sad. I might use the words "frustrated" or "irritated," but the more basic truth is I feel *sad*. I am sad because I wanted to communicate myself, my feelings or my soul but failed to do so adequately. Keep in mind that miscommunication happens all the time. We need to be patient with ourselves and with others in any communication. We need to trust the "just being sad" when we fail in this important endeavor of self-communication. Players, you need be sad when your playful action offends. Caretakers, when you get too busy and dismiss someone for your concern of property, it is sad. Analysts need to face up to the routine sadness of miscommunicating unintentionality. Lovers, you need to feel sad when someone doesn't want your hug. Remember, we are always inclined to first express ourselves through our nature, and then, when we add words in an attempt to communicate ourselves, we are in murky waters, the waters of feelings. We need to work hard to communicate our feelings but we never communicate perfectly. This is sad, not bad.

Whatever your temperament, and however you choose to communicate yourself, take pleasure in the times when you have succeeded in communication as well as the disappointment when you have failed to communicate. When you allow yourself to simply be sad when you haven't adequately communicated, you will learn to govern your expression of feeling. Governing your expression doesn't mean repressing these feelings. It means taking a step back from what you said or did to communicate and find a newer and better way to communicate. When you work at communicating your feelings, you will find that both the joy of successfully communicating and the sadness of a failure to communicate are born of love: love for yourself and love for other people. You can really love other people when you really love yourself. You learn to love yourself somewhat by understanding and valuing your own temperament among other ways of understanding yourself. We think that you can love other people better by understanding and valuing their temperaments. In understanding and valuing the other temperaments you will be "killing two birds with one stone," as the old adage goes. You will discover that you are adding the essential elements of the other temperaments to your own and you begin to learn how to speak in the other temperaments' language.

ADDING TO YOUR BASIC TEMPERAMENT

Once you have succeeded in your first task of understanding, accepting, and valuing your own temperament and have learned to communicate yourself in your own language, the next task is to understand other people's temperaments and learn to appreciate what they have to offer: which eventually includes learning their language. The final addition is incorporating the characteristics of the other temperaments into your own nature. All of this is essential if you wish to be mature and be content in life whether with friends, family, work or play.

Adding to Your Temperament Is Not Subtracting from Yourself

While we have suggested that you need to understand, accept, communicate, and govern your own temperament, which is the foundation of your personhood, it is not the pinnacle of maturity. It just isn't enough to engage the world singularly through your own temperament. When you are really settled in your own temperament, you have the basic foundation for engaging in life. This foundation is the basis from which you engage the world, but it is insufficient to simply know your own temperament, speak your own temperament-based language, and approach life with the idea that you have the privilege to behave singularly out of your own temperament. You need to broaden your horizons if you are to succeed in life. With your temperament as a foundation, we would suggest that you need to build onto this foundation: a living room where you talk, a kitchen where you work together on a recipe, a back yard where you play together, and a bedroom where you are most intimate in connection. Adding to your foundation the other elements of a house can be a challenge because it means you have to expand beyond your temperamental foundation. You can't live in your basement if you're to have a good life. Maturity is always about adding to who you are, not changing or forfeiting who you are. You will never lose your temperament and all that goes with it, like the passion, the purpose, and the people in your life. It is natural for people who are truly grounded in their own temperaments to engage in broadening and adding to themselves. Adding to your temperament, whether in words or actions, is the heart of social maturity. There will be growing pains. You will have to take risks, make mistakes and learn to offer many apologies along the way. You will need to embrace humility.

Humility

Humility is a wonderful virtue, and it is necessary to find genuine personal humility in order to have a satisfying life. Humility is often misunderstood as feeling "lower than other people" or somehow inadequate. Humility is not feeling shame, which is the undue fear of others' disapproval. Humility is quite the opposite of shame. Humility is also completely different from *humiliation,* which is the feeling that occurs when someone attacks your very essence. A person who is truly humble first has a good foundation of self-love, which then naturally leads to seeing other people's gifts, valuing their gifts, and a deeper love of other people. Genuine humility is the understanding that the package of life is about doing your best at something, yet, falling short of success, or perhaps failing entirely. It is humbling to fail at something, but humility most naturally leads to an appreciation of others' accomplishments, and just possibly towards seeing how you can improve at life in some way. Humility is a central ingredient of success in life, whether in work, play, or relationships. Humility comes from being okay with yourself in both success and failure. Recall, however, that failure and criticism are always hurtful and always lead naturally to sadness, not to defense, and not to anger. Sadness is recognizing you have made a mistake; humility is letting yourself mature from the mistake.

The most important and delicate procedure of good psychotherapy is to help people "love themselves first and love others second." The matter of "loving yourself" is often misunderstood because people conflate loving and liking. The essence of self-love is, quite simply, seeing who you are and accepting who you are. This naturally would grow into self-liking. Self-love needs to be grounded in all of us; in times of self-approval and in times of self-disapproval. It is important to recognize when we don't like ourselves. For me, Deb, it is generally an indicator that I need to mature in some matter or to simply be disappointed in some limitation that I have. Liking or not liking should not alter self-love. Observe how toddlers display their self-love as they engage the world with exploration. They simply go about discovering themselves though the world around them. They do not yet have a sense of self-disappointment, and certainly not self-judgment. Toddlers do not distinguish self-love and self-liking. Loving oneself and liking what one does often become conflated in later life. Personal success or others' approval can become predominant, which is about liking, not loving. Good psychotherapy helps people re-discover their natural self-love and then carefully separate self-love from self-approval and the approval of others. When people come to understand their basic self-esteem is built on their natural self-love, they are more willing to accept their mistakes and the judgments of others by just feeling sad, not afraid. They feel humbled and sad, not ashamed and afraid. Then, and only then can people develop a genuine love for other people, which enhances both self-confidence and humility. Along the way in this confidence-humility building we find one of the most humbling… and instructing…things: times when you hurt someone else.

Hurting Other People Is Inevitable
Both of us have hurt people many times, almost never intending to do so. Most of the times we have hurt people have had to do with what we have said, sometimes with the analyst temperament that is dominant with Deb or the caretaker temperament that is dominant with me, Ron. We have also hurt people because of actions or words that typifies the player nature that is a part of both of us. We often wish we could take back the words we have said to people with the intention of playing and friendly teasing because these words were not playful and friendly to the person hearing them. Once when Deb and I were co-presenting a seminar, she was interjected something to what I was saying and without a blink I (joking, so I thought) said, "Shut up, I am speaking." She did "shut up" and simply nodded her head as I went on with my lecture. Later, she told me that she was greatly offended by my "shut up" comment even though she knew that I meant no harm in it and was simply enjoying my momentary time on stage. Some of my clients who were in the audience commented to me in private that I had sounded harsh with my "shut up" comment. I would never tell Deb to "shut up" in real life, but at that moment on the stage, I was playing. I hurt Deb, and I hurt many people

who I try to serve, all because I was "just playing." I feel sad at this moment as I remember this incident where I meant to be playful.

"Sticks and stones can break my bones, but words can never hurt me" is palpably false. Words cause deeper hurt and more lasting hurt than any stick or stone might do. As we have hopefully clearly pointed out, we cannot just *express* ourselves out of our temperament, we must add the skill of communicating with words that speak to the other temperaments. Our words and our ways have hurt people at every turn of our lives, and we dearly wish we could turn back the clock and prevent the hurt that we have inflicted on people, so much of it temperament-based. To be able to courageously look at what you have said or done that has hurt people, completely without intending to hurt them, helps you grasp the whole of what it means to *be you* and for them to *be them*. Your temperament-based behavior and words are, as Dickens says, "the best of times and the worst of times." We look back at the raising of our player daughter Krissie and our lover daughter Jenny and see how we did not serve them as well as we should have. While we did our best, our best was often not good enough simply because we were not yet mature enough to engage beyond our temperament. In short, we indulged Krissie's player nature to a fault because we have a player nature as well and neglected to truly appreciate Jenny's lover nature because that has been the least of both of our natures.

It is painful for us to look back at what we did wrong and what we didn't do right but admitting to our errors assuages this pain as Shakespeare said, "One's pain is lessoned by another's anguish" (Romeo and Juliet). We can look at our mistakes with a deeper appreciation of how people suffered at our hands. We spent an entire chapter in *The Positive Power of Sadness* on the centrality of hurt in human relationships. To face the fact that I hurt people when I am just trying to do the best thing is central in personal maturation and ultimate life contentment.

Seeing someone's hurt is to see someone's loss. To see someone's loss means you understand their value system; seeing what they love. This is why humility is such an intricate part of maturity. To effectively get beyond feeling hurt, whether due to your own regret or the effect you had on someone else, you have to understand your values and the values of other people. *Seeing someone else's values is first an emotional effort, then a cognitive task, and then a spiritual phenomenon.* It is grasping the vastness of what people value. Coming to understand what and how other people value is the heart of temperament awareness. If a caretaker can fully realize that he loves property above all else, he will be better at the other three loves: people, ideas, and play. Likewise, true of the other three temperaments. If players, lovers, and analysts can see their own loves, they will be able to see the significantly different loves that others have. You will be all the more accepting and appreciative of your own gift without demanding that other people have the same gift. You will see that everyone's value system is intrinsically good, if different.

The remarkable thing about humbly approaching mistakes and the hurts we render others is that it breeds self-confidence, particularly in the business of communicating the values implicit in our temperament. When we feel this important combination of humility and self-confidence, we will be better able to put time into understanding the other temperament-based languages. I sometimes have a client ask me, "Dr. Deb, can you say that in a different way?" In these cases, I am fully aware that my analyst language didn't communicate to my client. Because of my having self-confidence as both analyst and therapist, I can respond with something like, "certainly," and then proceed to break down what I said. I know that as an analyst I can easily make a quantum leap statement because I might have collapsed a lot of information into one statement. My statement might make sense to me but not to my client. Most of the time I am able to communicate pretty well but I am always aware of the possibility that I might be using "analyst language" with a caretaker, lover, or player. I often have to pull back from my own preferred language in order to adequately communicate. In these instances, I am humbled because despite my best effort and good intention I fail to communicate. There is nothing wrong with me for making the error. There is no shame or humiliation involved, just good honest humility that reminds me that we are all different and my task is to meet my clients where they are and to speak their language.

You Won't Be Good at It

We having been discussing the importance of humility, which is something that can come only with facing your own mistakes and the criticisms you hear from other people. The other aspect of humility is appreciating how someone else does well in an area of life that is not your gift. I, Ron, often tell patients that I have several areas of life where I am unskilled. I am not good at art. I am not particularly good at music. I am certainly not good at appreciating nature. I'm not particularly good at playing basketball, and as a result, I am often the worst player on the court. I can face these limitations and inadequacies because my self-esteem is not based on art, music, nature, or basketball. My self-esteem as a caretaker is based primarily on my work and secondarily on how I relate to people. As a result of my acknowledging to myself that I am less than good at such things as music, nature, and basketball, I can appreciate people who are good at them. I am amazed at people who can strum a guitar, play a flute, or direct a choir. I am sometimes transfixed when I see certain artistic creations, whether long-lasting creations like those of Monet or Michelangelo's *David* or the short-lived creations of a well-played shot on the basketball court. I am certainly appreciative of Deb's understanding and engagement of nature. I do a bit of nature-engagement with Deb, dabble in a bit of artistic endeavors, and play a bit on my Irish tin whistle. Because I don't expect to be good at these things, I can work at it a bit, but more easily appreciate other people's giftedness that is largely out of my reach.

Appreciating other people's gifts of art, music, nature, reading, math, or gardening is a lot easier than to appreciate their temperament-based value systems, which makes those things more important to them than doing/caretaking is for me. It is hard to see the world as others see it. It is hard for people to do something that they are not good at. It's not necessary that you learn to play music, create art, or play basketball, but it is absolutely necessary that you learn the rudiments of all four temperaments starting with your own. When you start to think, feel, talk, and otherwise engage the world from a different temperamental perspective, you will not be good at it to begin with. Here is where humility again comes to the rescue.

Players are generally not good at such things as swinging a hammer, and even less good at filling the dishwasher because such things are "boring" to them. But if a player is to mature and find contentment in life, s/he will need to do these things, get better at them, and possibly even enjoy them a bit. I remember an analyst/player whom I saw decades ago telling me that he never felt any kind of feeling of accomplishment when he did some kind of physical task. As a caretaker I feel accomplishment all the time because I am usually doing something all the time. I also feel disappointment frequently because I fail to do things right or have too many things on my plate to do. Caretakers really don't like to "waste time" playing because there are always things to repair and restore. If they don't learn to play in life, they will never succeed in work and in relationships because play is an essential ingredient in life. Lovers are not good at analyzing for the most part, and analysts are usually not so good at connecting. However, when lovers learn to analyze, they might just think before they jump into a relationship, and analysts might realize that speaking truth and finding meaning are not cornerstones of human connection. All of these people will feel inadequate when they are trying to engage in behavior that is not of their temperamental nature, but if they take the plunge, they will get better at things not natural to them. More importantly, they will find the contentment of being more mature people, deeper people, humbled people, and people with ever-increasing self-confidence.

Most people are not like you. Only about a quarter of the population has one of these temperaments. Consider yourself fortunate when you have multiple people in your life that are very much like you. Keeping this in mind might help you get better at things that are not in your nature, as well as, help you get better at communicating yourself and understanding other people as they communicate themselves. You already have relationships with some people who share your way of life, your value system, and your purpose in life. Friends like these are a true treasure in life. As you broaden yourself, particularly in understanding the other three temperaments and learning the value of these other ways of life, you will find great joy.

Broadening Yourself

Being bold enough to add to your own temperament and trusting the value of humility in the process will substantially fortify your own foundation so that you can continue in the maturing of broadening yourself and adding elements of the other temperaments to your own. This is the transition from personal maturity to social maturity. When you add elements of the other temperaments to your basic temperament, you enhance your ability to be yourself. If you're a player, you will engage the world with an equal amount of verve but with a greater ability to experience the world in ways other than play. For example, you will begin to be more familiar with allowing some of the doldrums of care-taking so that you can become more productive. This add-on can make your play all the more exciting because there will be a layer of anticipation of the play while you are doing chores. You will begin to experience more of the intrinsic value of delayed reward. Likewise, caretakers can continue doing all that they want to do but, do it better, or do things with more discretion of when they do things and how much they do. They might find that people appreciate them better if they are available to more talk and work less. Analysts can continue to see all the problems that needs to be solved but not be lost in the problems by being more open to other's suggestions and correction. They will begin to appreciate more the various perspectives that the other temperaments have and experience a delight in what they had missed as they add the new perspectives to their own considerations. Lovers can connect all the better with people because they know that there is more in life than connecting and many people don't actually want to connect, however odd that might seem to them. They can breathe easier in the absence of others with the joy of knowing connections exist without always having to be immediate or permanent. Ron has complimented me over the years by acknowledging that (some of) my analytical challenging of him has assisted him in developing more discipline. Likewise, Ron has taught me the most valuable lesson of recognizing my own mistakes and speaking them without fear of self-recrimination. Learning from the basic nature, passion, and soul of the other temperaments helps you quell your fear of being inadequate.

When we are infants and throughout much of childhood, we are inadequate to care for ourselves. We learn to do things for ourselves by developing the skills of talking, walking, working, and playing. In a similar way, we mature as we learn how to walk, talk, work, and play in new ways. This is the essence of maturity: adding to what we already do naturally. We have already noted that the great psychoanalyst, Carl Jung, confidently suggested that real maturity is based first on self-knowledge and acceptance but that it is necessary to add to one's basic nature additional factors in personality and personal functioning. Adding an understanding and appreciation will naturally lead to learning the other temperament's languages as well.

Adding a New Language

When you really understand your own temperament and have come to truly appreciate people who are gifted with the other temperaments, you will find a drive to speak the other temperament-based languages. Leaning to speak another temperament language can be very exciting, like learning any foreign language. If you have ever attempted to learn a foreign language, you know that it is challenging because you have to learn words, grammar, and idioms that are specific to that language. It is hard, for instance, to really master the rolled "R" sound that is typical of Spanish-speakers and Russian-speakers, but with work, you might learn how to do it. At first, when you are just learning the new language, you translate everything in your mind before you speak, and may even be careful with every word you speak. Eventually, if you stick with learning a language that is new for you, speaking this new language begins to feel more natural, and you even start to think in your new language. The same is true for learning the language of another temperament: You start to *feel* the way someone else feels because *feelings* are always underneath a temperament-based language. When you begin to feel the way other people feel, you are well on the way to be a good communicator and a good friend.

Leaning another language takes a lot of listening, fumbling and practicing over and over again. It is hard enough to learn the vocabulary of another language and culture, but it is especially hard to learn the nuances of another language. If you put a concerted effort into understanding and eventually speaking another language, you begin to see how people of other cultures think and feel. Ron and I were in Scotland some years ago and while at the book store at Lock Ness, I happened to say something about the Gaelic language to the cashier. Immediately, the cashier corrected my pronunciation of the word "Gaelic." The cashier said that Scottish Gaelic was not pronounced "Gay-lick" as we Americans (or Irish) might pronounce the word, but rather something like, "Gah-lick." Being the analyst, wanting to understand more, I asked the woman "What then is the difference between "Gah-lick" (Gaelic) and the herb garlic? Big mistake! The dear woman provided alternate pronunciations that were completely indistinguishable to me, apparently because the "R" sound in British English is *soft* rather than the *hard* "R" most Americans use. Again, the woman emphasized the difference but the subtleties fell on my "deaf ears." After a couple of more tries it became a language battle for a few minutes, with me twisting my lips and repositioning my tongue to no avail. I'm sure I was a bit irritating to this woman. Finally, I paid for the books I had picked up in the store and walked outside. Ron and I rolled our eyes at one another knowing that we simply didn't hear the difference between the Scottish pronunciation of garlic and Gaelic. We could recognize that the cashier was saying two different words with clearly different pronunciations and meanings to her, but we simply couldn't hear the difference. The same is true of temperament-languages. A person might use words like connection, excitement, truth, or production, with a very different meaning than you use the word. For an analyst "connection" will almost always first mean cognitive comprehension. The analyst will be every bit as thrilled with a cognitive connection as a lover is with an emotional connection. How very different is the lover's understanding of connection from the analyst's understanding of that word. If you're a player, your language will be that of *experience*. Using the word "experience" a player can come home from an adventure and excitedly relate his fantastic experience of seeing several bobcats in the redwood forest. The caretaker might say to his player wife what a good "experience" it was to finally clean out his file cabinet only for the player wife to cross her eyes and shake her head thinking what a boring way to spend the afternoon. If you're a lover, your language will be about *connection* and "we-ness", i.e., how we operate together. If you're a player, your language will be about experience or excitement. If you're a caretaker, your language will be about *doing* something, and if you're an analyst, your language will be predominantly about *thinking* something. These are very different languages, and they are all temperament-based. In addition to the actual words that have different meanings to different people, the nuances of our respective vocabularies make a difference in communication.

Speaking a temperament-based language is not just about the words. It is about feelings and behavior. We suggest that by learning the other temperament languages, you will intrinsically learn to embrace the other temperaments' characteristics and begin to blend them onto your own temperament foundation. Learning the other temperament-based languages is about the feelings and passion that generate words. Lovers who feel compelled to put their arms around you are "speaking" their connection-based language just as you might be speaking caretaker-based language when you would rather put the dishes into the dishwasher than have a hug. The lover could easily feel hurt by what he feels is your rejection, while you, as a caretaker, may be offended by what you perceive as the lover's intrusion on your productivity. Learning the languages each temperament speaks brings you closer to personal and social maturity, but it is no easy task and fraught with misunderstanding, offense, and hurt. If you listen and watch carefully to friends with the other temperaments, you will begin to understand them better, communicate to them better, and be better at loving each other.

Learning another language is a hard thing to do for most people. Yet, when you do learn another language something "magical" happens. All of a sudden, your world is bigger; there are more things you can do, there are more connections to make and enjoy, you understand more than you did before. You build on what you have already known, experienced, treasured and understood. You become bigger. You mature.

MATURITY AND CONTENTMENT

"If it's good for you…really good for you…, it will be good for the people in your life." This is something we say to people in our offices when we are trying to help them find the right thing to do or find the right words to say. This is a philosophical perspective we have about life that also has profound psychological implications. Or we might dare to call it a spiritual perspective because we often interchange the terms philosophy, spirituality, psychology, and relationships. We believe these elements of life are intrinsically intertwined. The essence of good psychotherapy, as we see it, is first to establish self-awareness to build confidence and self-esteem, and second to become increasingly aware of other people's perspectives of life and thus build social-esteem. We could say that the initial part of therapy is geared to be selfish and the second part of therapy is to become increasingly selfless. People who are truly selfless have a good grasp of their basic goodness, including their temperament, and realize that there is a lot more to life than what they see, what they know, what they feel, and what they want.

We want to conclude our discussion on temperament by reviewing what we think is the most important component for all temperaments and how it leads to contentment in life: maturity. Remember, personal maturity is really a form of self-love. Social maturity is a form of other-love. Some of the earliest philosophers focused on self-love based on self-awareness. Socrates said, "The unexamined life is not worth living." Other philosophers, like Epicurus, suggested that the first thing that one needs to do is to find pleasure which comes best from experience. We might suggest that he had a bit of the player temperament. All the great philosophers, whether classical or modern, have suggested that self-love, while basic in life, is not sufficient to develop a meaningful life.

The ancient Greek philosopher Diotima suggested that social maturity is like a beginning: first understanding one person, then understanding other people, then understanding the rest of the physical word, and ultimately the universe, or Creator. Diotima went on to suggest that when we love something, whether animate or inanimate, we are seeing the intrinsic beauty in it. We think that if people can see their own beauty first, they are prepared to see the beauty in others. If, as a player, you can see the true beauty in yourself and in experience, you will naturally be drawn to see beauty in other things and other temperaments. We certainly appreciate the caretakers every time we drive and the roads are in good shape. We always appreciate the players when we have a bowl of popcorn watching a game, or a glass of wine listening to good music. It is easy to appreciate the lover who, when your mother has just died is the first one on your doorstep with a sad smile, a hug and a pan of lasagna. Certainly, in the midst of a pandemic, we appreciate the analysts who bear down and develop a vaccine so quickly. We see in these day-to-day experiences the beauty in each of the other temperaments. If our foundation of self-awareness and self-love is firmly established, we can spend the rest of life becoming increasingly aware of the value of others, particularly people of different temperaments. Narcissism is conceived as selfishness, but in fact narcissism is a *lack* of self-love that always leads to attempting to find meaning in acquiring property and people's approval. It is paradoxical that you can only obtain this virtue of maturity by engaging with the virtue we spoke of earlier: humility.

Maturity leads to contentment in life because it has two elements: yourself and other people. Humility comes about not only from seeing that you will always need to improve yourself, but also from an always deepening understanding of other people's gifts and abilities. Groundedness in self-understanding allows you to move towards groundedness in social maturity. Social maturity does not imply that you have to actually *like* a person in order to relate to them, but you need to understand and value the other person without comparison to your own values. As Max Ehrmann instructs us in his wise collection, Desiderata, comparisons bring about vanity and bitterness. In context of temperaments, there will always be someone who is better gifted in their temperament than you and less skilled than you in your temperament. Maturity allows self-accepting and other-accepting without comparative judgment.

As a truly mature person you will be able to communicate yourself successfully by having an always-improving understanding of yourself, which then leads to expressing yourself effectively. When you effectively communicate yourself, others will be more interested, challenged, accepting and appreciative of you. In turn, they will be more trusting to communicate themselves to you. Remember, communication does not end with expressing yourself. Mature communication includes knowing your preferences and then translating your expression of feeling into a language that others can grasp.

Good living is based on the execution of self-value, which is based in self-perception and in successful communication. Truly *contented living* comes from being able to forget about yourself. *You can forget about yourself only when you are certain that you are a good person* and that you are capable of communicating yourself. "Forgetting about yourself" does not mean that you are not important; quite the opposite. You can forget about yourself when you know that you are important, but you don't have to let anyone know that fact. Simply put, when you develop the self-confidence that comes with the elements of self-acceptance, you do not have to concern yourself with what others think of you all the while striving to be understood. When you have the personal solidity and assurance of your basic goodness, you can then engage in the business of relating to other people. Psychotherapy, if it is executed correctly, is first about establishing *self*, and then understanding *other people*. Unfortunately, much counseling focuses on other people too quickly, before the individual has a good sense of self. When you are to the place of understanding and successfully communicating yourself, you will do an extremely important thing: you will spend energy understanding and accepting other people. Unfortunately, there are not many people who are self-assured enough to forget about themselves. Lovers, caretakers, analysts, and players, when yet immature, are usually so focused on their passions in life that they have not found ways to engage people of different temperaments.

We started this book with sharing the temperaments of our own family. Each of us has had to learn to add to our foundational temperament. We suggest that you will mature and find contentment in your life by adding to your basic temperament as we continue to do with our own temperaments. Deb, the analyst, can honestly say that she is much swifter to just listen to Jenny or me without offering solutions to apparent problems. A few months ago, we were visiting daughter Jenny in Iowa helping her move into a new apartment. Deb was so excited to help Jenny decorate, something she has a real gift for, yet was aware that Jenny is much more easily satisfied with simple things compared to Deb's own desire for the "perfect coordination" of furniture and surroundings. So, when we all three were shopping for some furniture, Deb offered opinions but was just as quick to encourage Jenny to "make her own choices." When we were all walking the barstool aisle, Deb was far ahead of Jenny and me, when she turned around and waved at us grinning and said, "I found them, but I am going to wait until you finishing looking. You tell me what you like before I tell you what I think will work well in your new space." As an analyst, Deb certainly had a good vision for what would fit in Jenny's apartment, but she recognized that Jenny wanted to pick them out herself. Deb admits she wasn't good at this when the kids were younger and it brought the household some painful moments when she insisted on what was *right* in her eyes. Deb can now actually enjoy waiting for someone to discover what they want rather than telling them what the best is and then appreciate someone else's style even if it doesn't fit her analytical criteria.

Our early years were a plethora of my (Ron) doing anything and everything on the 100-year-old office building where we lived and worked. Restoring the building fit my caretaking/doing nature well. I can look back at those 20 years of hard work on this property as good in itself, but not always good for Deb and our daughters because I was "always working," as the girls would often say to me. I can now see that lover-based Jenny did not get enough connection and player-based Krissie did not get enough play even though

I connected and played as much as I thought I could. I just wasn't mature enough to value my caretaking nature and add a good bit of connecting and playing that my daughters needed during their crucial growing up years. I remember many times of tolerating shopping with the girls wanting to just get it done, not realizing that my daughters needed me with them more than they needed me to buy something for them. When Deb and I were in Iowa with Jenny walking around most every aisle of the home goods store, I found myself musing that even though it wasn't productive, I actually found a tender pleasure in just being with Jenny and Deb. Just being with them? Being with them as in connecting. I was connecting with these two wonderful women in my life without doing a single thing that was productive. Now, I understand better what Jenny or Krissie meant when they said they were "just hanging out with friends," something that eluded me when I was 40. I don't think that Deb understood the "hanging out" phenomenon any better than I did. These days, (don't tell anyone) Deb and I actually just hang out on occasion, sometimes alone, sometimes together. It is a bit odd to see that we first understand something in our mid-sixties and seventies that our daughters understood when they were children. Maturing, and the contentment that comes with it doesn't ever have to stop.

Having just recently vacationed with daughter, Jenny, we had the opportunity to see how she has grown beyond her lover-based nature…without ever giving up on her desire for connection. She is able to engage in conflict without anger and without despair that so often keeps people in dependent relationships far too long. Jenny has chosen to depart from her longtime partner without anger or resentment, and has faced the sadness that this separation has brought. Jenny's former partner is a very good and matured person so, together, they grieved though the parting as partners and have been able to return to the friendship that has been the core of their relationship. Recently, Jenny has finished a law-based degree at age 43. She reads about world events, political matters, and history more than she ever did in high school or her earlier college years and has developed her analytical ability to discern and make wiser life choices. When we held the celebration of life for her sister, Krissie, we were pleasantly surprised to see Jenny stand up in front of a crowd of friends and family in our back yard and acknowledge the conflict that was so prevalent between Krissie and her, all without defense or fear. She was able to speak tenderly about Krissie as well as the many difficult years she had with her sister without shame or rebuke, but only with understanding and forgiveness. Many people spoke to us about what a remarkable person Jenny has become.

Krissie remained the player person that she was born to be with all the experience-seeking, excitement-seeking, and adventure that is so typical of players. I believe that as she now looks "down" at life with the privilege of understanding more than we do, she sees the joys and sorrows that come with all people and with all temperaments. I trust that she can laugh at the wonder as well as the excesses of experience, excitement, and adventure that she had in life. We remember how she joyfully skipped across the hallway from one room to another, how she loved anything new and different, and was always ready for another experience, however challenging. We remember her breaking her foot while jumping off one living room chair to another, getting married at 17 and divorced at 18, and then married and divorced again in her 30's. None of that matters to us anymore, thankfully. We also see the way she pushed herself into caretaking, especially with her children, but also in her profession and her own household because as a young mother, that was essential more than her playing. We have a picture of her blowing insulation into her attic doing what needed to be done for her home and her kids, yet with the biggest grin on her player face.

The four of us are quite imperfect…and continue to be so. Some of our imperfections have been trivial and unimportant while others have had life-altering consequences. The four of us are happy to be how we were created and now, more than ever, are glad that we are different and happy that we can accept each other more easily, more lovingly, with more understanding and joy. We would wish for you the freedom to look at yourself carefully and wisely, find true self-acceptance, particularly of your temperament, and then add to that the ingredient of personal development of the other three temperaments with curiosity and genuine interest. We hope you will expand your own foundation and begin to engage and create a larger, greater family of temperaments for yourself.

Chapter 10

Connections and Conversations

WE NOW HAVE COME to the practical part of this book: How do we use our understanding of temperament to enhance our lives, the lives of others around us, and the relationships we have with other people. It is one thing to understand that you have a certain temperament, but it is quite another to know how you can effectively communicate yourself with this understanding. We have placed a primary emphasis on knowing your temperament with the implicit values, ways of learning, ways of working, and ways of speaking that erupt from your temperament. You are always speaking from your temperamental orientation and you are always acting out of your temperamental values. We grant that there are other important aspects of your psychological structure, namely your personality type, your intelligence, your cultural and subcultural background, your philosophical, religious, spiritual and ethical values, and other factors. In fact, the more you know about all these factors that are a part of you, the better you will be at living as you should, communicating yourself, and finding happiness and satisfaction in life. We always do a psychological assessment of the people who come to us. We examine temperament as well as all these other factors so as to arrive at what we call a "friendly diagnosis," namely what is right about someone. It is only from this positive psychology perspective that we are able to help people find life satisfaction in work, play, and relationships. We have found the concept of temperament particularly helpful in its simplicity and practicality.

In addition to a self-understanding based on temperament we have suggested that you will succeed in relationships better the more you understand how people of other temperaments function and what their value systems are. This means understanding the people that you like, love, live with, work with, play with, or just talk to. The more you understand them, the more you will be able to watch, listen, and learn about how to engage them. You can privately and lovingly make a "friendly diagnosis" of someone if you carefully watch, listen, and learn. You will see their values, the joys, the hopes, the successes, and their failures are all related to how they engage the world. Specifically, you will see that people of various temperaments are doing what seems right to them even if it seems wrong to you.

In this chapter, we will look at various people that we know, be they friends or clients, and attempt to illustrate how temperament is central in their lives and in their relationships. We want to highlight two elements that exist in all people: what they *say* and what they *do*. We have suggested that temperament is predominately demonstrated in our speech and in our activity. We will give examples of how you can listen carefully to what people say and watch carefully what they do from a perspective of temperament so you can more effectively relate to them. More importantly, we will give examples of how you talk and act out of your temperament in order to make you more effective in life. In the examples that follow, know that all of the people we describe, all the conversations we report, and all the challenges that occur are from real people. We have changed the details in order to keep the identities of these people confidential, but the nature of what they say and what they do is always real.

Let me (Ron) give you an example that occurred not hours ago. On this day, I have been writing this very chapter of the book and it has taken most of the day. When I am writing, I am feeling, thinking, considering words that I should use, and then actually writing something. I work pretty fast in this writing process as it is a strength of mine to produce, in this case producing the first edition of this last chapter of our book. I am good at this kind of producing. Recall that I am a caretaker by temperament, namely a person who produces things, in this case a chapter of a book. Deb certainly does her share of caretaking, some which she cherishes, like working in her greenhouse today doing all that she needs to do on this late February day so that her flowers and vegetables will be ready on time. On the other hand, Deb is not as productive in writing as I am. The kind of writing that I do is not her gift. However, as an analyst, she works just as hard on this book as I do but in quite a different way. After I finish the draft of this chapter, I will put it on Deb's desk for her scrutiny. She will then do the very difficult work of reading, feeling, thinking, and editing this chapter. Before we ever finish this book, including this chapter, it will pass back and forth between our desks multiple times: I as a caretaker "producing" and Deb as an analyst "perfecting". We have done this back-and-forth editing for years and it has served us well, and hopefully serves our readership well. That having been said, it is always a challenge for us to engage in this process because we have different basic temperaments: she an analyst first and player second; I, a caretaker first and player second. What this means in terms of our writing is that I write furiously and speedily, and Deb does the painstaking process of reviewing, correcting, and suggesting. I am good at writing 50 pages. She is good at reducing that 50 to 20 to make the writing more meaningful, readable, and practical.

After I had an idea of how I might proceed with this chapter and had worked on the introduction, Deb and I took a drive during which time I told her a couple of ideas that we should include in this chapter. My idea at the time was for there to be three or four sections in which we would give examples of the various temperaments talking and doing things that were a reflection of each person's temperament. I began by describing one section, and Deb almost immediately said that she didn't like the approach I was taking. I was mildly offended, or perhaps mildly hurt. Why? Because I had been working for several hours feeling, thinking, and writing only to be met with Deb's almost immediate challenge to my idea. She said something like this, "When I hear what you are writing, it seems that there is too much negativity to it. I would like the introduction to this chapter be largely positive." Having heard Deb's comment, I followed the instruction we have made throughout the years in our work and in our various writing: feel first, think second, and then decide whether to speak or not. I felt hurt, for sure, not particularly important or deep hurt, but hurt nevertheless. I thought about several things: Her suggestion had real merit, and I know as a psychologist it is woefully too easy to identify what is wrong more than what is right. Then, I thought about Deb's basic nature, that of an analyst and her player nature second. Her analyst nature is to take a "critical look at things," which is what she did with her comment. Then, I thought about her player nature, which is to jump right in when an experience presents itself. So, I concluded that she had exercised these two temperamental operations, and it was more important for me to hear her suggestions than for me to express my minimal amount of hurt. It seemed best to avoid speaking about this incident because the hurt was minor, while the content was important. Note that coming to the conclusion to *not speak* about hurt was based on the fact that I had first felt, second thought, and third took action, in this case saying something like, "The focus on being positive is important." This is but one example of how we hope you have learned to respond when engaging someone of a different temperament.

I have read Ron's report above and found myself so glad that he included this. Indeed, I can recognize that I did go right to correcting his work albeit with no intention of hurting him. Also, and importantly, I can recognize that Ron's response to me was kind in that I felt heard and that we could work on this project with my suggestions valued. I was not aware of his containing his feelings, which attests to how well he dealt with my offensive suggestions. I can bear testimony to the fact that his consideration of my temperament was very helpful and that it paved a way for us to come to a conclusion on how to proceed. We hope that the following scenarios will further illustrate how successful "temperamental" conversations can be a part of your life.

TEMPERAMENT DISPLAYED BY BEHAVIOR

The following scenarios are of real people who have matured in their understanding of their temperaments and often of other elements of personality and values. We have constructed real-life people speaking to one another about who they are, specifically about their temperaments. Note how the people speaking and the people listening are emotionally mature and socially mature, something that is evident in the way they talk about feelings and thoughts. While we present these real-life experiences with real people, keep in mind that these people have often gone through the arduous therapeutic process of self-discovery and self-understanding in order to communicate successfully. The result of this process is that they have arrived at places where they could truly understand and communicate with people who are different from them.

Lover and Analyst

This is one of the most difficult combinations. This combination is difficult because the loves of lovers and the loves of analyst are so significantly different. We start with this combination to demonstrate that such difficult relational combinations can come to a place of respect and compatibility in some cases, and in other situations, they can come to respect the vastness of difference and find alternate paths. Lovers seek connections, while analysts seek separations. Lovers want agreement, but analysts want debate. There is obvious value in both harmony and agreement because they are intrinsic social elements, especially for lovers because harmony is a central part of connection, but there is equal value in debate because it is in real debate, especially for analysts because it is debate that they find truth that is so central to their way of life. Understandably, these two very different ways of looking at the world make the lover-analyst connection quite challenging. Both of these orientations are good and godly, and both are necessary for the world to work, but when put together, they don't always work well. Max and Susie are such a couple, Max being the analyst and Susie being the lover.

There is much relevant history to Susie and Max's 30-some year marriage but it might be fairest to say that while it seems that Susie was genuinely in love with Max, he might not have been truly in love with her. In fact, marrying her was more of a "good idea" rather than a desire. He was certainly taken by Susie's lover nature with all the ingredients of generosity, kindness, and sexuality. However, the central ingredient that all lovers have is connectedness, and this was not part of Max's basic makeup. It came as a complete surprise to Susie when Max moved out of the house and quickly sought a divorce.

We had a good deal of individual therapeutic contact with these people over several months but it seemed unlikely that they could, or perhaps should stay together. Despite the fact that they have lived together all of those years and were successful by some standards, in the end, they just weren't happy and satisfied together. Understandably, this decision was devastating to lover Susie even though she knew they were not happy and had not been for years. For Max the analyst, it was finally a relief to state the obvious and "face the truth". He was courageous enough to tell Susie that the divorce was "100% his fault" because he had not been honest with himself, and hence not honest with her when they got married. Looking back at their courtship and engagement, he admitted that he had doubts about the marriage from the inception of their relationship but couldn't justify breaking up with her. Fortunately, their impending divorce is amicable as their children are out of the house and there is no outstanding financial matter that could be difficult. It has been a painful end to a marriage that should never have happened. In the end, even Susie acknowledged that she was relieved, having felt that something must have been wrong with her given she gave her best, loved her best, yet it never seemed enough. It was helpful for her to realize that her loving, generous, and connecting nature kept her reasonably satisfied but never truly fulfilled. We assisted them in grasping the significance of their differences and saw them through the pain of the separation and divorce. Now, they are both in different relationships that seem more honest and compatible and they are each living more fulfilled. Having faced their great differences, they have remained friends, and good parents and now good grandparents.

Ted and Mary also display the lover-analyst marriage, but in their case, Ted is the lover and Mary the analyst. This couple came to us earlier in their marriage, just about the time when most marriages start to unravel as young couples are trying to manage finishing their education, establishing themselves in their vocations, building houses, and raising children. Difficult as these things are in every marriage, these challenges are exacerbated by differences in temperament. Typically, Ted, as a lover, found that Mary was "always finding fault" with him and "not able to connect" with her. He saw that she was very efficient in her work, with the household duties, in child-rearing, and finances, but she just "never seemed to have time" for him and was somewhat sharp or stern in her management of the children and the household. On Mary's part, she felt "pressured" by Ted's lover nature wanting "to be together all the time" while not being particularly interested in things that interested her. She got "bored" sitting around watching sitcoms and "romance movies" while Ted was bored with the History channel. Predictably, Ted was more interested in sex and felt abandoned when days or weeks passed without such intimate contact. Mary saw sex as "good but not central in life." There was nothing wrong with their values and loves, but they hadn't found ways to connect and disconnect, to agree and disagree, and have a good life together.

As is true with most couples that we see, we focused on helping them understand themselves first, each other next, and then find ways to be together with respect of one another. Ted admitted that he, as a lover, had "put too much stock" into thinking that Mary needed to be his sole source of connection. He began to find other people who were more like him in temperament with whom he could enjoy times together in the coffee house, on walks in the neighborhood, and Facebook; things that simply were not in Mary's nature. Mary did the same, i.e., found people with whom she could have philosophical conversations, discuss what they had been reading, and engage in debate about political, religious, and cultural matters. They came to a genuine understanding that their sex life needed to be a reflection of how they felt in life, so when they came to see their differences more profoundly, they found good common ground for sex not based on frequency but on intimacy and meaning. It was good for Ted as a lover to have found other people with whom he can have a "deep connection" while remaining sexually faithful to Mary. He doesn't want another lover, but having learned to trust that he can be intimate in conversation and enjoy others more deeply has freed him from his fear of "loving means sex". Now he finds it rewarding to come home from a coffee time with a friend and tell Mary that he feels heard and enjoyed compared to his previous complaints that she doesn't enjoy him or understand him. This recognition of their differences and his trusting that he can enjoy other connections was significant. Ted came to recognize that a relationship is based on both coming together and going apart. To his great delight, he discovered that the going apart is what often brought them closer together. Mary learned to be much more accepting of Ted's affection and recognized that her alternate engagements that provide more analytic stimulation gives her the space she needs from Ted so she can "come back to him" and enjoy and appreciate his desire for more intense connection. They recently came in for one of their last sessions and where Max bounced into the office and said somewhat jokingly that Mary was seeming "a little hornier" these days. Ted said that her desiring him more that was the greatest gift he could think of. Mary reported that she was enjoying the pleasure of wanting Ted more and that it was good for her to "think" about wanting him and then going home to enjoy him regardless of it being sexual, conversational, or just being near him in the house. These two people are maturing in their own natures. They have found ways to serve their basic temperaments without insisting that their partners need to be different. As we noted to start with, this combination of lovers and analysts can be a good fix for random engagements, but to mature in a lasting relationship requires a lot of hard honest work. Good for analyst Mary and lover Ted.

Analyst and Player

This is an interesting combination. For all the depth of thinking and considering that analysts do and the playing with abandon that players do, it might seem that this combination is an impossibility. In truth, this combination doesn't work in many cases. Players are just too "irresponsible" for analysts and analysts are just to "stuck on themselves" for players. Many analysts and players simply find one another grossly offensive. Let us tell you about Lawrence and his supervisor Maryann. Lawrence is about as analytical as you can get. He is all about what is real, what is true, what is right and how to get there, primarily through the means of problem-solving and problem-preventing. We've actually never met Maryann but from what we hear from Lawrence, she seems to be a player analyst combination. When Lawrence first came to see me, I had to admit to Deb that I wasn't sure I would be able to assist him because he seemed so rigid in his intention to examine all possibilities and seek to always do the right thing. Anything that I suggested was countered with retorts such as "I have already thought of that", "that won't work for me", and "no, I think you are wrong about that." Not easy to assist someone who has come to you asking for help but seemingly unable to consider any suggestion you offer. Nevertheless, I did work with Lawrence over several months attempting to help him come to some understanding about the typical complaint that people make about analysts: appearing to be always "critical." Ever so slowly it seemed he was lightening up a bit. He had begun a new job and was quite excited thinking that he had finally found a place where he could use his best skill-analysis. He did mention that he didn't like his supervisor, Maryann, very much. Sure, she was smart, but she was rather silly and annoying and he wondered why she was in a supervisory role given her somewhat flippant nature. He was glad for the job and was feeling good about being there, doing the work he was doing for a company that had an altruistic mission and a promising future. I didn't see Lawrence for a couple of months and then got a call that he needed to see me as soon as possible. I thought to myself that he probably got himself fired by being too rigid and seeming too critical. I got him in for an appointment that week. When he entered my office, I had to do a double take because his countenance was very different. He didn't seem distressed, anxious, and he certainly didn't seem angry and critical. As soon as he sat down, he jumped right in and said "you are going to love what I have to tell you!"

Before I tell you his report, note that when we started this description of the analyst-player combination, we noted that they often they don't get along. There is however, an intriguing element that make these two temperaments compatible: when the player finds fun in understanding and the analyst finds meaning in fun. Lawrence takes great pride in his ability to examine and find solutions at work. His boss, Maryann, who seemed flippant and irritating to him, is not only a player; she is a consummate player, very intelligent, very capable, but a player who has matured enough to succeed in the responsible position she holds in the company. Despite the responsible way she goes about work and life, she often teases and jokes to relieve the people whom she supervises to give them a respite from the grind that they all have in the laboratory where they work. Maryann has somehow managed not only to be responsible and instill responsibility in her employees, but also works to have the work interesting and exciting. I surmise that in some previous work she has learned to be her player self while also being responsible. So, when she teases and cajoles her employees, she is simultaneously encouraging them and challenging them. When Lawrence began to work for Maryann, he was appalled at what appeared to be her nonchalance in the midst of the exacting and sometimes tedious nature of scientific research. Lawrence had frequently complained about her seemingly frivolous nature, but now had come to notice that she was equally aware of the exacting nature of the work that they were all doing. But on this particular day Lawrence was excited to tell me about work including an encounter he had had with Maryann. A summary of what he told me is this: "So, I went to work last week thinking that if this crazy lady, my supervisor, makes one more joke, I am going to through a vile of chemical at her. Sure enough, she did make some jokes and I got so angry I couldn't keep my mind on my task. I tried over again to ignore her, but I kept thinking about the stupid joke she told that morning in the coffee room and found myself just throwing some of my lab equipment on the floor! (Lawrence laughed as he told me this). He continued his story by telling me that he *knew* immediately, namely that he was probably not only going to lose this ideal job but also that he would probably never be able to repair his exquisite reputation as a lab tech. Then he asked me, "Do you know what my supervisor did?" I shook my head, truly baffled with both the story and his apparent delight in telling it. He said that within moments Maryann approached him and just smiled at him. At first, he thought she was mocking him and began to defend himself. Maryann, without any retort went to the floor and began to pick up the pieces of this and that which had smashed on the floor. Then with a bit of a chuckle she motioned for Lawrence and the others to join her on the floor. The other team members, apparently more familiar with the antics of their supervisor, just got on the floor but only with great hesitation did Lawrence join them and began to apologize. Maryann quickly hushed him and said, "Hey, I know this is hard, but what I am going to ask you to do is even harder. I want you to sing your apology to the team and me. Seriously, I am not making fun of you, but I do want you to sing your apology. The team members just nodded their heads as if this was the most logical and acceptable thing to do. "Poor Lawrence," I thought. By this time as he sat down in my office, I was afraid of what he his response to his supervisor's odd suggestion might be. Lawrence continued talking while he chuckled and said "I sang! I f…ing sang! I have never sung in front of anyone before and it felt so good. I don't know what tune or what words I used, but I did sing that I was sorry for my outburst in the lab. When I finished, everyone just clapped and then I did something else I have never done: I took bow. Doctor, I have never felt so good in all of my life! Thank you for helping me be the wonderful analyst that I am but even more so, for helping me lighten up. Now, when Maryann does her silly jokes in the coffee room, I am the first to laugh. I just love this job!" Lawrence left, and he hasn't come back to see me. He doesn't need to. He has found a way to find meaning in fun, just as his supervisor, Maryann apparently had already found fun in the important meaning of the lab work.

Caretaker and Player

In some ways this is a combination that might have great potential because, as you might remember, both caretakers and players are quite physical. Remember, however, that their physicality is quite different with the caretaker valuing property and hence the engagement with property while the player uses property as a means of experience. Simplistically, the caretakers would be inclined to keep the car running with repair and upkeep, while the player would like to run with the car to places unknown. Prentice is a caretaker *par excellence* as has been evidenced all his life in the care of property and the care of people. His desk was always well ordered when he was in school. He worked hard in high school and finished college right afterward in four years and went directly into his graduate and post graduate programs. He married well and has been responsible in his professional, personal, and family life. Prentice's son, Samuel, a player, however, is not so inclined: His school desk is a disaster, he forgets to take homework home, never does more than half the dishes when it is his turn, his bed is never made, and he would really like to be outside with his friends riding bikes or inside playing video games. The operative word is "playing," always with something he describes as "fun." Doing dishes and homework is certainly not fun. Understandably, Prentice "brought" Samuel to me to get "fixed" or "straightened out" so he could be "responsible." He thought that his son suffered from ADHD, a diagnosis that is often rendered to players. I spent a number of hours with Prentice and Samuel individually and eventually together before I could really help them find ways to understand and respect each other. While Samuel was only 10, he was pretty bright, and the talks we had about his player nature were interesting to him, as were the illustrations about his father taking care of property being "fun" for him. In a situation with a parent and a child, however, the larger share of the responsibility for understanding and adapting lies with the parent. So, it was difficult for Prentice to accept that his son was a player and all that means. He admitted it had not occurred to him that his son wouldn't "be like him." This understanding helped lessen the criticism and concern he had for Samuel. Additionally, Prentice could understand how the terms he had been using for Samuel, like irresponsible, unacceptable, and disrespectful, were hurtful and potentially harmful.

Largely with Prentice's direction and work, father and son slowly became aware that they were quite different in many ways even if they were alike in other ways. It was easier for Prentice as a caretaker to reach beyond his nature than it was for his son to do so. It helped that he admitted that he also was quite player-like as a child and had also been criticized for being "irresponsible" and "disrespectful" which made him all the more determined to prove his accusers wrong. The more father and son learned about each other, the more they understood their differences as well as their similarities. They found a way to play together, more in line with play and rules that Prentice preferred, but also play that was "free play" that Samuel preferred. After a while, young player Samuel learned how to do some caretaking things like repairing cars and houses, and it actually became "fun" for him to do things that previously had been "boring." For example, Prentice bought Samuel a model car kit that they "had fun" putting together. When they had completed this project Prentice invited his brother to come for a visit from a distant state so that the three of them might spend a week working on an old car that belonged to Prentice's grandfather. This was quite "fun" for Samuel to "help" the adults with the treasured car. Never before had Dad let him do such things because he might do something wrong or break something. Samuel was able to grasp how important the old car was and found a tender respect for how to handle tools when he passed them to his father and uncle. He came in one session and was quite excited to tell me how he had used the tools "right" and even put them away which brought a smile to his father's face. Samuel then reported how much fun it was for his dad and he to go to the park and just play tag around the playground equipment. "Dad didn't use to like to play tag; now he knows how fun it is," he said. In addition to father and son finding common interests and adjusting to one another's values, they found that it was necessary to engage in their temperament-based activities with other people. Samuel as a player is learning that he doesn't need to demand everyone's attention to play all the time, a tendency that players have. Prentice as a caretaker has lessened his demand that Samuel do the dishes the way he thought they should be done. The last time I saw them they had just done their first rock climbing excursion, something that had enough excitement to please Samuel and yet required a good bit of practical skill and precision to please dad (not to mention enough protective head gear!)

Lover-Player/ Lover-Caretaker

The lover/player combination has the most passion of any combination, passion that can be remarkably joyful and sensual. Recall how both of these temperaments are highly physical, but their physicality is demonstrated quite differently. Players seek physical connection with anyone and everything as a means of *experience*, while the lover seeks *intimacy* through physical *connection*. This highly passionate combination can be true ecstasy for those involved, or it can be an all-out war when things go awry. When one person has both of these strong physical and passionate characteristics, as in a person with both player and lover strengths, it is always a task to establish and maintain a good relationship even if there is a mutual component. In the case we are going to present next, the other strong force is the caretaker temperament. Remember, caretakers value property, something that players often disregard or neglect. The task in this situation is for both parties to harness their physically passionate nature in their lover natures while balancing that strong mix of excitement and fun of the player with the "sensibility" of caretaking. Not an easy task.

Meet Sheila and Tom: Sheila, predominately a lover and player combination, is an especially attractive woman, and as such has had men interested in her since she was 12. She never had to work hard to get male attention because boys were competing with each other for her affection. Her physical beauty in addition to her sweet and connective nature made it easy for her to be in multiple relationships that were always intense and engaging. We should also note Sheila's secondary temperament of player, so she sought out intimate relationships as a reflection of her lover nature, and as a player, enjoyed the thrill of any new relationship. Lover/player people are extremely attractive in their demeanor because they are fun, entertaining, generous, and gracious. They can be playful and they can be comforting. The lover/player combination is one of the most powerful personalities. Because of her playful nature, together with her ability to "love the one you're with," Sheila was quite sexually active from middle adolescence onward, right up to the day she got married to Tom...and afterward.

Tom, also a lover was somehow different than all the other guys she dated and loved. He was pure lover, no doubt about that, he was particularly good at connecting, sacrificing, and generosity like most lovers are. Unfortunately, in the passion of them both having strong lover characteristics, some of Tom's caretaking simple crossed over into lover characteristics and was not differentiated. Tom gave Sheila that "lasting spark" that seemed to transcend long after they kissed (or other things) good night. She liked the fact that Tom was always taking care of her without expecting any response from her. He just enjoyed loving her. Tom was very much different from the guys she had been with before, many of whom shared her player nature. Tom didn't display the free and easy nature of player people, but provided instead, a certain stability, dependability and predictability that is so characteristic of a lover/caretaker. At first, it seemed that Sheila could finally settle down and trust Tom as a life's partner. No doubt about it, Sheila and Tom dearly loved each other. They had a wonderful romance together before and after they were married. Sex was a central part of their relationship and remained vibrant, at least for a time. But despite Tom's openness to sex and his other loving characteristics, Sheila began to be bored with Tom, sometimes in bed and sometimes in other situations. Unfortunately, Sheila was not able to govern her "love the one you're with" and ended up having a series of affairs over their first 10 or 15 years together, all of them brief encounters without any desire on her part to ever leave Tom or partner with someone else. She knew that she could never find a man better than Tom.

When Tom found out about these indiscretions, he was understandably devastated and didn't understand how such a thing could happen. He knew he loved Sheila and enjoyed "just taking care of things" for her, the house, and for the family. It didn't make sense to him that Sheila wanted something more than him. It didn't make sense to him that she would find it necessary to find another lover, much less several other lovers. He was stunned when Sheila admitted that she had become bored with their "routine sex life" and desired more playful and thrilling experiences. For Tom, their sexual connection, as well as the rest of their life's activities were "just fine." Things weren't any different for him than when they first fell in love. He had no clue that such basic things as daily household chores and even sex were less than satisfying for her. We saw this couple for some time, mostly individually, and somewhat jointly. They worked hard and began to find healing in their marriage. It took a long time to deal with the hurt, pain, and disappointment that they both felt, largely by learning about themselves individually so they could understand themselves as a couple.

Sharing the traits of lover was always easy for Tom and Sheila. It was easy to connect, primarily through sex, affection and other intimacies, which is always true for lovers. So, it wasn't their identical primary temperaments that caused difficulty; it was their secondary temperaments. They had had such an easy time connecting that they didn't realize that connection was insufficient for a lasting and faithful relationship. If they were to succeed together in the rest of their lives, they needed to add to their shared lover temperament an understanding of the rest of their personalities. Tom as a lover-caretaker had to work his way through the feelings of being "taken advantage of" as a caretaker as well as working through the hurt of Sheila's sexual indiscretions. Sheila as a lover-player had to work through reconciling that life was more than play. Sheila had a jump start in the therapeutic process when her mother took seriously ill and Tom, in true caretaker form, managed the house and the kids while Sheila sat beside her dying mother. While caretaking for her mother Sheila realized, more than ever before, how significant Tom's steady manner and reliability was in their relationship. This realization helped her recognize that while Tom and she shared loving together, it was his caretaking nature that set him apart from all the other guys where playful loving was the heart of the contact. Tom began to reconcile how Sheila's sense of adventure and playfulness made her so attractive to him…and to everyone else. It wasn't just her beauty and loving nature that he fell in love with. It was her playfulness too. She always put pizzazz in all they did. He loved that spontaneous and playful part of her and he had grown to miss it without realizing it was absent in the bedroom. He came to face that not all of life was about structure, predictability and daily routine.

In one very significant therapy session, several months after Sheila's mother died, they were both about to give up on the marriage when they came to recognize that loving each other was not enough: They had to understand each other better, particularly their differences in their secondarily temperaments. In their "new marriage," as they called it, Tom has learned to play a lot more, to engage Sheila with more invitations of random play, like bringing home flowers and airline tickets to some surprise romantic location on the spur of the moment. Tom is still as responsible as he has always been, but he has added to his strengths of caretaking and production more spontaneous play that gives Sheila such delight. Sheila is much more mindful of how much Tom does out of the simple pleasure of "just doing." She has voiced more appreciation for him and has become more patient in his busyness. They have come to terms that Sheila needs more spontaneity and Tom needs more verbal and "routine" affection and appreciation.

One important aspect of their reconciliation was the agreement to be more straightforward when Shelia became bored and when Tom felt taken advantage of. It took several months for them to "gulp" when they had to call out each of these emotions and a lot of practice to simply hear what sounded like criticism and to translate their respective feelings into the other's language. Once they became safer in being more honest in regards to their own needs, they began to learn how to use the other's language much more fluently. For example, Shelia began to acknowledge how much she appreciated Tom for his caretaking of the house and then added that she would really enjoy him "caretaking her." That was their way of recognizing that Shelia was longing for more excitement with Tom. Tom, on his part, began to use the word/concept "play" much more often. He came up with phrases like, "Sheila, would you play with me as I fix dinner?" or "Sweetheart, I have been doing so much caretaking, would you be willing to surprise me with something playful?" These were phases that helped him communicate that he adored her playfulness and was in need of it to balance his caretaking. It is important to note in this illustration that Sheila and Tom had to go through the confrontation of their differences before they were able to engage in learning about the other and eventually learn to speak the other's language so successfully.

Caretaker/Analyst

If the lover/player combination between people has the most passion of any combination, the caretaker/analyst combination has the least, at least if we look at what is *said* in the relationship. Both analysts and caretakers tend to talk in a somewhat dispassionate manner, or what might sound dispassionate to lovers and players. They neither express the sensual passion of lovers nor do they express the frequent excitement of players (unless of course, their secondary temperaments include these elements). The caretaker/analyst combination is good for production and accomplishment, partly because these two temperaments accentuate each other. There are people who marry with this combination, as we did, and it is the blend of our temperaments that make our relationship so enriched and productive. Additionally, you might recall, that both of us have a good bit of player temperament as well. We don't always play with abandon as players do, but playing is a very important part of our relationship, and it is a place where we often meet. Just minutes ago, we played a game of Triominoes, a game we often play when we need to break from our work. After playing the game for a few minutes, we both went back to our week end passions: Ron's with writing and Deb's with gardening. Given that it is Saturday, likely, Ron will help in some small way with the gardening like moving a rock, or lifting a heavy pot and Deb will help Ron with current writing albeit in small amounts of time throughout the day, but these are times of grace that we can afford one another because we both have our separate passions and meet in occasional play. Yet, it has been just as much of a challenge for the two of us to find ways to be true to our own natures and find commonality in life. We love each other dearly but we do not love as pure lovers do. Rather, we love each other in analysis, caretaking, and through our joint pleasure in playing.

Most frequently, we see the interaction between caretakers and analysts trying to find their way together in the world of work. Peter, an analyst, worked in IT where Sean, a caretaker, was his supervisor. Each of these men are quite bright and well-trained in IT, but they came to their trade from very different perspectives, and hence in quite different ways. As is often the case in business, caretakers find their way to supervisor or officer status more quickly than people of other temperaments simply because they do more, do anything, and seem to work harder, if not always efficiently. People end up in a trade for both good reasons, like passion, interest, and ability, or for bad reasons, like making as much money as they can make or meeting someone else's expectations. Fortunately, both Sean and Peter came into IT for good reasons and both were good at their work. They both were honest and hardworking, aspects that both liked about the other. They came to me because they had locked horns a number of times and couldn't seem to agree on *how* to get their work done. Sean supervised six people, Peter being one of them. He had some trouble with all of his supervisees but it troubled him most that he couldn't seem to connect with Peter in the work arena despite the fact that he liked Peter and respected him more than his other team members. Their differences were typical of this analyst/caretaker duet; the analyst wanting to seek meaning, work with a broad scope, and find the best ways to get the work done. Sean, caretaker that he was, just wanted the bottom line, namely make as much money for the company as possible by being efficient in what was produced. He often found Peter seemingly "playing" online with information that didn't seem relevant to the job. Analyst Peter was always researching ways to improve production that was "meaningful" as well as efficient. For his part, Peter thought that he was working by researching new and perhaps better options for production although such investigation looked frivolous to Sean because it didn't result in immediate production results.

In many ways, this combination is easier to deal with than many of the other combinations. It is easier because there doesn't tend to be the emotionalizing of feelings that the other temperaments tend towards. Peter and Sean came to see that they were quite alike in many ways, like getting the job done, but they went about the job in quite different ways. Peter explained that he often found information on internet sites that weren't directly related to the company work, but valuable nevertheless. He also admitted that he got "bored" with some of the routine of the IT work, and needed some time to do something in unique or unconventional ways. Sean helped Peter understand that he didn't want to take away his unique perspective, but that it was hard for him to see him in his cubicle doing something on the computer that didn't seem work-related. I advised Sean that he might actually sit down with Peter for an hour or two and watch how he went about work. That seemed to help Sean realize that Peter was working to stay interested in production but needed some distractions to stay interested in the work as well as discovering bits of information that would eventually be helpful to a current project. Sometimes,

Peter the analyst had to admit, his internet research was just frivolous, but other searches led to his coming up with ways to improve production. Peter came to see that production was the basis for Sean's life, and Sean came to see that curiosity and meaning was the basis of Peter's life. They realized more fully how they both loved work but that their love of work was quite different in its expression. Sean was able to let Peter "play around with new ideas" a bit because what he did produce was often higher in quality, albeit not always as high in quantity, than his other supervisees. In fact, Sean came to realize that what he didn't like about Peter was actually what prompted Peter towards his best production and did indeed serve the "the bottom line" in the company.

Peter realized that there were times where time was of an essence and something needed to be done by the end of the day even if it wasn't produced in perhaps the more ingenious way. He could do these tedious things, not so much to please Peter, but to grace him with work that wasn't exactly to his liking. Occasionally, Peter was able to go to Sean and acknowledge that he recognized it was an important day to "just get things done." This gave Sean the assurance of work production as well as a sense of being understood and appreciated in his role as supervisor. When they realized more fully how they both loved work but that their love of work was quite different in its expression, they came to a better understanding of each other, and ultimately worked more efficiently together.

Caretaker/Lover

No one has just one temperament. Rather, people tend to have a combination of a dominant temperament and one or more secondary temperaments, like in the case of Sheila and Tom noted above. You might recall that both of them were lovers but Sheila was also a strong player and Tom was a strong caretaker. We have pointed out that Deb is analyst first and player second, while Ron is caretaker first and player second. We want to give you another example of a couple who have two strong temperaments, in this case of Joseph and Judy, they both are strong caretakers and lovers.

Many people have this combination, which works quite well in most circumstances. This combination makes for the consummate parent at home, project manager at work, and community volunteer. With Joseph and Judy we might say that they had a kind of corporation in their marriage, their family, and their recreational activities because they worked together as a well-oiled machine almost knowing what the other person would do because they were so much alike. In many ways it is valuable for any two people who work or live together to find a way to develop this kind of cooperation because it makes doing the rudimentary elements of life so much more efficient. In many ways, Joseph and Judy's marriage has been easy, as is often the case with this blend of temperaments. In fact, caretakers and lovers often work very well together because they both have a focus on attending to the environment and the people within the environment. They both love and give and care for others and property. Both of these people are well educated, have done well in work, and have been particularly successful with their adult children. As they are now empty-nesters, it seems that they have fallen away from each other for some unknown reason. Likely, their marriage/corporation has been based so much on loving and doing that they never had any time left over to communicate their feelings and thoughts aside from the day-to-day necessities of raising children, going to work, and paying the mortgage. For some time now since the children are gone and the mortgage is paid, they seem to have a parallel life, but not a unified life. Previously, they were unified in caring for people and property, but those cares are not so important now. It is as if their life's goal of loving and caretaking is complete and that there is little else in life that seems important. To some extent, this couple got so lost in the doing and the caring for others that they neglected to care for each other, nor did they see the need to challenge each other to mature beyond connecting and property management. This couple is "satisfied" but they are no longer vibrant. Our work with these very good people has been to assist them in developing characteristics of the other temperaments both as individuals and as a couple.

We have already noted that the great psychologist Carl Jung suggested that a significant for all of us in later life is to mature what he called our "secondary functions" of personality. If we transfer Jung's concept into the matter of temperament, we would suggest that we need to add to our basic temperament the characteristics of all the other temperaments, something that we have reiterated throughout this book. With Joseph and Judy, it wasn't so much about adding the analyst nature as much as the player nature. As competent and mature lover and caretaker they knew the foundations of what was needed to take care of people and property. In their own way they had "analyzed" the needs of everyone around them and discerned how to meet them and found satisfying meaning and intention. But they seemingly had never just played, just experienced life without exact plans, meaning, or purpose. They had already engaged in conversations about meaning and truth. They had taken time to look back and notice how and when they were most honest, most successful, when life was most meaningful for them, but they were simply perplexed that there "seemed to be nothing more" on the horizon for them. We introduced them to the concept of experience and excitement that is central to players. They weren't initially interested in such things because it seemed, as they noted, a bit selfish. This couple had "done" life and all its responsibilities but hadn't experienced much beyond the requirements of family, house, and work. We worked with them for a while learning more about their individual passions, their skills, their hobbies and interests at large. One day, out of the blue, Judy said that she had always wanted to take a welding class. Joseph bolted, turned his head and said, "What? Welding? Where in the world did this come from?" She laughed out loud and said "Yes, I remember a movie I watched long ago, that tornado movie, where this group of young people go chasing tornados." Joseph interrupted her and said, "I thought you didn't like that movie. It scared you to even think about being in a tornado!" "Well, yes," Judy answered, "It is scary to think about people we love being in danger, but I am just thinking about those big artistic wind chimes that lady had in her yard and that she made them herself. I find myself wondering, well, wishing I could be creative like that and make big lovely things for the yard. I know it sounds silly, but I think if I could learn to do something creative rather than just practical, well, it might spice up my life."

That was about all this couple needed. They actually left that session and within two weeks' time they were both enrolled in a metal working shop class at the local community college. They came back to us and said that they were having so much fun and that they were both allowing themselves to not worry if or not what they worked would ever be used. And, they asked, "Does this qualify as adding the player part to our lives?" We laughed with them and enjoyed their playful discovery. They were "just playing" for the first time in many years. This couple can continue to be good as caretaker and lover without changing who they are and what they value but to truly fulfill their lives they needed to face the challenge of adding to their loving and productive goodness the elements of the player. This challenge is about true maturing. We had not heard from them in quite a while and then got a card from them with some pictures of yard art they were now selling at local craft markets. They noted that they were happy.

In all of these examples, we have looked first at how people with different temperaments act and then have suggested that everyone can build upon their basic natures in order to succeed in life. It takes some time to get used to seeing a person's temperament underneath his/her behavior, but eventually it is very helpful to do so. We call this a "friendly diagnosis." We find ourselves seeing such things with people and say something to each other like, "Oh, that's his player operating," "Isn't that interesting how she is such a good caretaker," or even, "It's a challenge to see that analyst nature because it is so critical, but I know she's right about what she's saying." This way of looking at people keeps us away from "diagnosing" people with some kind of disorder. We can see something that someone does that we don't understand, or perhaps don't like, but not get caught in complaining about the person or thinking that what someone does is irresponsible, unkind, or selfish. Most of the time people are doing their best to live in the world, very often a world that does not accommodate their temperament. Now, let's look at how people of these different temperaments *speak* about their feelings and their values.

TEMPERAMENT DISPLAYED IN WORDS

If it's hard to understand why people act in some way, it is even harder to understand why people speak the way they do. With few exceptions people speak primarily out of their temperament, and they speak thinking that the world understands them. Unfortunately, people are more often *misunderstood* than understood. In the following scenarios we present conversations among people who understand their temperaments and make an attempt to explain what they are saying from that perspective. We grant that there are many other elements that go into what one says, like the way a person has learned to think, one's belief system, one's vocabulary, and one's cultural background all of which come to bear when someone is speaking. All of this having been said, however, it is our *feelings* that influence our speech, and feelings are intrinsically tied to our different temperaments. Note how the following *emotionally mature* people express themselves in working diligently to communicate their feelings. Note also how these speakers are *socially mature*, which means they understand that we're not all alike, which requires us to communicate in ways that people can understand something, not just as we understand something. Finally, note how such people frequently use *qualifiers and gracious apologies* for what they say and what they hear.

Player Speaking to a Caretaker

Joe: Abraham, I want to tell you about myself, particularly what I have been learning about myself, particularly about my temperament. Interested?

Abraham: Of course, Joe. We've been friends for a long time and I know that you have been studying this temperament thing recently, so I'm all ears.

Joe: One of the interesting things about you and me, our relationship, is that we have a lot in common and we seem to approach life in much the same way.

Abraham: That's certainly true.

Joe: I've been thinking about how we look at property, which means that we both like property and use property. You know, like, when one of us has a new hammer, we enjoy showing it off and describing how we found it useful.

Abraham: Certainly true.

(Note at this point that Abraham is primarily listening, not speaking, and not interrupting. He sees that Joe is speaking and understands that his task is to listen.)

Joe: As good as we are with doing things together, and as good as we are enjoying things, there are times when something just doesn't feel quite right. I can't explain this feeling very well but when we are doing some kind of project, which is what we do best at, I feel a kind of separation from the project and a separation from you. Odd as it sounds, I almost feel a kind of irritation inside of me that I can't quite explain.

Abraham: This sounds very interesting, Joe. I think I have some understanding of what you're talking about, but please, go on.

Joe: Thanks, friend, because, I gotta tell ya', that I've been thinking about this for a while and I couldn't put my finger on it. I couldn't seem to label the feeling that I had because feeling "irritated" didn't feel quite right, but there was something that occurred inside of me at times when we're working on something. Let me explain a bit further with this temperament theory that I've been reading about.

Abraham: I'm with you. Please go on.

Joe: This "player" part of me seems to be operating a lot, and it doesn't always seem to mesh with what you are doing and how you go about things. Players, as I have been learning, are people who seek *experience* in life, usually physical experience in life, like doing something. In a way, you and I go into some project, usually building something or fixing something, both looking for some kind of physical engagement. But there is a difference between us with these projects. I get excited about doing something or whatever and see it as an experience to be enjoyed, almost like an adventure. Remember the time we looked at that bay window in my house and we stood back wondering how we could fix it, repair it, or replace it?

Abraham: Yup. I remember the very time. We stared at that window and talked about what we should do for 10 minutes before we picked up a hammer.

Joe: Right. You know what? Those 10 minutes were the best part of the project for me. I looked at the window and considered various possibilities. I saw us tearing the window out, or fixing it, and it was just fun to consider what we might do together.

Abraham: I remember. Then we went right at it.

Joe: Exactly, and that was an important moment for me because when we just went at tearing the window out, I somehow felt a bit…I don't know what to say…maybe, disappointed. We continued to work on the window and eventually got it done, and it was a good project, but it wasn't nearly as fun actually *doing* the window as it was *considering* doing it.

Abraham: You know, I remember that project, and I think I felt something wasn't quite right with you in the project. I didn't make much of it at the time. Try to explain this to me, Joe.

Joe: Right. That's exactly what I'm trying to do, and I'm having a duce of a time finding words to explain what I was feeling. I think it comes down to the difference between you and me. You just charge right in. You don't worry about a plan. You face problems as they come up and take a left turn or a right turn, and just keep on going. I admire the way you do things. But for me, it is not as fun, if I dare use that word, to just tear into something. It's more fun for me to sit back and muse about it, and then see the project as something that is a game, something to figure out, and something akin to playing more than working. Does that make sense?

Abraham: It sure does, Joe. Perfect sense. I'm beginning to understand how you look at a project. I don't think I ever understood this "player" part of you, like everything is play, a game, or something to be enjoyed, right?

Joe: Exactly. When something is a game, I'm all in, and I can work for hours as long as it is a game. But when it becomes "work," I lose energy. It's not important to get the job done as much as it is to be engaged in the "game" of fixing a window. Hell, to be honest with you, in those ten minutes, I even thought, what if that window were a door to another world, like in a sci-fi movie and we traveled to space. I know that sounds weird, even childish, but that was part of the play for me.

Abraham: Weird? Yes. Childish? No. Just playing and dreaming, I guess. This is a whole different way of understanding how a guy fixes a window. It begins to make sense to me.

Joe: I'm glad to hear that. I'm particularly glad that I haven't offended you telling you about how I go about the work we so often do together.

Abraham: Not at all. This is good stuff to know. To be honest, I was a bit curious as to why you sometimes seem hesitant when we get ready to actually do a project. I think I understand you better. So, shall we just charge right into a beer, or shall we consider it first?

Joe: Let's charge!

Note how this is a one-way conversation for the most part, i.e., Joe is telling Abraham how he feels. They are not particularly interacting, back and forth. Rather, Abraham is primarily listening and seeking to understand his friend, while Joe is struggling to find words that reflect his feelings. We discussed the challenge of expressing feelings and the much harder challenge of hearing feelings in *I Want to Tell You How I Feel*. Now let's consider how this conversation might have progressed if Abraham had started it with his perspective as caretaker speaking to a player:

Abraham: Hey Joe! Got a minute.

Joe: Sure, Abraham. What's up?

Abraham: You know that Lynn and I have been seeing that therapist. Well, we are learning about what the psychologists call "temperament" and I have found it helpful. Very usable.

Joe: I'm always interested in something that is fascinating. What does this temperament thing mean? Is it some kind of diagnosis, like ADHD or something?

Abraham: Actually, quite the opposite. It doesn't have anything to do with what's wrong with people, but what's right with them.

Joe: You mean, like, good people do good things, or something?

Abraham: Yah, a little like that but temperament theory has more to do with how we feel, what we value, how we act, and how we speak.

Joe: Wow, heavy stuff but I'm all ears. Let's have it.

Abraham: So, let me try to explain it by telling you what I learned about my own temperament.

Joe: I'm listening, but I don't have a grasp of this temperament thing yet. When I hear the word temperament, I think of good and bad, right and wrong. But you're saying that is not the idea. (Note here, that Joe is doing his best to stay with his friend Abraham but he is in his player nature and getting excited with something new).

Abraham: Yah, I know, when you hear the temperament word or a lot of psychological words, they seem to be referring to good and bad, right or wrong, or some kind of diagnosis. Temperament is not like that. It's a reference to how one thinks, feels, and values. And then it is about how a guy goes about engaging in life. You ready for me to explain?

Joe: Shoot. Enough of the introduction, already. (His player nature is showing.)

Abraham: Yes, yes, sorry. I am actually quite excited about this new idea. Here's the summary. There are four different temperaments that people have, and each one of them has different elements in it. The four temperaments are lover, caretaker, player, and analyst. Now, I know that temperament is not all that makes up a human being, like there are cultural things, education, family background, religious persuasion and a lot of other things. But the idea here is that each temperament has a basic value system, which we might say is a way the person sees life and goes about life.

Joe: Okay, this is sounding kinda fun. I'm with you so far.

Abraham: So, let me tell you what my temperament is and how it affects what I say and do. I am a "caretaker" by nature. Caretakers are "doers." They do things. They produce. Furthermore, they value property and take care of property. Give a caretaker something to do, and he is happy. This could almost be anything to do as long as he can do something productive, like fixing the window we fixed the other day, or working on the oil change in your car last week.

Joe: So, does this mean that we're both caretakers by temperament? Because we both do things and fix things.

Abraham: Yes and no. The "yes" part of my answer is what you just said: we both like to do things and fix things and work together. The "no" part of my answer is that we approach this doing very differently. Let me ask you something? How easily and how often do you get bored?

Joe: You're kidding, right? You know me, I am often bored.

Abraham: How often do I get bored?

Joe: Well, I suppose you get bored about the same amount as I do, but I don't actually remember your saying that you were bored.

Abraham: Exactly. You don't hear the "bored" word from me, pretty much ever. The truth: I never get bored.

Joe: That's a little hard to believe. Everyone gets bored, don't they? People have to do things that are intrinsically boring and just "bore through," Ha! Get it?

Abraham: Actually, Joe, people like me, caretakers as they call them, don't get bored, or rarely get bored. You know how long I can work on a project, like well into dinner time and then wish I could continue? Furthermore, you know that I always have another two or three things that I wish that I could do even while we're finishing some project.

Joe: I have noticed that. When we're working on some house or car project, I would want to pop a beer and sit back and look at the window and enjoy what we've done or tell each other some jokes.

Abraham: Exactly. And do we do that?

Joe: Rarely, now that you mention it. Sometimes, I want to put a chain around you and slow you down so we could have a bit of fun.

Abraham: I'll come back to the "fun" thing in a minute. But first, you mentioned something that is really important: I don't slow down, even when I'm dead tired. Even when I push through something and break something because I'm tired.

Joe: So, why don't you just stop and pop that beer and then go back at it? I don't get it.

Abraham: Right. I don't stop. There are a lot of times that I should have stopped, but I don't like to stop. I like the finished product. I love starting the project, but what I really enjoy more is finishing the project. If I would stop for that beer, I'd be wishing that I could be back swinging the hammer. So, this caretaker temperament is about working, doing, and finishing. Then, it's about having a product for all the work. But it's more than that, Joe. It's about valuing property.

Joe: Well, isn't property something to enjoy? Property isn't of any value in itself, is it? It's what you can do with it.

Abraham: Again, yes and no. The "yes" part of my answer is that I know that property isn't living, and I don't want to be materialistic thinking that property is somehow more important than people, or faith, or love. The "no" part of the answer is this: caretakers like me look at property as having intrinsic value. You know how I take care of things, like my tools and stuff?

Joe: Certainly. Your garage is the envy of the neighborhood. I can't seem to do what you do with tools, and I'm always forgetting where I put the hack saw.

Abraham: Good example. Yes, you see property, like the hack saw, as something to be used, or dare we say, even something to "play" with. I see the hack saw as almost sacred, odd as that sounds. It bothers me when I see property neglected or lost. It just seems wrong.

Joe: Sometimes, I wish I had your ability to care for property. It would save me a lot of money.

Abraham: That might be true, Joe, but then you would be like me and not like yourself. You have a great time going about life and dealing with property for what it can do, or even play with. You know how you once took the reciprocating blade and did some kind of dance to it following some radio song.

Joe. I'm embarrassed to even remember that moment. You must have thought that I was crazy.

Abraham. Not at all. I enjoyed the dance and it made the project more fun. You were playing, and it was great. I was working, and it was just as great.

Joe: So, if you're a caretaker, what temperament am I?

Abraham: From what I know of you, you'd be what they call a player. Simply put, work is play for you, and it is production for me. A project is something to play with for you, but it's something to get done for me. Both of these ways about going into a project are good but they are both different. So, sometimes when you're playing in a project, I might be a bit irritated, trying to keep it to myself. I suspect, you're playing because you're a bit bored with just working and want to have some fun at the same time.

Joe: Exactly. Makes sense. Now, you've got me interested in what this player temperament is all about.

Abraham: It is good stuff! But right now, I've got to replace a toilet.

Joe: Now, that is a good example of this playing/working thing. I guess I'll just have to wait. You've got me excited. I think I will kick off work for now and go see what the score is.

Abraham: True to your player nature, I might note.

Analyst Speaking to a Lover

Mary is an analyst and her daughter, Melody, is a lover. As we have noted, this lover/analyst combination is challenging because the value systems of these two temperaments are significantly different, which often leads to hurt on both sides of the equation. As a reminder, lovers seek connection more than anything else and analysts seek truth and understanding more than anything else. Let's begin this discussion with having Melody speak her feelings but then moving the discussion to the parent, who needs to take leadership in the discussion. Note the initial feelings expressed by Melody, which are those of a typical 12-year-old, and how Mary migrates into these emotionally charged waters. Again, we present this discussion from a parent mature in her self-understanding, which can then lead to helping a child understand herself.

We will suggest the background of this discussion is Melody expressing herself in a typically childlike manner as is only normal for a child to do.

Melody: Why do you like Alex more than me? You're always talking to him but you never want to talk to me the way you talk to him.

Mom: Melody, please tell me more about these feelings. This seems very important. I am so sorry that I have hurt you. (Please note that Mary does not explain how she loves Melody, nor does she explain what she says to Melody's brother, Alex. She asks her daughter to speak more about her feelings. Certainly, Mary doesn't love Alex more than Melody, but this is where the conversation has to start because Melody spoke her feelings first. This is one of our "rules of engagement" from our book, *I Want To Tell You How I Feel*: whoever starts talking about their feelings gets to finish expressing these feelings.)

Melody: You just don't spend much time with me. You don't even listen to me most of the time. But when you talk with Alex, you seem to be very interested in what he has to say. You don't seem to be interested in what I say. You just don't seem to care about my feelings.

Mom: I'm very sorry that I have not heard your feelings, Melody. Can you please tell me something right now about how you feel or what you feel?

Melody: I don't know what to say. I don't know, I guess I just have feelings and try to express them but you don't seem to care.

Mom: Again, I'm truly sorry for not hearing your feelings, Melody. Can you think of a time you were telling me something that was important to you where I didn't listen? Remind me.

Melody: Duh, like yesterday when I was telling you about how my best friend at school, Karen, didn't want to talk to me. Now she seems to have some other good friend. I saw the two of them talking together, and I was sure they were gossiping about me.

Mom: I remember that from yesterday. You told me just what you said. Did it seem to you that I wasn't listening? Or did it seem that I didn't care about your friendship?

Melody: Yes, I know you listened because you kept nodding your head, but you didn't say anything. It was like you didn't care at all about my feelings. I was really hurt seeing Karen talking to someone else the way she usually talks to me.

Mom: You know, Melody, I think you're exactly right about what I did. Now that you remind me about the Karen situation, I remember what I said... or didn't say. In fact, I remember not saying anything.

Melody: Why didn't you say anything about me or Karen? You talk and talk and talk with Alex about his schoolwork, some history thing that you think is interesting, but you never talk to me about what is important to me? You just don't seem to care about me.

Mom: I'm so sorry, Melody. I'm so sorry that I didn't talk to you like I should have. And I'm sorry I didn't listen to you the way I should have. I am sorry, sweetheart. Also, I am sorry that your friend Karen has disappointed you.

Melody: I hope Karen will still be my friend. I am glad you understand how she hurt me.

Mom: Now, for a couple of minutes, I would like to tell you something about me that has to do with my not listening the way I should. And it has to do with the way I talk to Alex.

Melody: I already know what you're going to say, or what you really feel. You think Alex is smarter than I am and you are interested in what he feels more than what I feel.

Mom: Again, I'm sorry for having hurt you, Melody. I will try to do much better with listening and talking to you. I promise. Right now, though, I would like to tell you something that is very important to me. Your brother and you have different kinds of smart. In fact, I have a different kind of smart. Everybody has some kind of smart but no one in our family is smarter than anyone else.

Melody: I don't get it. Smart is smart, right? If you do well in school, this means that you're smart, and if you don't do well, you're not so smart.

Mom: Let me get back to what I want to tell you about me, Melody.

Melody: Is this going to be some kind of lecture about how I need to do more homework or something? I've already heard that lecture.

Mom: Not at all, love. It's not about you whatsoever, and it's not about school. It is about how your mom feels. Because I have just as many feelings as you do, and Alex does, but I show my feelings differently than you do.

Melody: Mom, sometimes, it seems like you don't have any feelings.

Mom: I know that is how it seems. And by the way, that is the way it seems to a lot of people. So, let me explain how *I feel* and then we can talk about your feelings. I think what I have to tell you might make more sense to you when you talk to me about Karen, for instance.

Melody: Oh, mom, don't be hurt, I am sorry. I didn't mean to hurt you. I just wanted to tell you about Karen.

Mom: No, you didn't hurt me. Right now, I want to start by telling you what is really important to me.

Melody: Okay, I already know what you're going to say. You're going to say that family is important, Dad is important, Alex is important, and I am important.

Mom: You're right about that! You are important. There is something else that is as important though, and in some ways, more important.

Melody: What could be more important than family?

Mom: This is going to be hard to explain so give me a few seconds to say what I want to say. Of course, I love the three of you as much as I have ever loved anyone. But there is something that is actually as important as my loving you. I love truth.

Melody: I don't get it.

Mom: I know this must sound weird, to say that I love truth. Melody, let me tell you about my loving truth. This is hard to explain but it is very important to me. When I say that I love truth, it means that I look to find out what is true and then try to say things that I think are true. It also means that I am always looking to understand what really happened, what was really said, and other things that are real. Does this make any sense to you?

Melody: Maybe a little. But when I think of loving something, it is always people, not anything else.

Mom: Right. I know that you do this. In fact, that is the second thing I wanted to talk to you about, which is what you love. Yes, you love people more than anything. You love to be with people, talk with people, cuddle with people, and do things with people. All of this means that you really love to be connected with people. Right?

Melody: Mom, isn't everyone like this? Doesn't everyone want to love people and be with them? It seems that they should. What is more important than people? We are supposed to love people.

Mom: Nothing is more important than people, dear. But there are some things that are just as important as people. So, when I tell you that I love truth, this means that I love truth as much as I love people.

Melody: That is very hard to understand. People are real. "Truth" is just a word. How can you love a word as much as you love people?

Mom: Melody, it's not just the word "truth" that is important. It is what the word means. Truth means learning, listening, reading, watching, and a whole lot of other things. By the way, there are other ways of loving. You love connecting with people. I love connecting with truth. But your brother loves connecting with things, and you dad loves connecting with play. That is why your dad is so much better at playing with you than I am because he really loves playing. Your brother loving things is a little harder to understand, but you know how upset he gets when you have borrowed something of his and not returned it. This is not because he is selfish but because he loves his things. He feels connected to things like you often feel connected with people.

Melody: This is hard, Mom. I don't understand. It sounds like everyone in the family is different, and I want everyone to be the same. Why can't we all just love each other?

Mom: We all do love each other, but we love in different ways, and we love different things. We can still love each other and love other things too. Let's come back to when you said that I loved your brother more than you. I certainly don't love him more than you. I love you both the same amount. You are right, I do talk to him more than I do with you for a couple of reasons, one of which is that he is in high school and he is very interested in learning so he can do well in school. You're not so interested in school, but much more interested in friends and friendships and being with people. So, I am a bit more interested in what he talks about, which might be history or math, which you don't care about too much.

Melody: Well, if you don't love him more than me, it certainly sounds like you like him more than me.

Mom: Sweetheart, I like what he talks about, but I don't like him more.

Melody: So, you don't want to hear about what I am interested in, like friends, and friendships? I don't want to talk about history all the time. I want you to want to talk to me.

Mom: Here's where I need to be much better listening to you and understanding what you love, which is always connecting and feeling close to people. And it also means that when things don't go right with some friend, this is very hard on you. I have just always been better talking history and other academic truth-language than friends-language. Actually, I think your dad is better at such things. He can certainly talk "friends" language. I want to get better at it, so please give me a chance to listen to you, and I will work hard to learn your "talking friends" language. You keep telling me about Karen and your other friends and I will learn how to listen to what you love.

This discussion could have been derailed at any time if Mom had gone into any kind of defense of her analyst nature, like, "you're not hearing me," or "that's just not true," or "that's not what I said." While this is seen as a conversation between a parent and a child, it is a good reminder that when you discuss your temperament with someone else, you have to stick with your temperament. And when someone is explaining their temperament to you, you need to listen and try to understand, something that is exceedingly difficult to do. Hopefully Melody and Mom will continue to talk and listen, each learning, at their own appropriate pace about how differences in a family are very important and can be respected.

Melody and her mom is an exceptional example of one person, namely the parent, taking charge of the conversation and giving the child a lot of room to express emotional feelings. In an adult-to-adult conversation it is usually necessary for two people to talk back and forth a bit even if one person is the one initially speaking.

Analyst Speaking to a Lover

Jean and Randall have just begun to date after finding each other on social media. They did what most people do on dating sites, like email several times, that followed by texting, then sending pictures, and other items of interest like song links, and then deciding to meet. They seem to be a good match although they both come from unsuccessful relationships and are leery of starting again. They have shared their concerns about their previous relationships. Understandably, both of them tended to focus on the mistakes and wrongs of their former partners rather than saying much about their own mistakes, much less about their temperaments. However, Randall has been in therapy where he learned about his analyst temperament and has begun to think about personality differences and how they can affect relationships, both positively and negatively. After their second coffee shop date Randall took it upon himself to tell Jean what he had learned about being an analyst.

Randall: I've really enjoyed our contacts over these weeks, and I think we went about it carefully. I am glad for that. I didn't do that in my previous relationships. In the past I tended to focus on how much I liked the woman I was dating and didn't look very closely at how we might be different. I thought it would be good, if you don't mind, to share some of what I've learned and see what you think of it.

Jean: Why, sure. What have you learned and how did you learn it?

Randall: My first introduction to learning about myself came from finding a therapist who looks at personality differences more than he looks at diagnoses. I've continued to read, study, and think about what it means to be me, how I feel, and how I come across to other people.

Jean: It sounds like you've been developing self-esteem, right?

Randall: Yes, self-esteem is part of it, perhaps the most important part of it, but I've learned a lot more about how I actually go about life, what is important to me, and what I love. Then this all relates to how I communicate to people. The self-esteem part of the equation is related to my understanding myself before actually liking myself.

Jean: Yes, self-esteem seems to be a central issue with everyone. The guy I was married to didn't have good self-esteem and I had to try to please him all the time or he would get really upset.

Randall: Let me get to that in a moment, I mean the upsetting people, the anger, and all of that, because I think a lot of arguments that people have relate to the fact that they see the world differently, and value different things.

Jean: Isn't it all about love, I mean people loving each other?

Randall: Yes and no. The "yes" part of the answer is that if two people are in a relationship, they certainly need to love each other. But I have discovered that liking someone is equally important.

Jean: Well, if you love someone, won't you like them? Isn't the liking part of a relationship a result of loving someone?

Randall: Actually, I think it is the other way around, at least for me. Liking is really important because when I like someone, we can talk about the same things, do the same things, and find ways to be together.

Jean: That seems opposite to what I believe.

Randall: Yes, and I suspect that loving is first for you, and maybe liking second, but let me get to your "people loving each other" question. You suggested that a relationship is all about love, and I said "yes and no." The "yes" part of my answer is that a relationship has to have love in it to survive and to thrive. The "no" part of my answer is this: loving each other is not enough, at least for me.

Jean: Hey, what about all those songs we have been sharing, they all are about love being enough. And when something works out in a relationship in a movie, it seems to always be about loving each other. I know they are 'just movies" but isn't that the way it is supposed to be?

Randall: I want to emphasize that loving is central in a relationship but loving one another is not enough for a relationship to thrive.

Jean: Of course, there are other things, like, having a family and building a home together.

Randall: Actually, it's more than that.

Jean: I don't know what more there could be in a relationship than loving each other, loving kids, enjoying your home and neighborhood. Of course, friends are important and maybe religion.

Randall: To be honest, for me, truth is as important as those things you mentioned. For me, seeking truth, understanding where truth comes from, and speaking truth are all very important. (Note in this conversation so far that Randall is trying to state a case for his being an analyst, namely someone who seeks truth, like Mary was doing with her daughter Melody. Already in this conversation we can see the difference in how Jean and Randall see life: Randall is laying out a perspective of truth and analysis, while Jean's perspective is clearly that of a lover. It is also likely that Jean is feeling a bit uncomfortable in the conversation after having been very comfortable in their previous meetings.)

Randall: Let me try to explain because I don't think I'm doing a very good job of it, and I might be miscommunicating at this very moment. By the way, I have learned that I might not be the best communicator and have frequently been misunderstood. (This is the necessary apology part of any conversation.)

Jean: I'm sorry to hear that. You seem to be a good man and we've had good talks. I feel quite connected to you even in just these few weeks.

Randall: Thanks for saying that. I feel good about what we've started here and hope we can find a way to make it even better. But let me get more to the point because I said earlier that I've been learning about myself, and what psychologists call "temperament," which has been very helpful for me to understand what I've done right and what I've done wrong. I've learned, for instance, that what I've done wrong is not some terrible thing, or that I have some kind of diagnosis of anxiety or depression, but I have thought that everyone else was like me.

Jean: But we're all alike in the fact that we all need to be loved, right?

(Again, this is a comment coming from Jean's lover nature. She says this to find connection with Randall, i.e., agreement, because she feels some of the separation that is coming from Randall in what he's saying. This is the intuitive part of a lover. Randall is not trying to separate from Jean, but when he continues to try to express how he is different, he is, indeed, separating himself from people, which is what analysts do all the time, and what lovers feel when it happens.)

Randall: Yes, I agree. We all need to be loved, that's for sure. But what I'm talking about is a larger part of love than just loving each other. Let me keep trying to explain. So, I'll just jump right in: I have learned that my personality is described as an "analyst." There are other aspects to my personality and other important things in my life. We've talked about some of them over the weeks. But this "analyst" thing has had a good ring for me because it answered some of the questions I have had for a long time about what it means to be me. Simply stated, analysts love truth. They also love analysis, like figuring out problems, solving them and preventing them. They like discussion, and even like debate. Not argument, have you, but debate about things, like politics, and religion, and work. It's actually fun for me to spend time searching online for information about some topic, and then maybe to use that information to fix some problem, or perhaps to get into a discussion with a friend about it. The whole truth-seeking thing is very exciting for me because I love to understand how things work, be it mechanical things, the stock market, my dog, or people. So, I could say that my first love is for truth. Yes, I love people certainly, but I look for what is real, truthful, and meaningful, to understand it the best I can and then love to share that with someone that I like.

Jean: I don't want to be mean, but his sounds sort of "cold." Like, what is so important about ideas and meaning and this whole truth thing? It doesn't seem to relate to how we can love each other and be together.

Randall: Interesting that you should use the term "cold" describing what I have said because I have had many people say that I seem to be cold. By that I think they mean that my analysis and truth-seeking seems to leave them cold because truth doesn't always have to do with people or relationships.

Jean: Well, if we are going to be honest here, I hate to say it, but that seems right. So how do you relate to people if relating always has to do with meaning, information, and problem-solving? This sounds like a committee meeting more than two people loving each other.

Randall: This is the very reason I wanted to tell you about myself, particularly this "analyst" part of me because I have been misunderstood by many people over my years of life, and have hurt many people whom I didn't intend to hurt. In fact, I have only recently become aware of how important hurt is in a relationship. Previously, I thought of hurt as the result of someone being right and someone being wrong. I certainly don't want to ever hurt someone, but emotional hurt hasn't been on my mind and certainly not something that I would ever say to someone, like, "you hurt me" even though I have heard that from people I have hurt.

Jean: Well, that's a relief. The men I have known have never seemed to care that they have hurt me. I'm glad to hear that you would not want to hurt me.

Randall: Certainly true. I would never *want* to hurt you. But it seems clear to me that I hurt people without intending to hurt them, often by the very way I speak to them. "My talk language" is about ideas, problems, what went wrong, how someone can do better". I know that sounds impersonal.

Maybe that is the word I am looking for. I seem impersonal to a lot of people because I can get really excited about how something works and that I know how to make it even better. I certainly don't feel impersonal but when I'm on a roll of inquiring about something, I just get excited. And sometimes in my excitement it can seem that I don't care about people. Now that I understand this analyst temperament, I want to be better at communicating the things that I love, particularly truth and getting to the truth. An important part of "truth" is how I feel about myself and other people. I never used to pay much attention to someone telling me that I hurt them. Now, I'm much more aware of hurt, but it is still foreign to hear it and even more foreign to say it.

Jean: You mean that you don't get hurt.

Randall: Not at all. I get hurt and have been hurt, but I've never recognized hurt in me, much less said it. Instead, I would talk facts, information, and truth but miss the whole hurt thing.

Jean: Well, this is very interesting. I have to think about it after this conversation. Are there other temperaments? I wonder what I might be, I hope I get a chance to tell you about me sometime, with or without the "right words".

Randall: Yes, there are four temperaments, at least as I have learned about them. I can give you a couple of book titles that are helpful.

Jean: Well, okay. I look forward to it.

We could reverse this conversation, i.e., have Jean talk about being a lover to Randall who might have no clue about temperament. If you are a lover, think how that conversation might go explaining yourself to an analyst. As a lover, how would you manage the desire to be connected while talking about differences? How might you respond if the person you are wanting to share your temperament understanding with begins to debate or dismiss it?

Player Speaking to an Analyst
Consider this conversation between a player employee and an analyst employer, which is quite common in the world of work. Many players are bright, educated, and attractive to employers only to find at a later time that their love is not for truth and analysis but for experience. Linda and Steve are such a pair with Linda being the player employee. Too often, we associate

playing with men, but there are an equal number of player women as there are men; they just tend to engage their player natures differently than men do. As we have previously done, we are presenting this conversation from the perspective of a person who is emotionally mature and socially mature. Linda will attempt to communicate her understanding of her own temperament, which is the love for experience, and then relate this to the necessity of work. The setting is midday in the work day and Linda has asked to see Steve, her boss.

Linda: Thanks for taking the time to see me. I want to talk to you about my work in the company and how I might continue to improve in work.

Steve: Sure, I'm up for it. What do you have in mind?

Linda: I'm sure that you have noticed that I am not your typical actuary, right?

Steve: That would be an understatement.

Linda: Well for one thing, I'm not introverted as many actuaries are. I'm more outgoing and expressing as an extravert. My nature is to engage people rather than wait for them to engage me.

Steve: I've noticed that.

Linda: Actually, I've recently learned that I have another element to my personality, the way I go about life. I've been doing some reading and research on personality differences among people and I've run across an interesting way of looking at people, called "temperament."

Steve: Isn't temperament the way someone feels, like excited or dopey, or something.

Linda: That is the way most people use the term. But it is much more than "mood". What you're speaking of is that some people are temperamental, meaning that they get easily hurt and irritated. But there is another way of looking at temperament rather than seeing whether someone feels up or down, excited or depressed. The way I'm using the term temperament means something more basic to how a person operates based on their individual value system.

Steve: OK. I am interested. Go on, please.

Linda: The way my psychologist looks at temperament is to suggest that there are basically four different temperaments, which means the way people go about life, and each of these temperaments is quite different and unique. My temperament is what they call "player."

Steve: You mean like playing with video games, or playing with your pencil the way I sometimes see you doing.

Linda: That may be part of it, but temperament is more than playing the way we usually think of playing. Players, like me, look for experience, or possibly engagement, or even excitement. But mostly we look for experience.

Steve: Like having more experience so you can be better at something?

Linda: Not exactly. The idea of "experience" for a player is to be as totally involved in something as possible. This can be physically involved, emotionally involved, or intellectually involved. To experience something is to be part of it. The way I see it, I need to get into something in one of these three ways: intellectually, emotionally, or physically. I really like numbers, so I am lucky enough to have this job which intellectually engages me. But it is the physical engagement that I really wanted to talk to you about. So, sometimes you might see me intensely looking at my screen being totally involved in working out a problem. Or, you might see me twirling my pencil as I am looking at the screen as I am trying to see how I can proceed. Or, you might hear me sigh, or laugh, or yelp as I am working. All of these are my ways of experiencing something physically. Here, it happens to be work. But when I'm in another setting, it wouldn't be about work or the screen. When I go rock climbing for example, I am so into every minuet movement I make, not just for the safety of it, but for the thrill of it.

Steve: Linda, this is helpful. I have noticed all of those things, like twirling your pencil…or don't you also twirl your hair? And, bounce, sometimes I look over and think you are going to start dancing. Or getting up from your seat while you are looking at the screen. And, indeed, I have heard the laughs or…what did you call them…yelps, when you are working. So, these are all expressions of your needing to experience your work physically, as a player? How does it help for you to get out of your chair, twirl your hair, or laugh, bounce around when you are engaged in working? It seems that these things would only interrupt your work.

Linda: Good question. Yes, I'm sure it looks like these ways of experiencing would interrupt my work, but actually, they help me work, they give me ways of experiencing my work physically. Believe it or not, they help me keep focused. So, when I can't quite figure out a problem, if I get up, walk around my chair, twirl my pencil, or bounce around, this all helps me concentrate. These movements might look like distractions but actually, they give me energy. When I am at my best, I experience something in all three ways: intellectually, emotionally, and physically. Or we could call these three ways thinking, feeling, and doing.

Steve: I think that I do mostly thinking. I can get involved in something that I'm thinking about but I don't want anyone to interrupt me when I'm thinking because I'm all about solving the problem.

Linda: I see that about you, Steve, and it works for you.

Steve: So, is there anything I can do to make work better for you, so you can "experience" work the way you've expressed?

Linda: There is one thing: how I affect other people. So, if I'm dancing around my chair trying to figure out what I should do with work, this might offend or interrupt other people in the office. I don't want my needing to experience something physically interrupt someone else who is fully engaged with their work. I am wondering if maybe I should tell them about this part of my personality.

Steve: That might be the case. Maybe at our next group meeting, you might take a few minutes to describe how you get your work done. In fact, as I think about it, perhaps the better thing would be to have a morning "in house" dedicated to exploring how all of us on the floor prefer to engage our work. I will do a little research and see what resources I can find to make this happen.

Linda: Wow, that would be great, and it could be quite fun.

Steve: Thank you Linda. This helps me understand you. I think it will be good for all of us to understand each other a little better.

Lover Speaking to Caretaker

The lover/caretaker combination is quite common and it can work out quite well despite the differences in these two temperaments. While lovers love connection and caretakers love property, those two things can work together quite well. Let's consider a couple that I know that have this combination, but I will augment their relationship with a bit more emotional maturity that neither of them has at this moment. Laura is the lover and her wife is Jan, the caretaker. We present this as an early conversation that they might have when they are just beginning to utilize what they are learning in therapy. Note how important it is for one person to speak while the other listens.

Laura, I'd like to talk a little about what we are learning in therapy. Would that be alright?

Jan: Well, sure, but you know that I need to fix the dishwasher.

Laura: You are so good at fixing things, Jan. You are always taking care of things, and keeping things is order. Sometimes I just wonder at your ability to do so many things.

Jan: I've always been that way. You know, also, that I don't always do things the right way because I'm always trying to get something done so I can go on to the next project. Mostly, I just like to be busy and do things.

Laura: From what our therapist has told us so far, you certainly are the "caretaker" and I am interested in this "caretaker" temperament you have, but if you don't mind, I think it would be best for me to tell you what I've been learning about my own temperament. Then we can come back to you being a caretaker.

Jan: Sure, I didn't mean to interrupt. So, I am a caretaker and you are a lover, right?

Laura: Yes. I am about "connections." Coming to understand that my orientation to life is always about connections has helped me understand why I am so happy sometimes and so unhappy at other times.

Jan: I am glad you understand this better. My mom swears you are bipolar.

Laura: No, I am not bi-polar, but yes, I do feel things strongly. I can be so happy and so sad. But perhaps "sad" isn't quite right. It's more like disappointed.

Jan: So, tell me more about this, Laura. I was interested when I first heard that you were a "lover" in temperament, and it explained a lot to me, but I still don't quite get it. At first, I thought you being a lover was referencing your sex drive. Now I know it is more, but I am not fully understanding yet.

Laura: The first thing I should say about this lover thing is to remind us what we both heard about lovers: we lovers sometimes think that everyone should be a lover. Now, I suppose any temperament could say that about everyone else, like you as a caretaker thinking everyone should be a caretaker, or some player person or analyst person thinking the same thing. But what we heard and what I've read is that lovers have a particular problem with thinking everyone is like them and should be like them because that is what they think connection is, being the same. Actually, I like the idea that I am "better at loving people" than people of other temperaments, although that is a hard pill to swallow. I've always thought that everyone had the ability to connect and enjoyed all that goes with connections. I now see, painfully see, I must admit, that we're not all lovers and that we all don't need to be lovers.

Jan: There is no doubt, Laura, you are absolutely better than I am at this whole loving people thing. And in fact, I think you're better at it than anyone I know.

Laura: Thank you for saying that, Jan, but it's a little embarrassing because it sounds like I am better than other people, which I most certainly am not. But I can sheepishly admit that I'm perhaps better at this connecting thing and loving thing when it comes to people.

Jan: This is cool, Laura, that you can see your giftedness in the matter of loving people. I do envy you in this regard, but sometimes I feel all thumbs when it comes to loving people the way you do. I always want to fix something, but isn't *fixing things* different than *loving people*?

Laura: Let's get back to you for a minute, Jan. The fixing thing you do with property, like the dishwasher right in front of us, is truly wonderful. In fact, I see this is a way you love people, by taking care of their property. You know how you enjoy helping the kids out with their homework...between you and me, I think Adrian is a little lover like myself, and she kicks the chain off her bike just so she can be with you when you fix it. Or, like working every night last week on Jason and Jill's basement project. It is a work of love, but yes, it is a different kind of love. But let me get back to explaining how this looking for connection thing affects me.

Jan: Yes, that seems to be the heart of it. People are always saying that you are so good at listening to them and feeling what they feel. I can't seem to really do that. I can fix Jake's car, but I don't have no clue how to fix his relationship with Jill.

Laura: I know they are suffering, and it pains me, but let's wait on that so I can I can tell you what I can about this seeking connections thing that I have. And yes, I do connect with people a lot and it means a lot to me when I can be of help to people. Most of the time, as you must see, I connect with people who are in some kind of emotional pain, often relational pain. I have talked to Jake's wife, and she is in a great deal of pain. She says that she really loves Jake but they just don't seem to connect very well.

Jan: So, is Jill a lover too?

Laura: Maybe. I'm not sure. Maybe some kind of caretaker like you but also a lover like me.

Jan: That might be the best of all worlds.

Laura: It could be, but the combination puts a lot of strain on her because she is always loving everyone and always taking care of things. She gets exhausted and then gets irritable.

Jan: I've heard about her irritability.

Laura: I'm sure you have. But let me get back to explaining more of this lover thing, and if I dare, express what I feel when I can't seem to connect with you.

Jan: It must happen all the time.

Laura: Not all the time, but it does happen frequently. This is the way I see it: your love, your passion is for things, very often the care of things to help people. This is how you love people, or perhaps the world in general: you fix things, care for things, buy things, and give things away. Your love is about things. Or, maybe I can say your love is through things.

Jan: Hate to admit it. Sounds materialistic, like loving things more than people.

Laura: I don't think it is materialistic. I think it is your way to love. Most of the time I can stand back and admire your loving me by, say, fixing the dishwasher. On the other hand, there are many times when things like the dishwasher prevent my having a time of emotional or intimate connection with you. So, like when we started this conversation, which we might think as a time where we can "connect", you're first statement was that the dishwasher was staring you in the face. Now, I get this about you, that you feel compelled to fix something that we really need. But it seemed like an immediate example of how I feel in second place to things…sometimes. I hope this doesn't feel like a criticism because I don't want to criticize your nature. It's just that there are always things to do, always things that need repair, and always things that need to be cared for. I wish there were more times when we could just, you know, go for a walk without talking about how the house needed to be painted, or seeing you check your cell phone in case Jason called to ask you to come over to his place.

Jan: I get this. Those moments are difficult for you. And they are difficult for me. Like, if Jason calls, I feel compelled to help him. I don't realize that I am making a choice to be with him instead of you. You seem to take care of yourself pretty well. I don't think I realized that I was hurting you when I would, like, run off to Jason's place for four hours with hammer in hand.

Laura: Well, thanks for listening, Jan. I appreciate your hearing me with this stuff. I don't want to hurt you.

Jan: I am not hurt…as much as I understand "hurt," which isn't very much. Maybe I can just be more attentive to us and a bit less with things.

Laura: I will have to do my part, which means I need to simply say that I need time with you apart from the kids, fixing things, or doing things. Just us. I am learning not to simply expect it, but to make statements about what I need and want from you.

Jan: Sounds like a plan…I mean a "connection."

Laura: Both true.

While there are 24 possible combinations of temperament, it is simply too arduous to illustrate all of these combinations. We know that some of you might be wishing we had an example specific to you and your situation. We are sorry if we didn't meet you in this. We hope, though, that all of the descriptions, all of the illustrations, and references will give you the tools for you to examine your own temperament, or combination of your temperaments, as well as application to consider the temperament of those people who are significant in your life. We believe that as you consider all the characteristics, the values and the examples we have provided will be a spring board for you to at least shake hands with, if not full embrace the fullness of who you are and the fullness of those around you.

If everyone talked the way our examples of people did, we wouldn't be in business. Let us remind you that these conversations have been of emotionally and socially mature people. We have suggested that people can learn to talk about their feelings and hear other people talking about feelings without anger or defensiveness. We are well aware, however, that to get to the point where you are regularly speaking carefully and listening even more carefully takes a great deal of effort. The effort is in an ever-increasing understanding of feelings, something that takes time. You shorten the time with some good therapy, but it still takes time and effort fraught with frequent failures on communication. Temperament isn't all we talk about with the people who come to see us, but it a very important part, and a part that is simple enough, and profound enough to alter lives for the better. Clearly, we have suggested that this is the way people *could* talk to one another, but to be able to talk and listen the way Laura and Jan have done requires a great deal of self-awareness, self-acceptance, and emotional maturity, to say nothing of the hours it might take to get there.

We hope that you can profit from understanding yourself so you can understand other people. The heart of success in life is self-understanding. We like to think that real self-understanding and self-acceptance not only leads to good communication, it also leads to humility and deeper love for other people, a love that is based on understanding them, always more, always deeper. You can get to true acceptance and acceptance of other people. These things will never be perfect but you can find your way through these murky waters to a point where you find immense joy in your interpersonal life.

Appendix: Johnson Temperament Indicator

Instructions: Please indicate how true the following statements are for you according to the following scale:

0 = never
1 = seldom
2 = occasionally
3 = frequently
4 = very frequently

___ 1. I like to work.
___ 2. I like a lot of excitement in my life.
___ 3. I find it easy to love people.
___ 4. I like to analyze things
___ 5. I like to be busy.
___ 6. I often get bored.
___ 7. I try hard to develop harmony between myself and others.
___ 8. I really enjoy trying to figure people out.
___ 9. I usually have a list of things that need to be done.
___ 10. Playing is very important to me.
___ 11. Strong disagreements are very hard on me.
___ 12. Searching for the meaning of life is very important to me.
___ 13. I am usually very responsible.
___ 14. I really like to be spontaneous.
___ 15. I really enjoy emotional "connections" with people.
___ 16. I often take a critical look at things.

___ 17. I am good at taking care of people.
___ 18. I like adventurous or risky activities.
___ 19. I am very aware of other people's feelings.
___ 20. People often see me as odd or different.
___ 21. I take good care of property.
___ 22. My favorite movies are action movies.
___ 23. I find it easy to empathize with others.
___ 24. I like to be creative or original in thought.
___ 25. My days are usually orderly and planned.
___ 26. I often offend people without wanting to.
___ 27. I tend to believe people most of the time.
___ 28. It is very important for me to seek truth.
___ 29. When confronted with a problem, I usually jump right in and act.
___ 30. I often use street language or cursing.
___ 31. Cooperation among people is very important to me.
___ 32. I like to develop theories about things.
___ 33. When something needs to be done, it bothers me until it is done.
___ 34. I often leave projects unfinished because I get bored with them.
___ 35. I tend to interpret much of what people say.
___ 36. I like to avoid making mistakes by figuring things ahead of time.
___ 37. I am very practical about most things.
___ 38. I often think of myself as potentially the best at some activity.
___ 39. I am quite aware of emotional hurt when it occurs in others or me.
___ 40. I usually speak with qualifiers, like "possibly" or "maybe".
___ 41. I like things to be stable.
___ 42. Freedom is very important to me.
___ 43. I like infants very much.
___ 44. I am inventive (in thought or in action).
___ 45. I like things to be simple.
___ 46. Some people see me as impulsive.
___ 47. Relationships are most important to me.
___ 48. I consider myself a good thinker.
___ 49. It is fairly easy for me to accept the way things are.
___ 50. Some people see me as "hyper."
___ 51. I look to the future frequently.
___ 52. Scientific things fascinate me.
___ 53. I like to save and preserve things.
___ 54. I like to have a strong effect on people.
___ 55. I am very romantic.
___ 56. It is very important to me to understand things.

Appendix: Johnson Temperament Indicator   321

_   57. I am careful about how I spend money.
  _   58. I like powerful rock music.
    _   59. Sex is very important to me.
      _ 60. I am usually very logical and reasonable.
_   61. I like to know the rules for things.
  _   62. I really enjoy sports.
    _   63. I like music which is "touching."
      _ 64. I try very hard to be accurate.

_ _ _ _

Directions for scoring: Add all four columns. There will be 16 items in each column.

Column 1:   Your score for *Caretaker*:   _____
Column 2:   Your score for *Player*:   _____
Column 3:   Your score for *Lover*:   _____
Column 4:   Your score for *Analyst*:   _____

Annotated Bibliography

Bandler, S. & Grinder, G. (1976). *Structure of magic.* Palo Alto: Basic Science Books.
    An immensely popular book written to present the author's early development of "neuro-linguistic programming" system based on four basic ways of perceiving the world, each of these ways based on one of our physical senses.

Barrett, L.F. (2017). *How emotions are made: the secret life of the brain.* New York: Houghton Mifflin.
    The author, a neuropsychologist, believes that emotions are "made", or "constructed" as a necessity of survival and understanding how to engage the world, particularly the social world. She suggests that we are born with an innate ability to do this "construction." She challenges the more traditional view that emotions erupt naturally out of a need for physical survival and pleasure.

Bates, J.E. and Wachs, T.D. (Eds.) (1994). *Temperament: individual differences at the interface of biology and behavior.* Washington, D.C.: American Psychological Association.
    This is one of many books using the term "temperament" seeing this term as a descriptor of mood more than personality.

Bloom, P. (2016). *Against empathy: the case for rational compassion.* New York: HarperCollins.
    Makes a case for distinguishing "emotional empathy," i.e., feeling what someone else feels, and "cognitive empathy," understanding what someone

else feels. He notes the dangers of emotional empathy, you can't empathize with more than one person at a time, and distinguishes compassion from empathy. Recommends cognitive empathy because of the danger of meeting immediate wants but not long-term needs, whether individually or societally. Some neuropsychology related to empathy.

Briggs-Myers, I. (1980). *Gifts differing.* New York: Consulting Psychologists Press.
This is the premier work by Isabel Myers, together with her mother, Katharine Cook Briggs, who created Myers-Briggs Type Indicator (MBTI) used widely to understand "personality type.

Brock, D. (2004). Comparisons of personality type and temperament and psychopathological indicators between evangelical and mainline denomination women seeking counseling [Doctoral dissertation, Breyer State University]. Madison, WI: Midlands Psychological Associates.

Brock, D. and Johnson, R. (2011). "Narcissism and Evil." In *Evil: definitions and development, Vol. 1,* J.H. Ellens, editor. Santa Barbara, CA: Praeger Press.
A chapter suggesting that narcissism, usually seen as pathological selfishness, is more accurately a lack of self.

Buckingham, M. and Clifton, D. (2001). *Now, discover your strengths.* New York: Free Press.
Buckingham and Clifton, principals at the Gallup foundation have developed a system of identifying strengths that people have, called the StrengthsFinder, used primarily in business. They find 34 "themes" as strengths.

Chapman, G. (1992). *The five love languages: How to express heartfelt commitment to your mate.* Chicago: Northfield Publishing.
This very popular book suggests that there are five "love languages," namely ways that people express love and want love expressed to them: Words of appreciation; Physical touch; Receiving gifts; Quality time; and Acts of service. There are, of course, combinations of these gifts, but the larger

value is knowing that we do not love them the same, nor do we want to be loved the same.

Csikszentmihalyi, M. (1993). *The evolving self.* New York: HarperCollins.
One of his later volumes beginning with *Flow*, for which he is best known. He uses the concept of "flow" to discuss how the self develops.

Csikszentmihalyi, M. (1997). *Finding flow: the psychology of engagement with everyday life.* New York: Basic Books.
In this and other books the author proposes the experience of "flow" as central to human existence, the heart of emotion and feeling, and important in human relationships, flow being the optimal daily experience when life moves forward positively. Consciousness is composed of emotions, intentions, and thought, and his preference is for "concentration," which is essentially thinking ahead. Flow occurs when a person faces the future with forethought based on experience but not governed by emotions but by using "arousal and control." Happiness results when one can look back with pleasure on one's hard work and success.

Damasio, A. (1999). *The feeling of what happens: body and emotion in the making of consciousness.* NY: Harcourt Brace.
Deals with consciousness, again suggesting a biological substrate to it. He notes that consciousness and emotion are not separable, and that emotions are an integral part of reasoning. Discusses "core consciousness", which is primary, and extended consciousness, which is learned. Sense of self emerges from core consciousness. He distinguishes emotion and feeling, which is the "private mental experience." Believes there are 6 primary emotions (joy, sadness, fear, anger, surprise, and disgust).

Davidson, R.J. (2012). *The emotional life of the brain.* New York: Hudson Street Press.
A neuroscientist proposes that there are 4 "emotional styles," resilience, outlook, social intuition, self-awareness, sensitivity to context, and attention. He discusses both personality and pathology dimensions with each

of these. Reflects much on the PFC as perhaps more the center of emotion than the limbic system (amygdala, etc.). An important focus is particularly on self-awareness, and he has much experience and sees much value in meditation along with its neurological substrate.

DeBenedet, A.T. (2018). *Playful intelligence: the power of living lightly in a serious world.* Solana Beach, CA: Santa Monica Press.
A study, largely with people examples of what the author proposes are the "four qualities of play: imagination, sociability, humor, spontaneity, and wonder.

Ekman, P. (2003). *Emotions revealed: recognizing faces and feelings to improve communication and emotion life.* New York: Henry Holt.
Ekman is known mostly for studying faces and the feelings that are represented in faces. He identifies the basic emotions as joy, sadness, fear, and anger that we see as basic, but adds disgust, surprise. He advises emotional awareness to prevent premature expression or action based on emotions. He also studies other emotional experiences such as resentment and hatred erupting out of anger. He notes that fear always precedes anger. The feeling of joy can lead to contentment, excitement, relief, amusement, or wonder.

Ellens, J.H. (1982). *God's grace and human health.* New York: Abington.
One of the first of many hundreds of books and articles by the author who has been a central figure in spiritual-psychological integration. In this volume the author suggests that emotional health brings physical health.

Erikson, E. (1968). *Identity: youth and crisis.* New York: Norton.
Erickson is the first, perhaps the foremost student of development. He suggests stages of development from childhood to adulthood.

Freed, J. and Parson, L. (1998). *Right brained children in a left brained world.* New York: Fireside.
This is one of several books available of "left-brain/right-brain" differences. This volume identifies children (and possibly adults) who do not do well in traditional school, which is largely "left-brained," i.e., reading and writing.

Gardner, H. (1983). *Frames of mind: the theory of multiple intelligences.* New York: HarperCollins.

This is Gardner's first and prominent work on multiple intelligences (linguistic, kinesthetic, musical, etc.) adding much to understanding various intelligences.

Goleman, D. (1995). *Emotional intelligence: why it can matter more than IQ.* New York: Bantam Books.

This is the first of two works by the author, the second of which is "social intelligence" although in this volume he incorporates social with emotional "intelligence." Widely read and used, but not much in the psychological community.

Grant, R.D. & Miller, A.W. (1992). *Recovering connections.* NY, NY: Harper.

Grant is perhaps the most articulate author regarding temperaments. This work, written from a heavily Catholic perspective, as well as from a good understanding of temperament proposes a close connection between temperament and addiction-recovery. We find the work too co-dependency and pathology oriented, but valuable.

Gray, J.A. (1991). The neuropsychology of temperament. In J. Strelau & A. Angleitner (Eds.), *Explorations in temperament: international perspectives on theory and measurement* (pp. 105-128). New York: Plenum.

A study of the possible brain functions in personal functioning. Largely related to psychopathology but valuable.

Herbert, N. (1993). *The elemental mind.* New York: Dutton.

Examines consciousness from several perspectives. Considers that consciousness is "about me" while much of life is about others. Admits that a sense of self is impossible to quantify. The contents of consciousness are sensation, action, memory, emotion, and cognition. "Human spirit enters matter in some unknown way...." Notes that existence may be related to perception. Deals with the possibility principle and the random hypothesis to understand how this happens. A bit of study of minds connected in some way.

Hillman, J. (1960/1992). *Emotion: a comprehensive phenomenology of theories and their meanings for therapy.* Evanston, IL: Northwestern University Press.
> An older volume with 50-year dated references by one of the best known Jungians presents a comprehensive view of emotions including emotion as many things including: a distinct entity, accompaniment, energy, quantity, totality, situation, signification, conflict, disorder, creativity, and spirit. His last chapter, Integration is superb where he suggests that emotion is closest to the human core.

Hillman. J. (1971). *The feeling function.* Dallas TX: Spring Publications.
> Perhaps the best examination of Carl Jung's feeling function. The author reviews the earliest recorded understanding of feeling beginning with a quote from Moses Mendelsohn (1776): "We no longer feel as soon as we think. Our feelings are closest to our sense of self or soul, but they are stirred by the physical and social environment. "Self-realization is feeling realization." Feeling is related to the other Jungian functions of sensing, thinking, and intuition, but also related to physical sensation and emotion. For instance, we may feel our thoughts, and feeling often leads to emotion (or affect). The feeling function needs to develop in order to be useful in life. "Above all feeling provides the order and logic for love."

Jasanoff, A. (2018). *The biological mind.* New York: Basic Books.
> A focus on the neurological substrate of the mind. Author makes a point of noting the interplay of biology, brain, and environment to create the "mind." Some interesting notes regarding other elements of the body beyond the brain, and how physical environmental and social influences affect the mind.

Johnson, R. (1991). Making a friendly diagnosis. *Journal of Psychology and Christianity,* 9(1), 66-71.
> A summary of my "Friendly Diagnosis" system which I am completing in book form. A brief presentation of the elements of temperament, type, gender, and sub- cultural elements making up that system written from a Christian understanding.

Johnson, R. (1994). *What's your temperament?* Madison, WI: Midlands Associates.
A study of the four temperaments: player, caretaker, lover, and analyst. This laid the foundation for the present work.

Johnson, R. (2010). "Neurotheology: the interface of neuropsychology and theology." In *The healing power of spirituality: how faith helps humans thrive.* Santa Barbara, CA: Praeger Press.

Johnson, R. (2013). *Seen and not heard.* Madison, WI: Midlands Psychological Associates.
This book examines various elements of child-rearing with a focus on understanding children, including temperament, and avoiding indulgence while encouraging acceptance.

Johnson, R. and Brock, D. (2017). *The positive power of sadness: how good grief prevents and cures depression, anxiety, and anger.* Santa Barbara, CA: Praeger.
In this volume we discuss the centrality of the emotion and feeling of sadness. We suggest that sadness is the most important feeling we have because we lose everything we love. Understanding sadness and allowing its process prevents (or cures) depression, anxiety, and anger.

Jung, C.J. (1970). *Psychological Types.* Princeton, NJ: Bollingen Publishing.
Jung is without a doubt the central figure in understanding much about personality factors, which he referred to as psychological types. He focused on differences in energy (introversion and extraversion) and how we gather and process information (objectively or subjectively). It is the subjective element that we are studying in this book, which would include both perception and judgment.

Keirsey, D. and Bates, M. (1984). *Please understand me: character and temperament types.* Del Mar, CA: Prometheus Nemesis Book Company.
A wildly popular book among followers of personality type out of the MBTI tradition. Proposes temperament as combinations of some of the elements of the MBTI perspective.

Kohn, A. (1993). *Punished by rewards.* New York: Houghton Mifflin Company.
> The author's thesis is that rewards and punishments are "external" and hence do not truly help self-esteem, which is developed by trial and error, success and failure.

Kohut, H. (1971). *The analysis of the self.* New York: International Universities Press.
> This author is perhaps the preeminent author in the psychoanalytic realm who discusses self-development with great detail. Beware of his complexity, however.

Kroeger, O. and Thuesen, J.M. (1988). *Type talk: or how to determine your personality type and change your life.* New York: Delacorte Press.
> One of many books based on understanding personality from the perspective of type based on the Myers-Briggs Type Indicator.

Lowinsky, E.E. (1973). Musical genius. In *Dictionary of the history of ideas.* Charles Scribner's Sons.
> One of many books identifying intelligence out of the realm of linguistic intelligence.

Lazoni, S. (2018). *Empathy: a history.* Newhaven CN: Yale University Press.
> A good history of the term, its origins, and its development starting primarily with the German Einfühlung, meaning "feeling into".

Lutz, T. (1999). *Crying: the natural and cultural history of tears.* New York: Norton.
> A fine summary of the history, chemistry, biology, neurology, frequency, personal, and interpersonal elements related to crying. The author notes "the more loving we are, the more prone to tears," crying occurs not at the peak of an emotional experience but at some point, after the peak during the return to a "sense of self." He reviews the "cathartic therapies", gender differences, and cultural differences in crying.

Lowen, A. (1958). *The language of the body.* New York: Grune and Stratton.
One of several books by the author, Lowen, the principal follower of Wilhelm Reich, in which he "diagnoses" personality and recommends treatment by body analysis.

Mate', G. (2000). *Scattered: how attention deficit disorder originates and what you can do about it.* New York: Penguin.
A very helpful volume from a sufferer from ADD who postulates that the condition is caused by early childhood trauma and consequent neurological adjustment.

McGilchrist, I. (2019). *The master and his emissary: The divided brain and the making of the western world.* New Haven, CN: Yale University Press.
The author provides a well-researched document regarding many aspects of the differences in the two brain hemispheres with many references to neuroscientists, philosophers, and fiction writers. His point is that the Western world, and much of science, has been dominated by a belief that the left hemisphere is the "dominant" hemisphere. He makes a good case for understanding the right hemisphere as the housing for one's core self and "feelings." Read the extensive Chapter 2 and skim the rest where he departs into too much of a diatribe against left hemisphere dominance.

Myers, I.B. and McCauley, M.H. (1985). *Manual: a guide to the development and use of the Myers-Briggs Type Indicator.* Palo Alto, CA: Consulting Psychologists Press.

Myers, I.B. (1992), *Gifts differing.* Palo Alto CA: Consulting Psychologists Press.
This is one of the foundational books describing the Myers-Briggs understanding of personality type, namely the "16 personality types" composed of the four psychological operations. Particularly relevant to our discussion of is the "judging" dimension of "feeling and thinking" first described by Carl Jung.

Nardi, D. (2001). *Multiple intelligences and personality type.* Huntington Beach, CA: Telos Publications.

A volume dedicated to primarily study the Gardner's theory of multiple intelligences interfaced with personality type.

Niednagel, J.P. (1992). *Your best sport.* Laguna Niguel, CA: Laguna Press.

The author specializes in applying personality type to athletic endeavors.

J.E. Bates and T.D. Wachs: *Temperament: individual differences at the interface of biology and behavior.* Washington, D.C.: American Psychological Association.

Orstein, R. (1997). *The right mind: making sense of the hemispheres.* New York: Harcourt Brace & Company.

The author's primary purpose is to suggest that humans need to fully utilize both hemispheres, an idea running counter to much of education, which focuses largely on the left. He highlights some of the strengths of the right hemisphere, such as emotional and social development as well as music, but also notes the "global" perspective of the right side. Yet he notes how important it is for the two hemispheres to work together in all spheres of life. While the left hemisphere houses language, reading, math, and most cognitive capacities, the right side "makes sense" of things that can lead to meaningful action.

Peck, S. (1978). *The road less traveled: a new psychology of love, traditional values, and spiritual growth.* New York: Simon and Schuster.

A very popular book in the 1980's beginning with his now famous statement: "Life is difficult." A study of how to deal with unavoidable difficulties.

Pillard, N. (2015). *Jung and intuition.* London: Karnac.

An in-depth analysis of intuition as understood and presented in the works of Carl Jung. The author notes the intrinsic connection between feeling and intuition. Intuition starts with instinct, then moves into the unconscious, then into the "underconscious," and then appears in thought or feeling. He notes the difference between concrete and abstract intuition depending on one's personality. He discusses empathy, inspiration, imagination as related to intuition, and then touches on trauma as it relates to the discussion.

Power, J (1969). *Why am I afraid to tell you who I am?* Allen TX: Tabor Publishing.
An older, simple, largely Christian take on the apparent fact that people are quite simply afraid to reveal their thoughts and feelings. The author's suggestion is that there is a deep need in all humans to be "known" but a related fear of being judged. He suggests that self-knowledge and self-acceptance are enhanced in self-revelation. Furthermore, self- revelation enhances both self-love and love of others. He also deals somewhat with (emotional) hurt and suggests that awareness of emotions does not always suggest that they should be expressed or acted upon.

Rafalski, Monika (2018). *Empfinden, Intuieren, Fühlen, Denken: die Vier psychischen Grundfunktionen in Psychotherapie und Individuation.* Translation by Boris Matthews. Stuttgart: Verlag W. Kohlhammer.
A recent addition to C.J. Jung's understanding of psychological type with a focus on the feeling function. Note the physical and emotional components of feelings.

Reich, W. (1961). *Character analysis.* New York: Farrar, Straus, and Giroux.
Reich was an early proponent of what is being called "body work." In this framework he examined people's personalities from observation of their body structures.

Riso, D.R. and Hudson, R. (2003). *Discovering your personality type.* New York: Houghton Mifflin.
One of many books on the Enneagram.

Rohm, R.A. (2005). *Positive personality profiles: D-I-S-C-over: personality insights to understand yourself and others.* Emeryville, CA: Alibris Publishing.
One of many books on the DISC identifying four personality types: Dominance, Influence, Conscientiousness, and Steadfastness. Used frequently in business settings.

Russ, S.W. (2000). Assessing positive features of the personality. *SPA Exchange*, 10 (1), pp. 1-3.
    An early proponent of "positive psychology," i.e., looking at strengths rather than weaknesses.

Schore, A.N. (1994). *Affect regulation and the origin of the self: the neurobiology of emotional development.* Hillsdale, NJ: Lawrence Erlbaum Associates.
    This is a well-researched (2300 references) study of early infancy emotional development from a researcher familiar with neuropsychology, developmental psychology, psychoanalysis, and some psychotherapy. Particular attention is paid to "mother"-infant bonding, normal infantile narcissism, "moral" development, and play. Frequent references to the value and disvalue of shame as well as the importance of the PFC in the lateralization of emotions, the learning of control/inhibition, the ultimate development of self, and some examination of resultant psychopathology.

Schutz, W.C. (1967). *Joy: expanding human awareness.* New York: Grove Press.
    An author central to the experience-based psychotherapy of the 1960's and 1970's, his ideas, while dated and limited are marked by a body-based understanding of feelings. Somewhat a student of Alexander Lowen he proposed that creativity as the essence of joy beginning with experience, then association with other experiences and information, that followed by expression, evaluation, and production. He seems not to distinguish feeling from emotion.

Seligman, M.E.P. (2002). *Authentic happiness: using the new positive psychology to realize your potential for lasting fulfillment.* New York: The Free Press.
    The author is the co-founder of "Positive Psychology", which emphasized "what is right about people" rather than what is wrong with them. A number of strengths are examined, like optimism and hope that are well studied in the psychological community but also includes the philosophical "virtues" of wisdom, courage, love, justice, temperance, and spirituality that are less well studied but ones that the author believes lead to happiness. He deals with gratitude and forgiveness that are more relational in nature. His is essentially a

cognitive approach to life, particularity to adversity. He compares the "pleasures of the emotions" to the gratification that comes with utilizing one's strengths and virtues, but ventures into the realms of love, work, and relationships.

Steiner, R. (1908/1971). *The four temperaments*. Spring Valley, NY: Andromorphic.
Steiner presents his four-part temperament system from his "theosophy" perspective, which is allegedly a combination of theology and philosophy, but which also has a strong ingredient of reincarnation.

Stotland, E. (1969). *The psychology of hope*. San Francisco, CA: Jossey-Bass, Inc. Publishers.
An early work that is a thorough review of extant literature on hope until 1969, yet valuable as hope and resilience became central themes in positive psychology. He suggests that hope is the antithesis of anxiety, i.e. looking forward with fear or positive expectation, as well as the opposite of "learned helplessness" in depression. He also noes the importance of thoughtful planning, recovering from failures with a "schema," the value of social support. He examines hope and lack of hope in psychopathology.

Tangney, J.P. and Dearing, R.L (2002). *Shame and guilt*. New York: Guilford
The principal author, Tangney, developed the Test of Self-Conscious Affect, a very valuable instrument that distinguishes guilt and shame among other feelings. She has done extensive research in the area. This is perhaps the most valuable view of guilt and shame available.

Thompson, R.A. (1998). *The developing person through the life span*. New York: Worth Publishers.
An examination of some aspects of personhood throughout human development.

Tillich, P. (1952). *The courage to be*. New Haven, CN: Yale University Press.
A work by one of the century's most prominent theologians examining the importance of being true to oneself.

Tournier, P. (1958). *Guilt and grace*. New York: Harper and Row.
   A "Christian psychiatrist" early in the field writes eloquently about "false guilt" and "real guilt," the former being guilt as we see it, the latter as shame as we see it. A bit rambling, but a valuable distinction of guilt and shame.

Van der Kolk, B. (2004). *The body keeps the score: brain, mind, and the healing of trauma*. New York: Viking Press.
   The classic neuropsychological understanding of trauma with a focus on the effects on the right hemisphere, the primary housing for emotions.

Von Fronz, M. and Hillman, J. (1971). *Lectures on Jung's typology: the inferior function and the feeling function*. Dallas: Spring Publishing.
   This is an important examination of Jung's "feeling function," which is quite related to the lover temperament that we have presented.

Vitz, P. and Felch, S. (editors). *The self: beyond the postmodern crisis*. Wilmington, DE: Intercollegiate Studies Institute.
   A newer volume regarding self-development with several authors contributing to the discussion.

West, M. (2007). *Feeling, being, and the sense of self: a new perspective on identity, affect, and narcissistic disorders*. London: Karnac.
   Perhaps the best contemporary understanding of feeling and its cognates. He distinguishes a "sense of I" and a "sense of being," the former being the subjective sense of being, the latter an equally subjective sense of experience. The author relates these two elements of feeling into a right hemisphere, largely emotional, experience relating to the world and a left hemisphere, largely intellectual, experience of self separate from the world. He refers to this as the "identity-affect" model of feelings. One's sense of being tends to lead to subjective judgment of "sameness and difference," but prefers sameness and can lead to narcissism. Maturing comes from "affect regulation" without losing affect.

Wolf, F.A. (2002). *Matter into feeling: a new alchemy of science and spirit.* Portsmouth, NH: Moment Point Press.

> The author's basic tenet is shared by many other authors, some scientists, some psychologists, and some philosophical theorists, namely that the universe is founded not so much on matter as it is on feeling and thinking, which through perception creates matter as we know it. Love is at the heart of the universe. Much of his ensuing argument is related to how individuals connect with one another and the universe at large, which the author believes to be essential in successful life. "Ego arises as a spirit/matter interface." Feelings erupt into emotions, which in turn create somatic sensations. He proposes a continuing interaction of Jung's four functions.

Zuckerman, M. (1979). *Sensation seeking: Beyond the optimal level of arousal.* Hillsdale, NJ: Erlbaum.

> The "sensation-seeking" person that Zuckerman describes fits with much of what we present with the player temperament.

www.ingramcontent.com/pod-product-compliance
Lightning Source LLC
Chambersburg PA
CBHW071951070526
44583CB00015B/1150